Third edition

Arthur J. Hughes, Ph.D.

Glencoe Publishing Co., Inc.

Encino, California

ACKNOWLEDGMENTS

The author wishes to acknowledge the assistance of the persons who have helped him in the revision of this text. Thanks are due Mrs. Irene K. Hughes, Mr. James C. Hughes, Mrs. Josephine Joseph, Miss MaryAnne Gallagher, Mr. Dennis Canning, Miss Rose Baraba, Mrs. Rita Burke, and Miss Julie A. Hughes for their technical assistance in the production and completion of this manuscript. The St. Francis College Library, with its ever cheerful staff and ever available sources, deserves special thanks. Dr. James J. Flynn of the History and Political Science Department was the important factor in the creation of this work in the first place and his interest has sustained it through its first and second revisions. His death in 1977 has cost the author and St. Francis College a close friend and a valued mentor.

To Irene

THIRD EDITION

Glencoe Publishing Co., Inc.
17337 Ventura Boulevard
Encino, California 91316

Library of Congress Catalog Card Number: 69-10437
Printed in the United States of America

ISBN 0-02-644560-3
2 3 4 5 83 82

CONTENTS

Introduction

Did you ever notice that some combinations of letters of the alphabet mean a great deal to you? Take FBI, for example, which means far more than its three little letters would indicate; or FDIC, which means your bank account is protected; or FDA, which protects your breakfast table. Or take the CEA, which advises the President on economic matters and interprets the latest statistics from the BLS for him.

In newspapers and on radio and TV you are always learning about the latest announcement from the FCC, the IRS, the EPA, or some other alphabetical agency in Washington, D.C. It must seem that our government is a large, complex, and mysterious thing. It is large, and it is complex. But it is not mysterious. In fact, our government was created for reasons which are quite simple.

Writing on the purposes of government in the Declaration of Independence in 1776, Thomas Jefferson stated that God had endowed human beings with certain rights, among which were "Life, Liberty, and the pursuit of Happiness." The reason governments were created, Jefferson went on, was to "secure these rights." Thus, governments are designed to:

- Protect us from harm (life);
- Preserve our freedom (liberty);
- Leave us free to live our lives as we see fit, provided we do not harm others or prevent them from the equal enjoyment of their rights (pursuit of happiness).

Government, then, is the means human beings use to enable them to live in society with others. Without government, life would always be a bit like the schoolyard before the first bell rings—disorderly and dangerous, the strong taking advantage of the weak. With government, life is somewhat like a well-run classroom—orderly enough to permit you to learn, yet not so closely disciplined as to turn out puppets instead of well-educated thinkers.

To carry the classroom example further, you may have noticed that there are three usual types of classes in school:

- One in which there is too much order or discipline, making it difficult to exchange ideas;
- Another in which there is so much liberty that very little work is done;
- And a third in which there are sensible proportions of order and liberty.

The third type of class describes the best kind of government, one in which there is a proper balance between the forces of liberty and order. As you know, such classes are rare. Few governments in history have been able to achieve this balance, either. Yours is one of those few.

The Constitution which our nation's founders drew up almost two centuries ago was designed to be a set of rules to make sure Americans had the freedom to use their opportunities to the fullest. But, this use could not interfere with the rights of other Americans to pursue *their* opportunities.

A constitution, therefore, is simply a set of society's rules, similar to the rules which govern the classroom or the clubs you belong to, or the sports you take part in. If you belong to a club, you know that there are certain times for meetings, certain dues to be paid, and a whole set of rules and regulations. When these are written down, there is less chance for misunderstandings to occur.

As the club invites more members in and takes part in more activities, it becomes larger and more complex. It then needs more involved rules. Exactly the same is true of our government. It is a large and complex government simply because American society is large and complex. And it is getting even more so every year.

If the nation's founders returned to look at America today, they would find many changes in almost every area. In 1790, when the first census was taken, only about 3.9 million persons were counted. Today there are more than 220 million people in the United States. When George Washington was sworn in as our first President, he had but a handful of helpers to run the executive branch. The War Department had three clerks and the State Department had four. By the early 1970's, the Defense Department had a staff of more than one million and the Postal Service had approximately six hundred and fifty thousand.

Geographically, the United States in 1790 was confined to the area east of the Mississippi River. Economically, it was primarily a nation of farmers. Internationally, it was one of the least influential countries in the world. Today its borders extend far into the Pacific, it has the most diversified economy in the world, and it is the leader of the world's free nations.

The growth of this country in population, wealth, and area has given us a place of leadership in the world today. But even more important than our size and power are the ideals for which we stand. Throughout our history, we have made our land a refuge for mankind. The late President Kennedy called us a "nation of immigrants" in a book of that title, emphasizing the fact that more than forty million human beings have come from Europe and Africa to populate our land.

The subject you are about to study deals with the way this vast land is governed. We will try to answer three main questions:

- Where did the American government come from?
- What principles is it based on?
- How does it operate?

Chapters 1 and 2 will answer the first question and Chapter 3 the second. The rest of the book will deal with the operations of our government—its principal parts, the way in which each part functions, and the relationship of our government to the people.

One of the problems students encounter in studying government is their familiarity with some parts of the subject. After all, who has not heard of Thomas Jefferson and the Declaration of Independence or the "Founding Fathers" and the Constitution? Try not to be fooled by a superficial knowledge of our government. There is much that will be new to you in this book. You will find, for example, that a surprising num-

Population of the United States by census years

Year	Number of Persons	Percentage of Increase over Previous Census
1790	4,000,000	
1800	5,300,000	35
1810	7,200,000	36
1820	9,600,000	33
1830	12,900,000	33
1840	17,100,000	33
1850	23,200,000	36
1860	31,400,000	36
1870	39,800,000	27
1880	50,200,000	26
1890	63,000,000	26
1900	76,000,000	21
1910	92,000,000	21
1920	105,700,000	15
1930	122,800,000	16
1940	131,700,000	7
1950	151,300,000	15
1960	179,300,000	19
1970	203,200,000	13
1980 (estimated)	220,806,000	9

Source: U.S. Bureau of the Census.

ber of terms and abbreviations will be strange. For instance, try to translate the following sentences for a foreigner:

- The chief executive is constitutionally disqualified from taking a third term by the Twenty-second Amendment;
- Members of the upper house tried to log-roll some pork-barrel bills through, but a filibuster stopped them;
- The President almost always observes senatorial courtesy in the selection of appointees;
- The bill was bottled up in committee until a close vote brought it to the floor.

How did you do on the translation? Do you think you could have satisfied a curious stranger?

Or suppose you were asked to explain such terms as cloture, writ of certiorari, EOP, bill of attainder, or original jurisdiction? And, by the way, were you able to identify all the abbreviations in the first two paragraphs of this Introduction? If not, FBI means Federal Bureau of Investigation, FDIC means Federal Deposit Insurance Corporation, FDA means Food and Drug Administration, CEA is the Council of Economic Advisers, BLS is the Bureau of Labor Statistics, FCC means Federal Communications Commission, IRS means Internal Revenue Service, and EPA stands for Environmental Protection Agency. Also, from this present paragraph, EOP refers to the Executive Office of the President.

Like any other subject, then, government has its own specialized vocabulary. Sometimes different meanings are placed on words ordinarily familiar to us. The word "recall," for example, usually means to remember something. When used in government, however, it refers to a practice by which citizens of some states may force an unpopular public officeholder to stand for election before his or her term expires.

The special terms used in government will be explained fully the first time they appear in this book. If you find them used later on and are not sure of their meaning, refer to the original definition by using the Index.

The study of government is not easy. Your best abilities as a student will be required to master it. However, the government under which we live is such a wonderful one that you will find it well worth the effort. This does not mean there are no flaws in our system—there are, as there are in any human institution. Nor does it mean that our leaders are perfect. Far from it, they have faults as grave as our own.

But unlike the government and leaders of many other countries, ours is a system which can change peacefully and by democratic processes. *You* will decide who its leaders will be and what policies it will follow. *Your* activities as an intelligent citizen will determine its success or failure, for you are one of those rarest creatures in the history of humankind—a free person.

1

The Historical Background

If you could put all the people who have ever lived under freedom on one side of a scale and all who have ever lived under dictatorships of any kind on the other, you would see how few free people there have been in human history. Even today most people live under governments they did not choose and often do not like. A great many people are subject to the whims of a few dictators who tell them where they must work and live, what kind of food they must eat, and even how much food they are allowed. If a person commits an offense, in some countries he or she can be condemned to jail without even being present at the trial. In fact, a person can be imprisoned without being given a trial at all.

This is the way it has been throughout history. Rulers could exile or execute subjects without any valid reason. A person's property could be confiscated to enrich others. An offender's children could be made to suffer for the deeds of the parent. Debtors who were unable to pay their bills could be sold into slavery and in some places could be executed.

Freedom—the right to govern yourself, to live and work where you please, to marry whomever you wish, and to raise and educate your family as your conscience dictates—is a rare thing in history.

Our government did not just come into being in one leap. It evolved over a period of many centuries. Today it is like a great tree with many roots. An examination of some of these roots will show us how deep they go.

GREEK AND ROMAN ROOTS

We owe a great deal to the Greeks and Romans for our knowledge of forms of government. The Greeks lived in dozens of small political divisions known as city-states. These political units underwent many changes of government during their centuries of existence. The Greek philosopher Aristotle tried to classify these forms of government more than three hundred years before Christ was born.

The name of every form of government the Greeks had was usually made by adding a term to some form of the Greek words *krateo* and *archo*, both of which mean "rule." Thus, when they described rule by one person, they called it monarchy *(monos-archo)*. Rule by a few was oligarchy *(oligos-archo)*. When a class of people governed, it was called an aristocracy *(aristos-krateo)*. A government ruling by the will of all the free citizens was a democracy *(demos-krateo)*. Many of the words that we use in government today are of Greek origin. Aristotle thought the form a government took did not matter so much as the extent to which it ruled in behalf of all the people. He believed that a monarchy could be a good form if it governed in the interests of the public and that democracy could be bad if the majority thought only of its own interests and ignored the needs of minorities.

The Romans contributed another form of government to us. This is the republican form, from the Latin words *res publica*, meaning "the business of the people." Rome's population was so widely scattered that not all the citizens could get together to vote on every issue. So representatives came to the Forum to take care of the public's business.

Not everyone, of course, was represented in the Greek or Roman governments. Slavery was widespread, women had no political equality, and many free people lived all their lives without having any voice in their own government. In fairness to the Greeks and Romans, however, we should point out that slavery was abolished only a little more than a century ago in our own country, and that women have gained the right to vote only in this century.

The most serious defect of people in ancient civilizations was their inability to treat all human beings as equals. Greeks considered themselves more human than any other peoples—

not just more civilized, but more human. Free males in ancient societies felt that slaves and women were not as human as they. Thus, when these groups were badly treated, it did not seem so unjust. Legally, there were different rules for crimes committed against slaves and against free men. Children, too, were subject to great inequalities. Sometimes a child could be put to death at the order of the father with no reason being given.

EQUALITY AND THE JUDAEO-CHRISTIAN TRADITION

Into this environment came the Judaeo-Christian tradition with its deep spiritual contributions. The founder of Christianity, Jesus Christ, taught that all people were neighbors. He preached the equality of humankind. After Jesus' death, St. Paul continued this teaching when he wrote that all persons —slaves, women, children, and free men—were equal in the eyes of God. This was a revolutionary statement. How could society continue to treat various groups of people differently if all were born equal? This question was an important first step toward the idea that everyone must receive equality before the law.

When the Christian Church became powerful in Europe, it used its influence to raise the social level of women and children and to improve conditions among slaves. Later, through Christian influence, slavery was abolished in most parts of Europe. This was not done overnight. It took centuries. But the goals were there to be attained in the future.

During the Middle Ages many cornerstones of the American governmental system were set in place. The Magna Carta of 1215, for example, forecast many future liberties. This charter, while not very meaningful in its own day, was a symbol of political rights the English would demand in later centuries. Forced from King John by the nobles and clergy of England, it contains within it the germs of such ideas as:

- The right to be judged by one's peers (equals);
- Protection from unjust imprisonment;
- Protection against delays in bringing a person to trial.

During the same era, men like Thomas Aquinas were writing that rulers had an obligation to govern their subjects justly and that if they did not, the people had the right to revolt. In later centuries other philosophers elaborated on this topic, creating a great amount of literature on the rights and duties of people and their governments.

In the seventeenth and eighteenth centuries, when the English were colonizing North America, the dominant form of government in Europe was monarchy. In many cases these monarchies ruled only for the benefit of the few. Moreover, the kings made up their own rules as they went along, some good, some bad. Things were fine when the ruler was well intentioned and capable, but such was not often the case. Sometimes the worst tyrannies existed under well-meaning monarchs who somehow did all the wrong things.

THE POLITICAL PHILOSOPHERS

The idea that people could best govern themselves, instead of letting kings govern alone, took hold among some thinkers in England and France. John Locke, an English doctor turned political theorist, wrote his *Treatises on Government* with this end in view. He upheld the rights to life, liberty, and property for all. His influence on Thomas Jefferson and on other Americans was very great, even though he died almost three quarters of a century before the American Revolution occurred.

Charles de Secondat, a Frenchman who was usually called Baron Montesquieu, contributed his *Spirit of the Laws.* In this work he examined the political systems of several nations and tried to uncover the best qualities of each. The British system attracted him because of its checks and balances; that is, power was not concentrated in one branch of government but was dispersed among three—the legislative, executive, and judicial branches. These were fairly equal partners in the business of government and each, by maintaining its independence, acted as a check on the others to keep them from growing too strong.

Another Frenchman, Jean Jacques Rousseau, had an enormous influence on thought in his own time and also for many years after his death. He resented the controls which royal governments exercised over most of humankind and devoted his life to demanding that power be returned to the people. In his work, *The Social Contract,* Rousseau claimed

that people had once been their own masters but had entered into a kind of agreement with their neighbors for protection. The governments founded at this distant time had eventually come under the control of tyrants. By the eighteenth century, when Rousseau lived, all the gains people had made by uniting in society were outweighed by their loss of liberty. Therefore, Rousseau preached the overthrow of monarchies, which made life very difficult for him at the time.

Locke, Montesquieu, Rousseau, and other thinkers were not noted for doing anything especially important. They were not rulers or generals or anything like that. We honor them for what they thought and wrote, for their courage in doing this, and for the fact that their ideas guided those Americans courageous enough to make a new government for our country.

SELF-GOVERNMENT AND THE AMERICAN COLONISTS

But thinking and writing are not enough to guarantee good government. What is needed is the ability to apply these good theories to practical governing situations. In short, no amount of theorizing can substitute for actual experience. The American colonists acquired this experience by being forced to solve

An exact replica of the colonial Capitol at Williamsburg, Virginia, showing how the Capitol looked in the early 1700s. The House of Burgesses, America's first legislative assembly, met here.

Colonial Williamsburg

problems on their own. Since it took months to get an answer from Parliament on any given question, the colonists came to rely on their own elected officials for many of their decisions. As a result, by the time our country went to war with Britain to gain its independence, it had a reservoir of talented legislators, judges, and other experienced officials to draw on for leadership. These men had learned the craft of governing in thirteen of the toughest schools for experience in the world—the thirteen colonies.

Self-government, that right which Americans consider basic to achieving full freedom, had been part of colonial experience to a greater or lesser extent during the more than 150 years since the country was first settled. The General Assembly of Virginia had begun operations in 1619, giving some Virginians the opportunity to participate in governing themselves. In 1620, the Pilgrims drew up their Mayflower Compact, binding themselves to abide by the will of the majority.

Thus, the English settlers began to seek self-government almost before they had a toehold on the continent. This process included the establishment of local governing bodies, such as town meetings, and assemblies with broader responsibilities, such as the legislatures which all the colonies eventually had. Some of the colonies had charters granted by the king to individuals or to semi-private companies. These charters defined the boundaries and laid down other regulations such as guarantees of religious freedom.

All through the colonial period in American history—from 1607 to 1776—the settlers in America enjoyed varying degrees of self-government. Thus, by the time we declared for independence, much of our population was fairly well prepared to embark on the difficult task of self-government.

The question may arise, "Isn't everyone prepared for self-government?" The answer is a resounding "No!" At the time of the Revolution there were people in America who thought that freedom meant they would not have to pay their bills. Not everyone was, or is, prepared for self-government. Obviously, to make intelligent decisions about candidates and public issues, a citizen must be capable of reading about them. Education, therefore, is perhaps the most important key to self-government.

THE COLONIES REBEL

The issue of self-government was central to the American Revolution, as you can see by reading the Declaration of Independence at the end of this book. The king was condemned for closing or harassing colonial legislatures, for preventing justice from being carried out, and for other acts of political persecution.

Taxation by Parliament was another issue which caused discontent in the colonies, particularly when the hated taxes were combined with reminders from Parliament that it was supreme in all legislative matters. The colonists replied to these assertions by using a slogan often employed by a New Englander named James Otis: "Taxation without representation is tyranny." This statement referred to the fact that the colonies, which were unrepresented in Parliament, had no chance to speak out against laws affecting them. British

Yale University Art Gallery

A painting by the American artist, John Trumbull, (1756–1843), entitled *Battle of Bunker's Hill.* The Bunker Hill battle, which actually was fought on Breed's Hill, took place near Boston in June 1775, more than a year before the Declaration of Independence. Although the Americans eventually had to retreat, they succeeded in killing more than a thousand crack British troops. Since the American losses were about four hundred killed, the battle has always been considered a major American victory.

spokesmen answered by stating that the colonies had "virtual representation" in Parliament. A member of Parliament did not represent only the district he came from, they argued. He represented everyone in the empire. The Americans were not satisfied with this answer; they preferred "actual representation," whereby a delegate spoke directly for them in the legislature.

The colonists very shortly went beyond mere protest. They resented the taxes they were subjected to, and they were equally irritated by the presence of British troops among them. These troops had to be fed and quartered (housed), an expensive and annoying obligation. Incidents between soldiers and colonists occurred in New York and in Boston. The British policy on the tea trade brought forth reprisals from colonists in

Yale University Art Gallery

John Trumbull's famous painting, *The Declaration of Independence*, shows the committee appointed to prepare the Declaration—Benjamin Franklin, Thomas Jefferson, Roger Sherman, Robert R. Livingston, and John Adams—submitting the document to the Continental Congress. Actually, Jefferson alone turned the document over to Congress, but Trumbull's painting catches the solemn drama of the Declaration.

Boston, New York, and Philadelphia. Soon one string of events led to another. British measures brought American reprisals and this led in turn to British retaliation.

These incidents point to the fact that, during the 1770s, we were an "emerging nation." We have seen the pattern frequently in our own time in Asia and Africa. The native population feels capable of taking over functions once performed by non-natives. Native leaders agitate for independence. Violence often occurs, and is sometimes a prelude to revolutionary war.

In a very special sense, Americans can feel justly proud when a new nation in Africa or Asia earns its independence in this manner, for we pointed the way some two centuries ago. And the new nation has one great advantage we did not possess

Library of Congress

The great Seal of the United States, first adopted by the Continental Congress, later became the official symbol of the new federal government. The American eagle shows self-reliance, the thirteen stripes represent the original colonies, and the olive branch and arrows symbolize peace and war.

—the success of our form of government upon which to pattern its own. A new republic in today's world is in good company, with dozens of older, more experienced governments to draw strength and wisdom from.

When the United States gained its independence in 1783, it was an island of republicanism in a hostile sea of monarchy. Even its most ardent friends feared for its future. But it is not accurate to speak of the United States in 1783 as an island. It was more like thirteen sovereign islands, divided by rivers of discord that threatened to wash away the bridges of unity which common sacrifices in the war for independence had built.

THE ARTICLES OF CONFEDERATION

During the 1780s the states were held together by the Articles of Confederation and Perpetual Union, which were adopted in 1781. The government established under the Articles had many defects, the most important of which were:

- It could not force the states to contribute to the support of the central government; instead, it could only ask them and hope for the best;
- Each state had one vote, regardless of population;
- Nine of the thirteen states, instead of only a majority, had to approve legislation;
- All thirteen states had to give their approval to amendments radically changing the Articles;
- There was no federal court system. Congress passed the laws and the thirteen state courts interpreted them;
- Congress could not regulate commerce, and as a result the states competed with each other instead of cooperating.

These defects were very serious and, as you probably know, were remedied when the next government of the United States was devised.

In spite of these shortcomings, however, many people in America were satisfied with the government under the Articles. These people felt that the states themselves could take care of internal affairs, while the central government would act when all were affected by some external matter such as a war or a treaty. They did not think of the central government as ruling them so much as representing the individual states in solving problems too big for one state to handle.

For a while the system worked. Under the Articles, the states accomplished a number of worthwhile things. There was the problem of the western lands, for instance. Should these lands, mostly in the Ohio Valley, be treated as colonies of the states? "No," said the states through their central government. The newer lands should be divided into territories which eventually would be eligible for admission to the Union as sovereign states equal to their older sisters on the Atlantic coast.

Through their Congress, the thirteen independent states were thus like a thoughtful and optimistic parent who, with

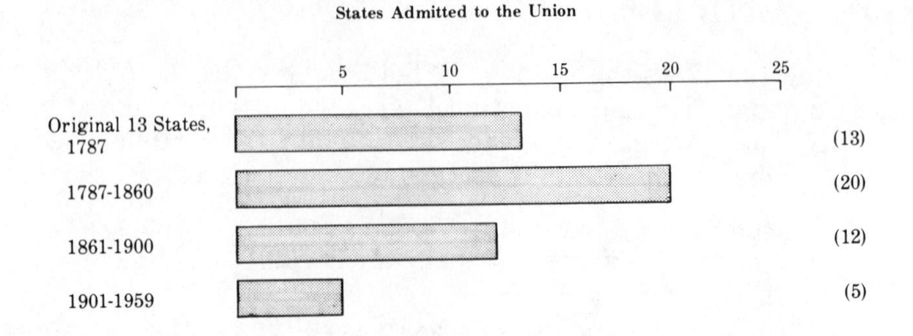

only one or two children, still built a large house with many rooms. As children were added to the family there was space enough for all of them. The United States has expanded from a small Atlantic coast cottage of thirteen rooms to a fifty-room mansion including, in Hawaii and Alaska, patios for summer and winter sports.

The key word to the understanding of this chapter is maturity. Although the government of the United States was young, American society itself was rich in the maturity which came from the traditions of the Western world—from the Greek, Roman, Judaeo-Christian, and British heritages. Added to this was the experience in self-government which the former colonies possessed. The traditions and the experience gave Americans the background necessary to produce a lasting government.

AFTER-CHAPTER REVIEW

REVIEW QUESTIONS

1. Define the following names, terms, or ideas in a few lines. If you do this consistently, chapter by chapter, you will soon build up a glossary of terms most often used in American government. At your teacher's instruction, keep these terms in a special section of your notebook.

monarchy	oligarchy	Mayflower Compact
democracy	Aristotle	Montesquieu
Rousseau	Locke	*res publica*
Magna Carta	aristocracy	

2. Vocabulary building. Throughout the course of this book, you will meet words which belong in the vocabulary of every educated person. You will no doubt know many of these from seeing them elsewhere, but they are offered to refresh your memory.

   Middle Ages   peer   quartering   "emerging nation"

3. Review of the text.
   a. What defects existed in ancient society which are not present in most societies today?
   b. Make a list of the main contributions of Greece and Rome to the origins of American government.
   c. What did the Judaeo-Christian culture add to the social and political life of human beings?
   d. What were the main issues which brought about the American Revolution?
   e. Name and explain the major problems confronting the new republic.
   f. List and discuss the defects of the government of the United States under the Articles of Confederation.
   g. Describe the main accomplishments of the United States under the Articles of Confederation.

DISCUSSION AND PROJECTS

1. Questions for discussion.
   a. Our system of self-government is often slow and inefficient. Should it be replaced by a streamlined dictatorship?
   b. How does life in America differ from life under a dictatorship?

c. Which side would you have been on during the events leading up to the Revolution: the tea parties, demonstrations, etc.?
d. Suppose the American Revolution had failed. What would the world be like today?

2. Debate topics.
   a. Resolved: The United States was not justified in declaring its independence.
   b. Resolved: The United States should have retained the Articles of Confederation.

3. Opinion polls. In this section, it is suggested that you take a poll of people on a variety of issues. If each member of the class asks the same question of five to ten different members of the community, a sample of opinion of your region's thinking may be gained. The first question might be:

   Do you think the American system of government will still exist one hundred year from now?

   Yes   No   No opinion

BIBLIOGRAPHY

Aikman, Lonnelle. "Women of the Revolution: Patriots in Petticoats," *National Geographic,* October 1975.

Archer, Jules. *They Made a Revolution.* New York: St. Martin's Press, 1973.

Becker, Carl. *The Declaration of Independence.* New York: Alfred A. Knopf, 1972.

Bridenbaugh, Carl. *The Spirit of '76.* New York: Oxford University Press, 1975.

Daugherty, James. *The Magna Carta.* New York: Random House, 1956.

Edwards, Mike W., and Bartlett, Linda. "Thomas Jefferson: Architect of Freedom," *National Geographic*, February 1976.

Goldston, Robert. *The American Wars of National Liberation.* New York: E. P. Dutton, 1976.

Hall, Alice J. "Benjamin Franklin: Philosopher of Dissent," *National Geographic*, July 1975.

LeFay, Howard, and Spiegel, Ted. "George Washington: The Man behind the Myth," *National Geographic*, July 1976.

Morison, Samuel Eliot. *The Oxford History of the American People.* New York: Oxford University Press, 1965. Chapters I, IV, V, VI, and XIV.

Morris, Richard B. *The Emerging Nations and the American Revolution.* New York: Harper & Row, 1970.

Michal Heron from Monkmeyer

Independence Hall, in Philadelphia. It was designed in the early 1700s by John Keorsley and Andrew Hamilton, neither of whom were architects. This red-brick building (its wooden tower was added in 1828) is intimately connected with the founding of our nation. Here the Continental Congress chose George Washington to be commander-in-chief in 1775. Here the Declaration of Independence was signed in 1776. And here the Constitution was drawn up in 1787.

2

The Constitution

In spite of the many accomplishments of the states acting individually and in unison during the 1780s, there was still much discontent over the disunity and the jealous rivalries among some of them. One big problem was commerce. Each state had its own policies toward trade and not only levied tariffs on goods imported from foreign nations but also on goods coming in from other American states. At the same time, the Confederation government was unable to raise money by placing a tariff on imported goods because the states would not unanimously approve an amendment to that effect.

In an effort to settle some navigation problems, delegates from Virginia and Maryland held the Mt. Vernon Conference at General Washington's estate in 1785. After the meeting James Madison of Virginia persuaded his state's legislature to invite delegates from all states to attend a commercial conference.

Thus, the Annapolis Convention was called and nine states agreed to send representatives. When the meeting was held in 1786, however, only five states were represented—New York, New Jersey, Delaware, Pennsylvania, and Virginia. The convention seemed doomed to failure until New York's delegate, Alexander Hamilton, called for still another meeting the following year to discuss not only commercial problems but also all other issues troubling the new nation. This last conference was the Philadelphia or Federal Convention which drafted the Constitution under which we are governed today.

The primary purposes of the Philadelphia Convention were to find means of revising the Articles of Confederation

Free Library of Philadelphia

BENJAMIN FRANKLIN GEORGE WASHINGTON

and to present these to the Confederation Congress and the state legislatures. In other words, the delegates were to be a kind of advisory committee to solve some of the problems of the country under the Articles.

It did not work out this way, of course. Instead of coming up with a few spare parts to make the old machine work, the nation's founders scrapped it and built an entirely new model.

THE NATION'S FOUNDERS

In May of 1787, delegates from the states met at Philadelphia to undertake the task. There were fifty-five of these "Founding Fathers," as they would come to be called, although not all of them were in attendance at all times. They were well-educated men, most of them having gone to college. A large number were lawyers, some had been teachers, and more than half had served as lawmakers in state legislatures or the Confederation Congress. More than fifteen percent of the delegates were foreign-born.

For "fathers" they were quite young. Ten percent of them were under thirty years of age, and their average age was a little over forty. The two greatest leaders, Alexander Hamilton and James Madison, were in their thirties. George Washington, at fifty-five, was one of the few older members, while Benjamin Franklin topped the list with his eighty-one years of wisdom, experience, and service to humanity.

Library of Congress

JAMES MADISON ALEXANDER HAMILTON

Americans can be proud of the distinguished group which drew up their Constitution. Many of them were men already widely known throughout the world. George Washington, without whose support the whole project might have failed, was the best-known freedom fighter in the eighteenth century. He was chosen to preside over the convention, and his calm perseverance and awe-inspiring presence kept the members hard at work. Benjamin Franklin was famous for his accomplishments in Europe and in America. His diplomatic ability had helped draw France into the Revolutionary War, which guaranteed our independence. His shrewd bargaining had helped to make the Treaty of Paris a triumph for the new republic in 1783.

While Washington and Franklin lent their reputations and their advice to the convention, Hamilton and Madison gave their brilliant and logical minds to the practical tasks ahead. Hamilton, who represented New York, had an enviable military career as a fighting soldier and as Washington's aide. Born in the West Indies, he had no special attachment to any one of the states. Instead, he saw the United States as one country and lamented the divisions which he thought prevented it from achieving greatness. Hamilton was not fond of democracy; he feared that a government run by the people might too easily fall into the hands of smooth-talking popular leaders who would use power for their own selfish purposes. Therefore, throughout the course of the convention, Hamilton stressed the need for keeping control in the hands of the better-educated classes.

James Madison, a scholarly Virginian with considerable experience in government, took such a keen interest in the convention that he has been called the "Father of the Constitution." The notes Madison took on the proceedings at Philadelphia have become our most important source of knowledge of what went on there. Like Hamilton, Madison was determined to create a government which balanced the interests of liberty and order.

Other delegates to the convention were equally well qualified. John Dickinson had drawn up the Articles of Confederation. Robert Morris had ingeniously managed the country's finances during the Revolution. Roger Sherman, Edmund Randolph, Elbridge Gerry, and William Paterson were also able and dedicated men.

THE DELEGATES' ATTITUDES TOWARD GOVERNMENT

For years, historians have tried to discover the motives behind the actions of the nation's founders. For example, what were their ideas on democracy? Did they want a government which *protected* everyone or one which *represented* everyone? Did they draft the Constitution to protect the interests of wealthier people? Did they want a powerful judiciary? These questions can never be completely answered, since the records of their ideas are sketchy.

We do know, however, that many delegates distrusted popular government. They felt that ordinary people were incapable of governing themselves wisely. A government based on the popular will would be very unstable, they thought, since it would be ruled by those best able to manipulate the lowest classes. To prevent this, the nation's founders provided for the indirect election of the President and the Senate, kept the judiciary out of popular hands, and made the amending process quite difficult. Only the House of Representatives could be called a popularly elected body. The delegates may have been right for their day, since popular control in such states as Rhode Island had not been a very satisfactory method of government.

Virginia State Library

EDMUND RANDOLPH WILLIAM PATERSON

Because many delegates were wealthy or were allied with the wealthier people in America, some critics have charged that the Constitution was designed to a large extent to protect the economic interests of the delegates and their class. This charge has never been adequately proved, since the critics overlooked the fact that in protecting their own property the delegates were also protecting the goods and lands of the less wealthy.

Thus it has been said that the nation's founders did not believe in complete democracy and that they tried to protect property rights. Whether or not these are serious criticisms depends on your knowledge of conditions in the eighteenth century when the Constitution was drawn up. It is true that our Constitution did not provide complete democratic rule, but compared with other countries of the Western world the United States was very radical in its emphasis on popular government. And if the delegates were interested in protecting private economic interests, we should remember that later on this worked to the advantage of the people by providing them with a financially stable government.

"A BUNDLE OF COMPROMISES"

Whatever else may be said of the delegates to the Philadelphia Convention, we can be sure of one thing: they were practical men who knew how to reach agreement by compromise. In fact, the Constitution has been called a "bundle of compromises." Sometimes the delegates debated various proposals for weeks until they reached agreement. When the Constitution was finished, many of the delegates thought that it was a weak and pale document which would not have the strength to stand for very long.

Of the many decisions they made, we will study the four which follow:

1. The decision to draw up a new Constitution;
2. The Connecticut Compromise;
3. The Three-fifths Compromise;
4. The Commerce Compromise.

When the delegates decided to ignore their original instructions merely to revise the Articles of Confederation, they took the first step in forming "a more perfect union," the goal they stated in the Preamble to the Constitution. They also decided to be guided by their consciences and, when they were finished, to let the people judge whether or not they had acted rightly. Their wisdom in this decision has been proven by the durability of the Constitution.

Before the convention was very old, Edmund Randolph of Virginia proposed the Virginia plan, a long series of suggestions offered by the Virginia delegation for consideration by the entire convention. The plan called for a bicameral (two-house) Congress, strong judicial and executive departments, and the recognition of the national government as more powerful than any individual state government.

This was quite a departure from the Articles of Confederation, and many delegates heartily approved of it. There were, however, disagreements over some of its parts. The Virginia plan would give great power to the larger states, for example, since representation in the proposed Congress would be based on state population. Delegates from smaller states were perturbed by this and soon offered a proposal different from the Virginia or "large-states" plan. This proposal was set forth by William Paterson and became known as the New Jersey or "small-states" plan. This plan brought the convention back much closer to the form of government under the Articles. There would be a unicameral (one-house) legislature, for instance, in which all states would be equally represented.

Debate on these plans continued until the Connecticut Compromise was reached. This called for a bicameral legislature, with representation based on population in one house and equal representation for all the states in the other. This is the system that was finally adopted. Thus in the Senate all states have two votes, while in the House of Representatives some states have dozens of votes and others have only a few.

The Connecticut Compromise, therefore, had the effect of bringing together the best parts of the Virginia and New Jersey plans. It helped to satisfy those who wanted a strong central government and at the same time it did not alienate those who tried to maintain the rights of the states.

Another source of friction among the delegates was smoothed over by the Three-fifths Compromise. Some of the states with large slave populations wished to have their slaves counted as persons in order to increase the number of representatives they would have in Congress. However, if Congress levied taxes on these states, the slaves would then have to be included as persons for this purpose, too. This was not satisfactory, so the delegates adopted an old formula whereby five slaves would be equal to three free persons for purposes of representation and taxation. This was not a very scientific solution, but it was practical and prevented quarrels between the free and slave-holding sections of the country.

Another debate between these two sections also ended in compromise. The northern section of the country was anxious to grant the national Congress power over commerce in order to avoid some of the difficulties experienced by commercial areas under the Articles. The southern states feared that this power might be used to discriminate against their trade in slaves or agricultural goods. The compromise over commerce and slavery provided Congress with the power to tax imports and to regulate commerce. However, Congress did not have the power to tax exports, nor could it interfere with the slave trade until 1807, another twenty years.

THE CONSTITUTION TAKES SHAPE

Day after day, week after week, in the spring and summer of 1787 the convention proposed, debated, voted, and amended. It worked in secrecy, in the belief that the deliberations would go more smoothly that way.

Slowly, after much deliberation, the surprisingly short document took shape, based on the experience and knowledge of the delegates. Every word they used counted for something. Everything had significance, every line could be traced back to some incident in history or to some practical principle which the delegates knew would work.

They insisted, for example, that a judge's salary could not be reduced during his term in office. The purpose of this was to free judges from fear of financial revenge by legislatures angry over their decisions. They permitted the President to adjourn Congress on only one occasion, when the two branches of the legislature could not agree on a time for adjournment. Although this clause seems to give the President power, in reality it limits him, since the nation's founders wanted a chief executive who could not dissolve Congress every time he felt like it as England's kings had done in the past with Parliament. The delegates forbade Congressmen to hold other offices while serving as legislators, in order to prevent conflicts of loyalty.

All in all, the Constitution is a carefully drawn legal document, providing the framework by which that delicate balance between order and liberty can be maintained. It is little wonder that so many people have praised it so highly. An English scholar has testified that it "ranks above every other written constitution," while an English statesman has called it "the most wonderful work ever struck off at a given time by the brain and purpose of man." But perhaps it is best summed up in the words of an American as "the work of plain, honest men."

On September 17, 1787, a day now designated as Constitution Day, most of the delegates signed the Constitution. Not many of them were of the opinion that their work would endure for the greater part of two centuries, but it was their best effort. Some of those who did not sign included Edmund Randolph, who had proposed the Virginia plan, and Elbridge Gerry, who later became Vice-President of the United States.

Having ignored their original instruction simply to revise the Articles, the delegates went one step further and provided for the adoption of the new Constitution when only nine states

Order of ratification of the Constitution of the U.S.

			For	Against
1	Delaware	Dec. 7, 1787	Unanimous	
2	Pennsylvania	Dec. 12, 1787	46	23
3	New Jersey	Dec. 18, 1787	Unanimous	
4	Georgia	Jan. 2, 1788	Unanimous	
5	Connecticut	Jan. 9, 1788	128	40
6	Massachusetts	Feb. 6, 1788	187	168
7	Maryland	Apr. 28, 1788	63	11
8	South Carolina	May 23, 1788	149	73
9	New Hampshire	June 21, 1788	57	46
10	Virginia	June 26, 1788	89	79
11	New York	July 26, 1788	30	27
12	North Carolina	Nov. 21, 1789	184	77
13	Rhode Island	May 29, 1790	34	32
14	Vermont	Mar. 4, 1791	105	4

ratified it, rather than after approval from all the states (as provided under the Articles).

RATIFICATION AND THE BILL OF RIGHTS

It was not easy to secure the support of even nine states, however. The country was badly split and, as should be the case in a free country, debate was loud, long, and boisterous. Farmers, storekeepers, and plantation owners voiced their opinions for and against ratification. Sometimes approval was unanimous, as in the case of Delaware, New Jersey, and Georgia. At other times it was quite close: Massachusetts ratified by a vote of 187 to 168, New York by 30 to 27, and Rhode Island by 34 to 32. The last two states were quite reluctant to ratify at first. New York was crucial, of course, because of its geographical and financial position. Among the factors influencing the slim favorable vote were *The Federalist Papers*, eighty-five documents written by Alexander Hamilton, James Madison, and John Jay to explain the Constitution.

Many voters throughout the country favored the Constitution but were worried about the lack of protection it gave to

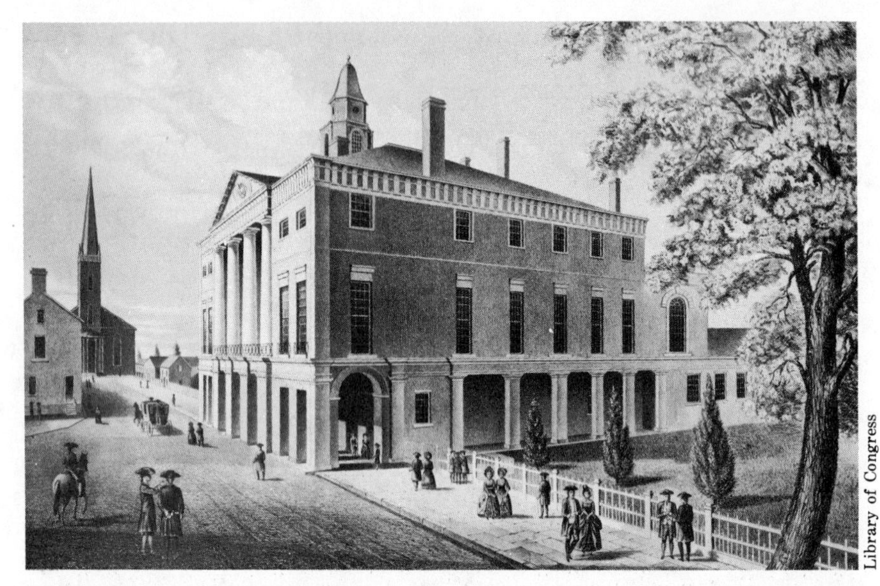

Library of Congress

Federal Hall, in New York City, as it looked in 1789. This building, on the corner of Wall and Nassau Streets, was originally the City Hall of New York. It was for a brief time the Capitol building of the new nation. George Washington was inaugurated on the balcony of this building as the nation's first President on April 30, 1789, and the first Congress of the United States convened here. In August of 1790, however, Philadelphia became the capital of the United States.

personal liberties. They wanted a bill of rights guaranteeing the individual against tyranny by the new government. Others pointed out that this was unnecessary because:

- The state constitutions had bills of rights already attached to them which would protect citizens;
- The Constitution provided for trial by jury, and forbade *ex post facto* laws (passing laws to make an act a crime after it was committed instead of before) and bills of attainder (judging a person guilty of a crime by a vote of a legislature instead of by a trial based on evidence).

But these protections were not enough for the holdouts, so some state conventions requested that the new Congress begin action on a bill of rights as soon as it met. This was done during the first session of Congress. By 1790, ten amendments had been approved, becoming what we call the Bill of Rights.

It may seem strange to you that there should have been any disagreement over whether or not the federal Constitution should protect individual liberties. Today a close relationship exists between the federal government and the citizen, but this was not the case in the eighteenth century. Instead, individual citizens were much more closely connected with their state governments. An example of this can be found in taxation. Before the Sixteenth Amendment to the Constitution was passed in 1913, Congress levied taxes for its support upon the states, which in turn collected them from the citizens. If people failed to pay these taxes or cheated in paying them, the state government would prosecute the offenders and the state constitution would protect their rights. Now the Sixteenth Amendment gives the federal government the power to tax the people directly, and to prosecute those who fail to pay. So the guarantees found in the federal Bill of Rights have become more important as the federal government has assumed more importance in our lives.

As a result of the action of 1790, a citizen had two bills of rights—one attached to the federal Constitution and another as part of the state constitution. What purposes did these serve?

At first it was thought that the federal bill would protect citizens when dealing with the federal government and that the state bill would protect them from their state governments. But what if a state ignored its bill of rights? Could the injured person seek protection under the federal Bill of Rights? "No," said the Supreme Court in 1833 in a lawsuit called *Barron* v. *Baltimore*. In this suit, a Baltimore man named Barron tried to collect several thousand dollars from his city for damages it had caused his business. The Maryland courts ruled against Mr. Barron so he went to the federal courts, claiming that the federal Bill of Rights protected him from injury by the state. The Supreme Court of the United States, under Chief Justice John Marshall, ruled that the federal Bill of Rights only protected an individual from injury by the federal government, not from state injury.

This decision has gradually been changed over a number of years as the federal government has become more active in the lives of the American people. In 1925, in the case of *Gitlow* v. *New York*, the Supreme Court ruled that part of the First

Amendment protected citizens from both state and federal injury. In the years since then, more and more parts of the federal Bill of Rights have been applied to the relationship between an individual and the state.

The reason for this change can be found in the Fourteenth Amendment, adopted in 1868, which forbids any state to "abridge the privileges or immunities of citizens" or to "deprive any person of life, liberty or property, without due process of law; nor deny to any person . . . the equal protection of the laws." These statements have been interpreted by the Supreme Court as giving it the power to protect a citizen of a state from state interference with his or her liberties.

PROTECTIONS FOR LIFE, LIBERTY, AND PROPERTY

What are the rights guaranteed by the Bill of Rights? These will be discussed more fully in later chapters, but for now a partial list will show you how extensive they are:

- The right to worship free from governmental interference;
- The right to freedom of speech and freedom of the press so long as these freedoms are not used to cause injury to others;
- The right to assemble so long as it is done peacefully;
- The right to petition the government to correct wrongs;
- The right to be safe in one's own home from unreasonable interference by government officials;
- Protection against being tried twice for the same crime;
- The right to refuse to testify against oneself in court;
- The government may not seize a person's property unless there is a good reason for it and then must pay a just price;
- A person accused of a crime has the right to a speedy and public trial;
- Cruel and unusual punishments may not be inflicted upon a person.

All persons in the United States enjoy many more rights, and these as well as the above will be explored later on. At this point, however, you should know that these rights are yours and will remain yours on two conditions:

1. That you recognize that every right you have carries with it a corresponding duty. Your right to freedom of speech, for example, obliges you to use restraint when you speak. You are not free to slander another person, which is to speak lies about that person. Your right to say what you think in writing is another example. This right does not give you permission to libel another person, which is to write lies about that person.
2. That you be willing to make sacrifices to protect the rights of others as well as your own. A famous Supreme Court justice, Oliver Wendell Holmes, once remarked that the true test of our belief in freedom to think as we please is whether we recognize not only freedom of thought for those we agree with but also "freedom for the thought we hate."

Although devised in 1787, the Constitution still governs the American people today. This alone should be proof of the wisdom of the nation's founders. They were moderate men, accustomed to working with others and to compromising rather than insisting on one way of doing things. Their work in producing the "bundle of compromises" we call the Constitution illustrates many truths about American society, but perhaps the most important of these is that cooperation gets better results than dictatorship does.

AFTER-CHAPTER REVIEW

REVIEW QUESTIONS

1. Define the following names, terms, or ideas.

Mt. Vernon Conference	Commerce Compromise
Annapolis Convention	Constitution Day
Virginia and New Jersey plans	*The Federalist Papers*
Connecticut Compromise	*ex post facto*
Three-fifths Compromise	bill of attainder

2. Vocabulary building.

bicameral   unicameral   libel   slander

3. Cases. Describe briefly the following cases by telling the circumstances surrounding them, the legal principles involved, and their overall significance to American government.

   Barron v. *Baltimore* *Gitlow* v. *New York*

4. Review of the text.
   a. Describe the parts played by Madison and Hamilton in the making of the Constitution.
   b. What were the qualifications and other characteristics of the nation's founders?
   c. What were the pitfalls which the members of the Philadelphia Convention tried to avoid?
   d. Discuss the following statement: The Constitution is a bundle of compromises.
   e. Discuss the ratification of the Constitution. How enthusiastic were the states about it?
   f. What were the major objections raised to the Constitution during the struggle for ratification?
   g. What was the relationship in 1790 between the federal government and the citizen which seemed to make a bill of rights unnecessary?

DISCUSSION AND PROJECTS

1. Questions for discussion.
   a. Did the delegates to the Philadelphia Convention exceed their authority unjustifiably in drafting a new constitution instead of modifying the old one?
   b. The Constitution was designed to provide a balance between liberty and order. How successful was this attempt?
   c. If you were drafting a Constitution for the United States today, what provisions would you add? Which would you delete?
   d. Discuss the significance of *Barron* v. *Baltimore* and *Gitlow* v. *New York* in the light of the Fourteenth Amendment.

2. Debate topics.
   a. Resolved: The nation's founders drew up the Constitution to protect their property and not to provide democratic government for all.
   b. Resolved: The American Constitution became the model for future constitutions as other nations came into being after the United States won its independence.
3. Opinion poll. Secure opinions on the following question:

   Is the American Constitution out of date?

BIBLIOGRAPHY

Corwin, Edward S.; Chase, Howard W.; and Ducat, Craig R. *The Constitution.* Princeton, N.J.: Princeton University Press, 1974.

Donovan, Frank. *Mr. Madison's Constitution.* New York: Dodd, Mead, 1965.

Hayman, Leroy. *What You Should Know about the U.S. Constitution and the Men Who Wrote It.* New York: Four Winds Press, 1968.

Jensen, Merrill. *The Making of the American Constitution.* Princeton, N.J.: Van Nostrand Reinhold, 1964.

McLaughlin, Andrew C. *The Confederation and the Constitution.* New York: Macmillan, Collier Books, 1965.

Morison, Samuel Eliot. *The Oxford History of the American People.* New York: Oxford University Press, 1965. Chapters XVIII and XX.

Peltason, J. W. *Understanding the Constitution.* Hinsdale, Ill.: Dryden Press, 1973.

Paul Conklin from Monkmeyer

Washington, D.C., with a view down Pennsylvania Avenue toward the Capitol. It is along this broad avenue that inaugural parades are held, since it connects the Capitol and the White House. Washington, D.C., was the nation's first planned city. In 1791, the French architect Pierre Charles L'Enfant drew up plans that included broad avenues like Pennsylvania branching out from the Capitol, many parks, magnificent vistas, and a checkerboard pattern of cross streets. The spacious and farsighted design of the Capitol may be considered a symbol of the American political system.

3

Ideas About American Government

The government of the United States is based upon certain principles and practices which you should know to understand it better. The principles are the rules upon which most people agree; the practices are the ways in which these principles are put into operation. In this chapter, you will study these principles and practices, which will be explained and illustrated by examples when possible. In addition, the chapter will conclude with a section on the trends or characteristics which can be found in American government today to distinguish it from our government in the past century.

Among the many principles underlying our government, let us look at the following:

- Federalism, or the division of powers;
- Checks and balances, or the separation of powers;
- Popular sovereignty and equality under the law;
- The principle of flexibility.

THE FEDERAL SYSTEM

Federalism is a term used to denote a system of government in which sovereignty (governing power) is shared between a federal government and a collection of states. Thus in America the terms "federalism" and "federal system" apply to fifty-one governments, not just to the one in Washington, D.C. We use the term "federal government," however, to denote the central or national government in Washington.

The federal system is not the only form a democratic republic can take. A democratic republic such as ours could have a "confederation" form. You will recall that we once did, under the Articles of Confederation: each state was supreme and gave to the central government what authority it thought might be needed. When the American people ratified the Constitution, they agreed to discard the confederation principle and adopt federalism.

Another form of government which might have been adopted is the "unitary" form. Under this system, all power is vested in a single central government which then divides the country into sections and grants some authority to the sections. Each of our individual states has a unitary system of government. All the power that the state has rests in the state government, which in turn divides the state into counties and gives these the authority to carry out local functions.

There are many reasons why we did not adopt a unitary system instead of the federal system. When the Constitution was adopted, the states already existed and were quite powerful. They had no intention of voting themselves out of existence to establish a unitary system. Besides, a unitary system must have smaller divisions anyway, so why not use those already in existence? In addition, a unitary system places very great powers in the hands of one government, while the federal system spreads the power around. Although a unitary system may at times be more efficient, a federal form keeps the people in closer touch with their government.

One serious problem arises under the federal system, however, which is not found in the unitary or confederation forms. Under the latter systems we know exactly where all the power resides; that is, it is either in the central government or the state governments exclusively. But in the federal system of shared sovereignty, we are continually trying to determine which division has what powers.

In studying this problem, students of government have discovered that roughly three types of powers exist under federalism: concurrent, delegated, and reserved. Concurrent powers are those which, like the power to tax, are shared by the federal and state governments. Delegated powers refer to those powers, such as the power to make war, which belong exclusively to the federal government. These are called delegated powers because they are specifically stated in the Constitution (Article I, Section 8). Reserved powers are those over which the states have primary control. An example of a reserved power would be a state's power to license marriages and certain occupations. This setup of shared power is illustrated in the following diagram:

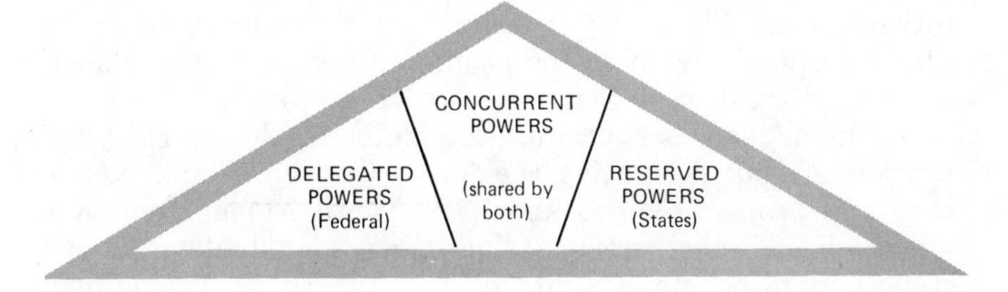

Remember that this diagram shows the theory of federalism. It does not always work out so neatly in practice. In fact, the history of the United States may be described as a struggle between the states and the federal government over the meaning of the Constitution about the extent of reserved and delegated powers.

When we turn to the Constitution itself, we find in Article I, Section 8, a listing of the delegated powers of the federal government. Some of these are quite specific: for example, the power to coin money, establish post offices, provide for an army and navy, and so on. But others are somewhat vague. For example: "Congress shall have Power to lay and collect Taxes, Duties, Imposts and Excises, to pay the Debts and provide for the common Defence and general Welfare of the United States. . . ." Now, how would you define "general welfare"? Would you say it was a broad power or a narrow power?

Again, if you look further into Article I, Section 8, you will find that it concludes with the clause: "To make all Laws which shall be necessary and proper for carrying into Execution the foregoing Powers." This "necessary and proper" clause is also called the "elastic clause" because it indicates that the specific powers of Congress may be stretched to cover necessary legislation not specifically provided for in the other powers.

Those who agree with a very loose interpretation of the term "necessary and proper" assert that it implies broad powers not specifically stated. Hence, this clause has created the "doctrine of implied powers." It would seem that the implied powers in the "general welfare" and "necessary and proper" clauses give Congress the right to do almost anything it wishes.

But when we turn to the Tenth Amendment, we read: "The powers not delegated to the United States by the Constitution, nor prohibited by it to the States, are reserved to the States respectively, or to the people." Judging by this clause, one would think that Congress is severely limited.

Which, then, is supreme—the nation or the states? Shall we be nationalists, placing the "general welfare" and "necessary and proper" clauses above the Tenth Amendment by a loose or broad construction of these terms? Or shall we adopt a states'-rights position by interpreting the Tenth Amendment to mean a strict or narrow limitation on the powers of Congress? The answer to this dilemma lies in the history of the United States which, you recall, is to a great extent the story of the struggle for power between the states and the federal government.

One of the first battles in this struggle, which is by no means over today, took place in the Supreme Court in the case of *McCulloch* v. *Maryland* in 1819. Here was a clear-cut case of the use of implied powers to justify an act of Congress.

Congress had chartered a national bank in 1816, and the state of Maryland placed a tax upon its transactions. The cashier of the bank, Mr. McCulloch, refused to pay the tax and Maryland sued for it. The case attracted wide interest in America. The bank was defended by Daniel Webster, the great American orator. The state's position was upheld by Luther Martin who, as a member of the Philadelphia Convention, had opposed the Constitution.

The Supreme Court, led by Chief Justice Marshall, ruled unanimously that Congress had the power to create a national bank. In its decision the Court wrote that even though the federal government was a limited one, "the Constitution must allow to the national legislature that discretion ... which will enable that body to perform the high duties assigned to it, in the manner most beneficial to the people." Here we see in the words "discretion" and "beneficial" a stretching of the Constitution by a broad interpretation of "necessary and proper" (discretion) and "general welfare" (beneficial).

Washington & Lee University, Lexington, Va.

John Marshall, the fourth chief justice of the Supreme Court.

The Court went on to deny Maryland the right to tax a federal agency on the basis "that the power to tax involves the power to destroy." Indeed, this power could have led to all sorts of mischief. The states might have taxed the mail, the courts, or anything else, and thereby paralyzed the federal government.

But the decision did not finally settle the question of whether or not the bank was constitutional. Some years later, when the bank applied for a renewal of its charter, President Andrew Jackson vetoed the bill which provided for this. He not only stated that he thought the bank was unconstitutional, but also that he had as much right to rule that it was not constitutional as the Court had to rule that it was. He believed that the Court should be respected not because it had power over Congress and the President but rather when and if its arguments were more convincing.

In his veto message President Jackson made two important points: first, when it came to an interpretation of the "necessary and proper" clause on the question of a bank, he

The Corcoran Gallery of Art

President Andrew Jackson's veto of the bank bill seemed to be not so much a personal act as an example of the spirit of opposition to monopoly and special privilege that was shared by many Americans—a spirit carried over from those colonists who had come from England.

supported the states'-rights position against the nationalist position; and second, he firmly believed that the three branches of the federal government were independent and that no one of them was superior to another.

Perhaps as significant as the problem caused by the conflict between states' rights and nationalist positions is the problem posed by the growth of urban areas in the United States. Since the 1920s, the United States has been an urban nation, meaning that the population has become concentrated in large urban centers. The largest of these are called SMSAs, or Standard Metropolitan Statistical Areas. These centers have spread across state boundaries and therefore do not fit easily into the neat federal pattern. City governments have serious problems which are not similar to those of state governments, yet state governments are responsible for the creation of cities under the authority of state constitutions. These problems of "natural" differences are aggravated by the different political structures which run state and city governments. Sometimes the differences arise out of differing political party control, and at other times out of different policies of members of the same party in the control of both governments. While there is a great deal of intergovernmental cooperation between city and state governments and between the national and city governments, there is also much rivalry for the tax dollars of citizens in these areas and much disagreement over how these dollars should be spent. Cities, in a sense, are the third partner in a dance written for two.

CHECKS AND BALANCES

We come now to the second great principle of American government, known as the checks and balances system or the separation of powers. The "plain, honest men" who drew up the Constitution were surprisingly suspicious in their outlook on human nature and government. They had high ideals, but they were not star-gazing innocents. They knew human nature had its faults and did their utmost to safeguard the people from those of evil intentions. To do this they separated the powers of the new government into legislative, executive, and judicial. As far as possible they tried to make sure that no single branch could control the others. However, they made the three branches *interdependent,* rather than independent of one another.

This system enables each branch to check the others to prevent abuse of power. No one branch may act without in some way securing the consent of the others. When Congress approves a bill, for example, it does not automatically become a law. Instead, it is sent to the President, who may do one of four things:

1. Sign it into law;
2. Leave it alone for ten days, after which it is automatically a law without his signature. This applies, however, only when Congress is in session for those ten days;
3. Leave it alone for ten days and, if Congress goes out of session before the ten days have elapsed, the bill "dies." This is called a "pocket" veto;

4. Veto it, returning it to Congress accompanied by a note explaining why he vetoed it. This is called a "message" veto and is required of the President under the Constitution.

If the President vetoes a bill, it is an example of the operation of the checks and balances system. Congress still has a word to say, however. It may vote again on the bill. If two-thirds of those present and voting approve, the bill becomes a law in spite of the veto. In this case the President has been checked by Congress.[1]

If Congress itself should abuse its power, there is a branch left to check it. The Supreme Court, by its power of judicial review, can declare part or all of an act of Congress unconstitutional. To prevent usurpation by the Supreme Court, the Constitution provides for the appointment of justices for life by the President, with the consent of the Senate.

The three branches of government were not intentionally designed to work at cross purposes with each other. They were designed primarily to insure the people against any form of tyranny. You will remember, from Chapter 1, Aristotle's remarks about tyranny. It does not matter whether a majority, a few, or only one tyrannizes; tyranny is tyranny. Thus, if fifty-one percent of the people agreed to persecute the other forty-nine percent in some way, it would be tyranny by majority. The checks and balances system safeguards against this by providing for staggered times of election for federal officials. The President has a four-year term, while a Representative serves for two years and a Senator for six. It is difficult, then for a majority of the people to capture the Presidency and Congress in a single election. In addition to this, Supreme Court justices serve for life on good behavior.

These and many other built-in safeguards protect the people from the abuse of power. The nation's founders wisely diffused power into interdependent branches instead of concentrating it into one agency, where it might be abused more easily.

---

1. The word *veto* comes from the Latin, meaning "I forbid." Since the President's veto is not absolute but only suspends action on the bill, it is called a "suspensive" veto.

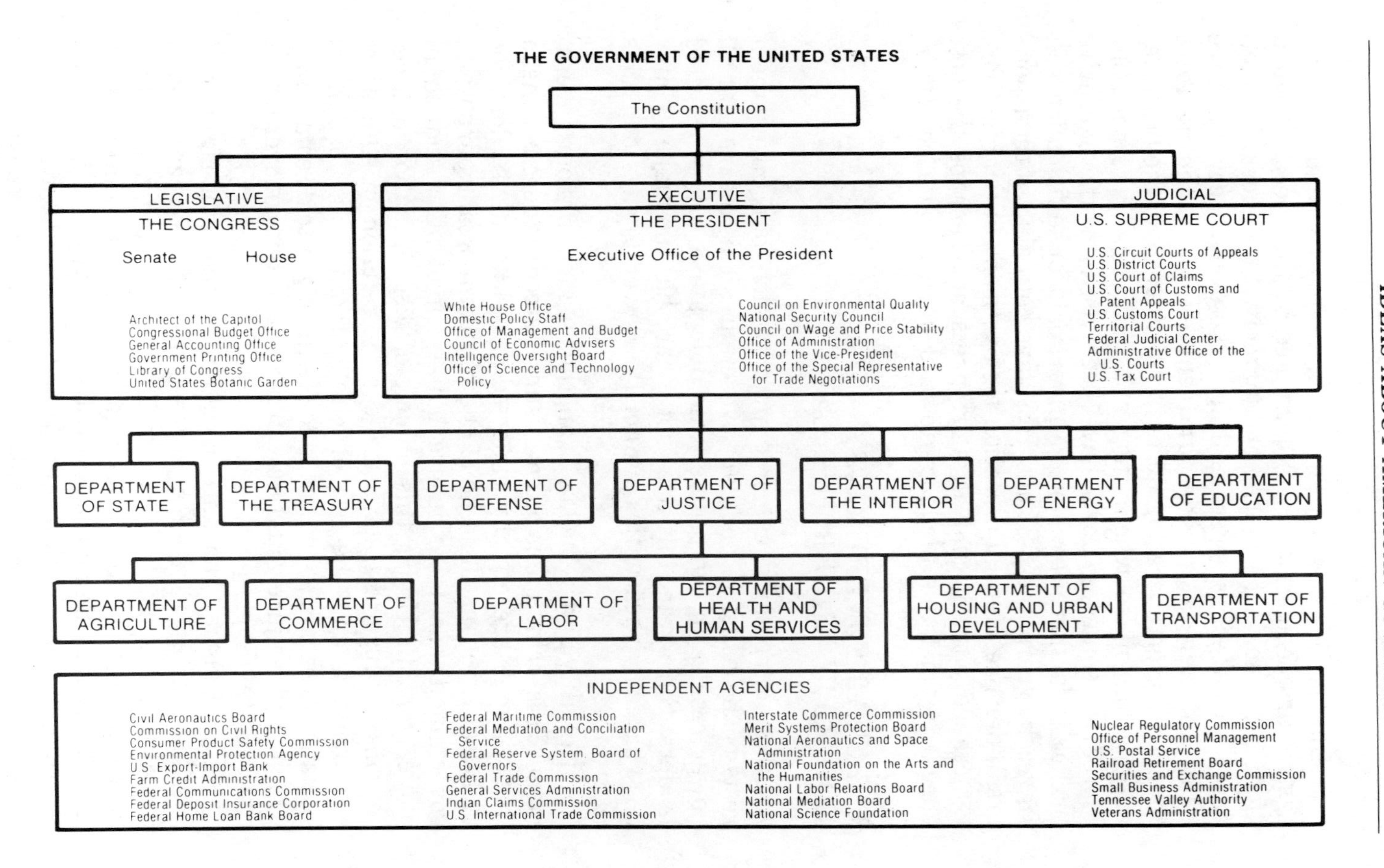
THE GOVERNMENT OF THE UNITED STATES
The Constitution
LEGISLATIVE
THE CONGRESS
Senate
House
Architect of the Capitol
Congressional Budget Office
General Accounting Office
Government Printing Office
Library of Congress
United States Botanic Garden
EXECUTIVE
THE PRESIDENT
Executive Office of the President
White House Office
Domestic Policy Staff
Office of Management and Budget
Council of Economic Advisers
Intelligence Oversight Board
Office of Science and Technology Policy
Council on Environmental Quality
National Security Council
Council on Wage and Price Stability
Office of Administration
Office of the Vice-President
Office of the Special Representative for Trade Negotiations
JUDICIAL
U.S. SUPREME COURT
U.S. Circuit Courts of Appeals
U.S. District Courts
U.S. Court of Claims
U.S. Court of Customs and Patent Appeals
U.S. Customs Court
Territorial Courts
Federal Judicial Center
Administrative Office of the U.S. Courts
U.S. Tax Court
DEPARTMENT OF STATE
DEPARTMENT OF THE TREASURY
DEPARTMENT OF DEFENSE
DEPARTMENT OF JUSTICE
DEPARTMENT OF THE INTERIOR
DEPARTMENT OF ENERGY
DEPARTMENT OF EDUCATION
DEPARTMENT OF AGRICULTURE
DEPARTMENT OF COMMERCE
DEPARTMENT OF LABOR
DEPARTMENT OF HEALTH AND HUMAN SERVICES
DEPARTMENT OF HOUSING AND URBAN DEVELOPMENT
DEPARTMENT OF TRANSPORTATION
INDEPENDENT AGENCIES
Civil Aeronautics Board
Commission on Civil Rights
Consumer Product Safety Commission
Environmental Protection Agency
U.S. Export-Import Bank
Farm Credit Administration
Federal Communications Commission
Federal Deposit Insurance Corporation
Federal Home Loan Bank Board
Federal Maritime Commission
Federal Mediation and Conciliation Service
Federal Reserve System, Board of Governors
Federal Trade Commission
General Services Administration
Indian Claims Commission
U.S. International Trade Commission
Interstate Commerce Commission
Merit Systems Protection Board
National Aeronautics and Space Administration
National Foundation on the Arts and the Humanities
National Labor Relations Board
National Mediation Board
National Science Foundation
Nuclear Regulatory Commission
Office of Personnel Management
U.S. Postal Service
Railroad Retirement Board
Securities and Exchange Commission
Small Business Administration
Tennessee Valley Authority
Veterans Administration

During this century, however, the checks and balances system has been seriously undermined by the appearance of a "fourth branch" of government, namely, the federal bureaucracy. Numbering several million, these civil servants have come to exercise powers undreamed of by the nation's founders, often operating quite independently of the branches of government to whom they are theoretically responsible. Moreover, some agencies have been used by the executive branch to further illegal or unethical goals for selfish purposes. In recent years, the FBI and IRS have both abused their powers under presidential direction for partisan political motives. Concerned citizens and an alert press are perhaps the best checks against this tendency toward bureaucratic power.

POPULAR SOVEREIGNTY AND EQUALITY UNDER THE LAW

Another important principle upon which our government rests is the belief in popular sovereignty. This means that all power resides in the people, who delegate it to their elected leaders. But again, this does not mean that the majority may do what it wishes with a minority. Power always demands restraint.

Equality under the law is another principle of our government. This principle is often misunderstood; it does not mean that all men are equally endowed with the same talents or abilities. It means that one of the most important purposes a government has is to insure equal opportunity and equal justice for all. Under this principle, discrimination against persons because of color, race, sex, or religion in education, employment, and the use of public facilities is forbidden. Equality does not, of course, give me the right to do something which might injure you. I may drive a car—but not over where you are standing.

Equal justice guarantees one person the same rights and privileges as another when accused of a crime, regardless of the differences of wealth or influence. It would not be fair, for example, to make a person go into court without a lawyer simply because he or she could not afford to hire one, while an accused person who could afford one could have this advantage. In a Supreme Court decision known as *Gideon* v.

Wainwright, the state of Florida was informed that failure to provide an attorney for a penniless defendant was an abridgment of constitutional rights.

In the same vein, as we shall see later on in a chapter on civil rights, there are two other principles which underlie our system of law. We believe:

- In doubtful cases it is better to let the guilty go free than to punish the innocent;
- A person is innocent until proven guilty. Thus, no matter how grave the charge may be or how sure we feel of a person's guilt, we cannot assume this until the courts have decided on the question.

This last principle may seem a hard one, but if we remember the motto that ours is a government of laws and not of men, it will help us understand and accept it more easily. In our society, we agree on certain rules (as in the case of the Constitution), the observance of which will provide for orderly lives. Among these are the jury system and our whole legal system in general.

While these principles stand today as unchanging guideposts toward which we should aspire, realistically we must also recognize that financial condition, racial background, and even social status give great advantages to one person over another. Most persons who go to jail for crimes tend to be poor, from minority backgrounds, without family or friends in a position to help them. Affluent white persons of distinguished background may be charged and even convicted of crimes, but will have a much greater chance of avoiding prison or, if sent to prison, of going to a minimum security facility far different from an ordinary prison. Many Americans believe that facts such as these dilute the overriding principles of equality under the law. Equal justice, they think, should mean equal opportunity for defense against charges as well as equality of punishment—taking extenuating circumstances into consideration—if the defense fails.

CONSTITUTIONAL FLEXIBILITY

One final principle remains, that of flexibility—the willingness and ability in our government and people to accept change and to deal with it. Change is one of the most important aspects of all life, one which we see all around us in our daily lives. Nature constantly changes, people change the face of the earth, we change our ideas, our bodies grow and change. So it is with government. A flexible one must adapt itself to meet the everchanging needs of its people.

President Jefferson would no doubt be shocked to learn that the federal government punishes people for selling impure margarine and forbids butter makers to use certain chemicals in processing that food. Yet President Jefferson could adapt himself to change. He sent three men to Paris to discuss the purchase of New Orleans with Napoleon Bonaparte. Instead, Napoleon offered to sell us the entire Louisiana territory. There was nothing specific in the Constitution which permitted such a purchase, but Jefferson and his supporters argued that it would aid in America's defense and would certainly be for the general welfare. Thus, a flexible interpretation of the Constitution doubled the size of the United States.

Flexibility does not mean that *anything* can be done so long as some excuse is found for it. It does mean that government must adapt itself to new conditions and must support orderly change. In other words, the principles we have just studied can be put into effect by flexible practices.

CHANGING THE CONSTITUTION

In the American government, change has been provided for in many ways. The nation's founders recognized the need for flexibility by providing for the amending process in Article V. An amendment can be *proposed* in one of two ways:

1. Congress may recommend an amendment to the states by a two-thirds vote of both houses;
2. Two-thirds of the state legislatures may ask Congress to call a constitutional convention to draft and approve an amendment. (This method has never been used.)

The amendment must then be *ratified* in one of two ways:

1. The legislatures of three-fourths of the states (thirty-eight of the fifty states) must approve the amendment;

Library of Congress

An early view of the Rocky Mountains. This region was explored by Meriwether Lewis and William Clark in 1805, two years after the Louisiana Purchase vastly expanded the territory of the United States.

2. Special ratification conventions held in three-fourths of the states must approve it.

Congress has the right to determine which of the above methods of ratification will be adopted. Only once, when the Twenty-first Amendment repealed the Eighteenth, has the second method been employed.

Securing the consent of two-thirds of the Congress and three-fourths of the states is a difficult task, as it was intended to be. Altering the Constitution is a very serious matter and should be undertaken only after much deliberation. It is like altering the foundation of a building once all the upper floors are completed. The amending process thus changes the structure of the government as, for example, when the Seventeenth Amendment was adopted providing for the direct election of Senators by the people instead of by the state legislatures as had formerly been the case.

INTERPRETING THE CONSTITUTION

Amendment is not the only way by which structural change can take place. Each branch of government brings about change in one way or another by its interpretation of the powers which flow to it from the Constitution. Here is an example of how all branches are involved in the process of change:

Change by amendment:

When the Sixteenth Amendment was adopted, Congress was given the power to tax individuals directly.

Change by the executive branch:

The President requests income tax legislation from the Congress.

Change by the legislative branch:

Congress approves a bill setting tax rates, indicating what deductions individuals may take, designating methods and times of payment, and so on. This bill is signed by the President.

Change by the judicial branch:

The Supreme Court may hear cases involving the new tax law and may declare parts of it unconstitutional.

Thus, change is by no means limited to constitutional amendment. Nor is the power under which a branch brings about a change always as specific as in the example just given. We have seen that Jefferson used a broad interpretation of the vague phrases of the Constitution to justify the Louisiana Purchase.

The nation's founders could not, obviously, specify all the duties of Congress. They gave it broad powers and expected it to use them to solve any other problems which arose. Congress has created a court system, enacted Social Security legislation, and determined the size of the House of Representatives, all under its delegated or implied powers.

The President and the executive branch in general have brought about change in their own right, too. When, in the 1840s, Vice-President John Tyler succeeded to the Presidency on the death of President William Henry Harrison, the question arose whether he would really be President or whether he would just act as President as the words of the Constitution seem to indicate. Tyler insisted that he was President in his own right and settled the question for future Vice-Presidents who assumed the highest office. But to prevent possible misunderstandings, Congress wrote Tyler's interpretation into the Twenty-first Amendment in 1967.

THE ROLE OF THE SUPREME COURT

The role of the Supreme Court in interpreting the Constitution makes the judiciary enormously important in the scheme of change. Judicial review, the power to review acts of Congress to determine their constitutionality, was not written into the Constitution. Earlier in our history, some critics stated that the Supreme Court could only decide on the rights and wrongs of specific cases. In other words, if *A* and *B* were involved in a lawsuit and the Court ruled in favor of *B*, the decision applied only to these two disputants, not to the whole population.

However, most scholars today agree that this limits the Court too severely. They accept the doctrine of judicial review as inherent in the court system of the United States. This view was first put into federal use by Chief Justice Marshall in an 1803 decision called *Marbury* v. *Madison*. Although the background of this case is somewhat involved, it is important to the issue of judicial review and to an understanding of the Supreme Court's procedure in general.

Under the Constitution, Congress was given the power to create a court system. This it did by the Judiciary Act of 1789. In drafting the act, Congress listed some of the powers which it thought the courts should have, including that of issuing writs of mandamus (court orders) directing officials of the federal government to perform certain actions. According to the act, in instances of this sort the Supreme Court had original jurisdiction, that is, the right to hear the case initially and not when it came on appeal from a lower court.

Later, when he was going out of office, President John Adams appointed a number of officials to positions in the government. One of these was William Marbury, who was to

Independence National Historical Park Collection

Thomas Jefferson remarked in his first inaugural address, "We are all Republicans—we are all Federalists." Yet shortly after taking office, he allowed party politics to influence his relations with the Federalist-appointed judiciary.

become a minor judicial official. Adams left office, however, before Marbury's commission could be delivered. When Thomas Jefferson became President, he decided not to deliver the commissions to the officials Adams had named because they did not support Jefferson's political party. Marbury sued for his commission, asking the Supreme Court to order Jefferson's Secretary of State, James Madison, to deliver the commission.

The Supreme Court reviewed the case and declared that it could not issue the writ of mandamus since Congress did not have the right to grant this power in connection with a case which the Court was to hear originally. The Constitution (Article III) listed the instances in which the Court had original jurisdiction, and Congress could not add to these. That part of the Judiciary Act was therefore unconstitutional. Thus, by refusing to accept a small power given to it, the Supreme Court asserted the much greater authority to review congressional legislation.

In the early days of our history, however, the subject of judicial review was a debatable one and the Court used it sparingly. More than half a century passed before it was used again, in the famous *Dred Scott* decision.

However, the Court more frequently asserted its right to review state laws to determine whether or not they violated the Constitution. In *Fletcher* v. *Peck,* it declared a state law invalid for the first time. This and other decisions which followed reinforced the words of Article VI of the Constitution, which says that the Constitution, Acts of Congress, and treaties "shall be the supreme law of the land." And this, of course, would apply to Supreme Court decisions interpreting these documents.

THE GROWTH OF THE FEDERAL GOVERNMENT

The practices of Congress, the Supreme Court, and the executive branch over the years have considerably altered the structure of the Constitution. This has usually been in the direction of increasing the power of the federal government in the federal system.

Why is this so? How do we account for this growth? Is it a threat to us?

Answers to these questions are not easy and those which will be given are by no means complete. Please bear this in mind and see if you can think of any other reasons.

Usually, federal governmental power has grown when various needs for it have arisen. These needs can be classified as follows:

- Needs of the public in general,
- Needs of minority groups;
- Needs arising from scientific advancements.

Take the federal Social Security program as an example of the first type. By the 1930s few states had adequate programs to provide support for older people who had passed their working years. Federal Social Security was enacted to satisfy this need. On the other hand, some years before this an amendment was proposed to give the federal government control over child labor at a time when young children worked in factories for very low wages and under poor conditions. The federal pro-

A federal employee explaining "Los Beneficios del Seguro Social"—social security benefits—to a Spanish-speaking citizen. It was not until the 1960s that the federal and state governments began general programs to serve the nation's large Spanish-speaking population by issuing pamphlets in that language on voting rights and other prerogatives of citizenship.

gram was never adopted, since the states did a very good job of eliminating child labor on their own.

Again, federal power has grown to protect the rights of minority groups in our country. The term "minority group" is used to describe a group which does not enjoy the full benefits of American life either politically, socially, or economically.

For years black people did not enjoy the benefits of American life in many ways. Restrictive state laws prevented them from voting, from living in certain areas, and even from eating in certain restaurants, or using washrooms or other public facilities set aside for whites. Through the action of Congress, the Court, and the President, many of these laws have been overruled by federal laws or legal decisions. The federal government has also tried to improve the lives of blacks and other minorities economically and socially by forbidding discrimination in employment, and by building apartment house projects to replace the slums in which some of them have lived.

The third type of need satisfied by the federal government is that arising from the great technological advances made in the past 150 years. The aviation industry is an example. Federal regulation of this activity is absolutely necessary to provide uniform standards of safety and to insure proper operation of airlines. Can you imagine the confusion which might arise if New York had an aviation agency with one set of rules and every other state had its own agency with its own rules? Some activities must be centralized, a situation which has led to the expansion of the federal sphere. The TVA or Tennessee Valley Authority is another case in point. No state had the money or other resources needed to harness the raging rivers which once caused havoc over seven states of the South. The TVA built an enormous dam system which has provided the area with flood control, electric power, and many other benefits.

Thus, the federal government acts upon need. It steps in when the job is too big for individual states or for a few states acting in concert. Is this a potentially dangerous situation? Could it lead to a reduction in the usefulness of the states, thereby removing control farther away from the hands of the people? The answer to this is "Yes, it could be dangerous." Government is best controlled at the local level. The United States federal government is a powerful force, possibly the most powerful and efficient institution in history. It operates huge businesses all over the world. It owns the largest publishing company (the Government Printing Office) and the biggest chain store (the military post exchange or PX system) in America. It distributes practically every product on a small or large scale. In the wrong hands, it could be the worst instrument for tyranny the world has ever known. So far this has been prevented because of two groups of people and one important factor:

- The dedicated American citizen, who votes regularly, communicates his or her ideas to public officials, takes part in political activity, and insists that government officials adhere to the same high standards they set for the citizen;
- The overwhelming majority of civil servants, who do their jobs vigorously but with restraint;
- The existence of an ever-increasing body of laws which require all government workers, from the President and

Library of Congress

Norris Dam, on the Tennessee River, one of the many dams operated by the TVA. It was named for Senator George W. Norris of Nebraska, who for many years fought for government development of the Tennessee Valley.

the members of Congress to the newest employee in the federal work force, to avoid illegal or unethical abuse of their powers.

As long as these conditions continue to exist, the republic will stand.

Philosophers know that the best kind of government is a well-balanced one in which the duties of citizens are clearly defined and their rights are firmly protected. But noble words cannot secure good government; only people can do that. The task of enjoying good government is much like bicycling up a hill: if you stop pedaling, you automatically start slipping back. Only through observing Jefferson's valuable advice, "Eternal vigilance is the price of liberty," can we be sure of success.

AFTER-CHAPTER REVIEW

REVIEW QUESTIONS

1. Define the following names, terms, or ideas.

federalism
confederation
reserved powers
concurrent powers
delegated powers
"necessary and proper" clause
implied powers
unwritten Constitution
separation of powers
"general welfare" clause
judicial review
writ of mandamus

2. Vocabulary building.

unitary concurrent mandate

3. Cases.

McCulloch v. *Maryland*
Marbury v. *Madison*
Gideon v. *Wainwright*
Fletcher v. *Peck*

4. Review of the text.

a. Distinguish between the federal, confederate, and unitary systems of government.
b. Name the various types of power existing under federalism and give examples of each.
c. Explain the power a President has over a bill.
d. Describe the amending process.
e. List and explain the other methods (aside from amendment) by which the Constitution may be modified.
f. How may the growth of federal power be explained?
g. What factors have prevented the federal government from exercising excessive control over its citizens?

DISCUSSION AND PROJECTS

1. Questions for discussion.

a. Discuss Andrew Jackson's veto message on the National Bank Bill. Would an American President today agree with his attitude toward the Supreme Court? Explain your answer.

b. Why is flexibility necessary to any form of government?

c. Write an essay on the separation of powers, examining whether the three branches of our national government are independent or interdependent.

d. Discuss the concepts: better to let the guilty go free than to punish the innocent; a person is innocent until proven guilty.

2. Debate topics.

a. Resolved: The Tenth Amendment has abolished the "elastic clause."

b. Resolved: The power to tax involves the power to destroy. If this be so, then the taxing powers of our government must be limited to prevent our destruction.

3. Opinion poll.

Is the federal government too big for comfort?

BIBLIOGRAPHY

Boorstin, Daniel J. "Political Technology, Reflections on the Continuing American Experiment," *Harper's*, March 1978.

Dutton, Frederick G. *Changing Sources of Power: American Politics in the 1970s.* New York: McGraw-Hill, 1971.

"Five Noted Thinkers Explore the Future," *National Geographic*, July 1976.

Kristol, Irving. *On the Democratic Idea in America.* New York: Harper & Row, 1972.

Morris, Richard B. *Basic Documents in American History.* Princeton, N.J.: Van Nostrand Reinhold, 1956.

Morris, Richard B. *The Basic Ideas of Alexander Hamilton.* New York: Pocket Books, 1957.

Moynihan, Daniel P. "The Politics of Human Rights," *Reader's Digest*, December 1977.

Olander, Joseph D.; Greenberg, Martin H.; and Warrick, Patricia, eds. *American Government through Science Fiction.* Chicago: Rand McNally, 1974.

Padover, Saul K. *Thomas Jefferson on Democracy.* New York: New American Library, 1939.

Said, Abdul A., ed. *America's World Role in the 70's.* Englewood Cliffs, N.J.: Prentice-Hall, 1970.

Paul Conklin from Monkmeyer

The dome of the Capitol. This cast-iron structure was designed by Thomas U. Walter, and was completed in 1863. The 19½-foot bronze statue on top is called *Freedom*, and was sculpted by Thomas Crawford. The Capitol dome has come to be a symbol for legislative bodies; as a result, most state capitols built after the Civil War have domes.

4

Congress: What It Is

Leaf through the pages of the average daily newspaper and you will find references to Congress and its members almost everywhere. "Congress will investigate . . ."; "Congress grants funds . . ."; "Congress warns people . . ."; "Congressman tells constituents . . ."; "Congresswoman back from Latin America says. . . ." The interests of Congress are as broad as its powers. The life of a member of Congress is never dull.

In the course of a given day, a legislator may attend a committee hearing, make a nationwide speech, vote approval of a presidential Senate appointment, or recommend a young person to the Air Force Academy. He or she may be in Moscow, Tokyo, or Brasilia investigating conditions which vitally affect America's interests. No matter where a member of Congress is, he or she is engaged in the nation's business and is wearing one of his or her many official hats.

An Ohio Senator reported to his constituents recently on his activities since taking office. He said a "typical day" might "range from my casting a vote on the Senate floor on something as historically significant as the Nuclear Non-Proliferation Treaty, to meeting the press in my office, to hosting my state's delegates to Boys' or Girls' Nation." During one year, the Senator stated, his office received 125,000 letters on a wide variety of subjects. Most of these letters had to be answered. Hundreds of them required the Senator or members of his staff to spend hours solving social security or veterans' problems for his fellow Ohioans.

A Wisconsin Congressman, reporting to the voters of his district, pointed out that he had received about 48,000 letters in the previous year. He also remarked that he had made sixty trips between Washington and Wisconsin, a fact which shows the great pains legislators take to keep in close contact with their home states and districts. This kind of activity is known as "fence-mending."

Many members of Congress find the demands on their time to be very tiring. Every two years, perhaps one out of every ten or twelve members of the legislature retires voluntarily because of pressures from family or constituents, or because the job seems unrewarding after a time. One Congressman from the Northeast announced his retirement in 1978 because, he said, "People bug me more than they used to." He also said that he did not want to make a lifetime career out of the Congress. Yet, in recent years the tendency has been for members of Congress to remain in office longer than in earlier days. In the House of Representatives, terms of forty and even fifty years are not that uncommon.

Before beginning the study of our national legislature, read over Article I of the Constitution to get an idea of the extensive powers Congress has. In that article you will find general rules laid down governing such things as terms in office, eligibility requirements, powers, and limitations of Congress. You will find that this branch of government is treated before the other two and is dealt with in much more detail. This is because of the special importance of our legislature. Obviously, if the President is to carry out the laws and the judiciary to interpret them, it is reasonable to conclude that these officials would not have much to do if Congress did not first make the laws.

THE DUTIES OF MEMBERS OF CONGRESS

To say that our 535 lawmakers simply legislate is to list only part of their duties. In the course of their terms, members of Congress can be called upon to do all or most of the following things:

- Amend the Constitution (subject, of course, to state approval);
- Elect a President or Vice-President under certain circumstances;

- Discipline federal officials through Congress's impeachment power;
- Advise the executive branch on such matters as foreign policy and the appointment of federal officials;
- Inform their constituents (the residents of their districts or states) and the American people generally of situations they should be aware of;
- Investigate persons, industries, activities, or situations through the committee system to see what laws are needed to make the nation function better;
- Punish fellow members of Congress by censuring, excluding, or expelling them for activities detrimental to the nation;
- Represent their constituents before the federal government by trying to solve individual or group problems.

The average lawmaker, therefore, is a very busy person, busier than most Americans. In a recent Congress, in addition to the duties listed above, more than 26,000 bills and resolutions were considered. Congress studied, investigated, debated, and voted on these measures, finally approving more than one thousand of them.

Very often bills are lengthy, involved documents. The Medicare program, for example, was embodied in a document of 138 pages of closely packed type. The document, by the way, was not called the Medicare Act. This was a nickname given to:

> Public Law 89–97
> An Act
> To provide a hospital insurance program for the aged under the Social Security Act with a supplementary medical benefits program and an expanded program of medical assistance, to increase benefits under the Old-Age, Survivors, and Disability Insurance System, to improve the Federal-State public assistance program, and for other purposes.

Although the title may seem clumsy and even confusing, there is a reason for spelling laws out in such detail. Legislators, who are acting in your interests, must be certain that

Brown Brothers

Jeannette Rankin was the first woman to be elected to the U.S. House of Representatives. A Republican from Montana, she served from 1917 to 1919 (a time when women in most states had not yet gained the right to vote) and again from 1941 to 1943. She was the only member of Congress to vote against American participation in both world wars.

bills do just what they are intended to do, neither more nor less. If a bill is vaguely worded, it can do more harm than good, since lawyers may be able to find "loopholes," or clauses in the law which will help their clients defeat the purpose for which the bill was drawn. This is perfectly proper for lawyers to do; indeed, they would be remiss in their duties if they did not try to help their clients in every legal way.

An example of a vaguely worded law is the famous Sherman Anti-Trust Act of 1890. This act forbade combinations "in restraint of trade" and was designed to curb the large business trusts which were trying to eliminate competition. Using the above clause, lawyers insisted that the act should be applied to unions which went on strike against business firms, since a strike restrained trade. The argument was accepted and the act was used against labor unions as well as business trusts. In drafting what seems to be even a simple measure, then, Congress must be very wary of side effects it does not intend.

THE MEMBERS OF CONGRESS: SENATORS AND REPRESENTATIVES

No doubt you have seen a Senator or Representative in pictures, on TV, or even in person. Have you ever wondered what kind of person he or she is? Is there such a thing as an "average" member of Congress? The answer to this is that legislators come in all ages, religions, and occupations. In a recent Congress, the Ninety-fifth (1977–1979), the members ranged in age from the middle twenties to the high seventies. The average age was fifty-four in the Senate, and just over fifty in the House. The overwhelming majority of both houses were white, Protestant men in their fifties or older. Only seventeen women served in the House, while the lone woman in the Senate was Muriel Humphrey, the widow of Senator Hubert H. Humphrey. A mere sixteen blacks served in Congress, with Puerto Ricans, Chicanos, Asians, and other minority groups having even fewer representatives.[1] Although most members of Congress belonged to the Protestant faith, about 120 were Catholics. Of the 535 members of Congress, about 500 were married. Previous occupations were remarkably varied and included prize fighting, house painting, electrical work, and even riverboat piloting.[2] However, most legislators had more conventional occupations, principally in law, business, and education. The Ninety-fifth Congress had 64 lawyers in the Senate and more than 200 in the House.

---

1. *New York Times*, 5 December 1976, p. 79. No blacks had been elected to the Senate since the 1880s until Massachusetts elected Edward Brooke, a Republican, in 1966. A "first" was achieved in 1968 when a black woman, Shirley Chisholm of Brooklyn, New York, was elected to the House. In 1972, the South sent its first blacks to Congress since Reconstruction in the persons of Barbara Jordan of Texas and Andrew Young of Georgia.

2. *New York Times*, 25 June 1977, p. 8.

UPI

Margaret Chase Smith, a Republican from Maine, was the first woman to be elected to both houses of Congress. She served in the House of Representatives from 1940 to 1948 and in the Senate from 1949 to 1973.

When a person becomes a member of Congress, he or she is entitled to certain benefits as compensation. These are guaranteed by the Constitution, although Congress decides what form they will take. The most recent salary scale calls for a basic wage of $57,502. Voted in 1977 (by a slim 214-to-213 margin in the House of Representatives), this was a 29 percent increase over the $44,625 that legislators had been getting previously. This sum compares very favorably with the pay scales of legislators in other nations. British members of the House of Commons received an increase in 1975 which brought their salaries to $12,650; in the same year, Canadian legislators received a raise which gave them $24,000 plus an untaxed allowance of $10,600.

Officers of the House and Senate receive greater compensation than ordinary members do and also enjoy such expensive fringe benefits as chauffeur-driven limousines. Excellent pension benefits, inexpensive and complete health care, high insurance protection, and free parking are among the other emoluments of the office of national legislators. Once a benefit is voted, Congress rarely refuses to renew it, although Senators recently denied themselves combs and free mugs for shaving. However, they did this as part of a bill which raised their salaries by almost $12,900 a year, so it was a sacrifice they could well afford.[3]

In fairness to our national lawmakers, it should be noted that these material compensations are offered to help them maintain a comfortable standard of living, and to meet the extraordinary expenses their positions entail. The salary is designed to permit persons of moderate income to hold office. At the same time raises were being given, Congress also voted to limit the extra income that members could earn based on their positions in the legislature or on special legislative committees. In the past, members of Congress often accepted large fees for speaking before business, labor, or other groups, and questions were raised over whether gratitude might be shown by preferential voting on matters concerning these groups. The amount of money which may be earned as outside income has now been sharply reduced. We must be extremely careful, however, to avoid the condition which once existed in Britain when members of Parliament served without pay. Only rich people, or those who were supported by wealthy patrons, could serve.

As it is, many members of Congress are quite affluent. More than forty members qualify as millionaires, and a large proportion enjoy several hundred thousand dollars in assets. Quite unusual is the house painter who never earned more than $9,000 a year before entering the House of Representatives.

Members of Congress are subject to criminal laws but need not worry about serving on juries or as witnesses while in the execution of their duties. This guarantee is provided for in Article I, Section 6, of the Constitution, along with the right to speak out on any matter the legislator deems fit without

3. *New York Times,* 19 July 1977, p. 17.

being "questioned in any other place." There has been some criticism of this very broad power on the grounds that a person's reputation could be ruined in an instant if a legislator had it in mind to do this. A suggestion has been made to permit persons who feel they have been unjustly accused of some act or association to reply to the charges. Legislators, however, have shown remarkable restraint in their use of this power. It has rarely been abused. In those cases where the question of abuse has been raised, many felt that the members of Congress who spoke out were entirely justified.

Moreover, if a legislator were to abuse this almost unlimited freedom of speech, it is within the power of either house to censure him or even to expel him from Congress. A two-thirds vote is needed however, to expel a person. Another important power of Congress is exclusion, that is, refusing to let a member sit even after being elected. In the past, Congress has used this power, which requires a majority vote, to exclude a polygamist, a Socialist (temporarily), and several others whose elections seemed to have been won by the use of bribes. In 1967, one New York Representative was excluded from the House of Representatives and a Connecticut Senator was censured by the Senate, the two men being accused of misconduct by their peers. Since that time, a few members of Congress have gone to prison or paid substantial fines for such crimes as bribery, perjury, income tax evasion, influence peddling, and other illegal acts. And some members have been forced to resign or have been defeated for re-election over other forms of unethical or inappropriate behavior.

The most frequent instances of congressional wrongdoing occur in connection with the election process. Election campaigns can cost enormous sums of money, particularly in districts where both major parties are strongly represented. And every economic group, professional association, labor organization, and so on, has some kind of ax to grind. A powerful interest group can win an important friend on a key committee by contributing to his or her election war chest. Under some circumstances this is legal, but in other cases it breaks the law. In recent years, some large corporations have been fined heavily for campaign contributions made illegally. Even foreign influence groups play this game. A South Korean

National Portrait Gallery, Smithsonian

JOHN C. CALHOUN

DANIEL WEBSTER

businessman, for example, gave generous sums of money and other gifts to large numbers of lawmakers to win friends for South Korea's foreign policy position.

ELECTING SENATORS AND REPRESENTATIVES

The House and Senate, you recall, are part of our checks and balances system. Both must approve legislation before it becomes law; yet each house is elected differently.

The Constitution provides for two Senators from every state regardless of its population. This, of course, illustrates the importance of the states in our federal system. During most of our history, Senators were elected by the state legislatures, thus removing the Senate from direct popular control. This system produced some extraordinarily gifted men, including Senators Daniel Webster, Henry Clay, and John Calhoun. It

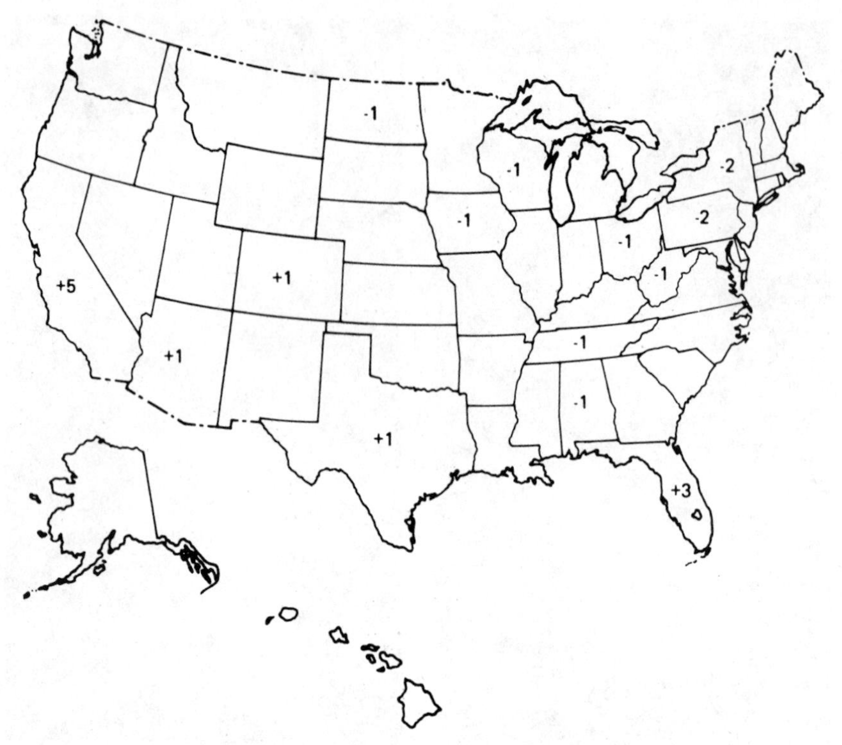

States which gained and lost representation in the House of Representatives as a result of the 1970 census.

also produced many mediocre men and, what is more important, was considered too undemocratic early in the twentieth century. By that time, more than half the states had revised their electoral laws to permit the voters to state their preference for Senator. Then the legislature would simply go through the motions of electing the person. Even this was not enough for reformers, however, and so the Seventeenth Amendment was adopted, making popular election of Senators mandatory for all states.

Senators must be at least thirty years of age, citizens of the United States for nine years or more, and inhabitants of the state from which they are elected. Each state decides what the term "inhabitant" means, that is, how long a person must live in the state to be eligible to run for public office there. Senators serve six-year terms, with one-third of the

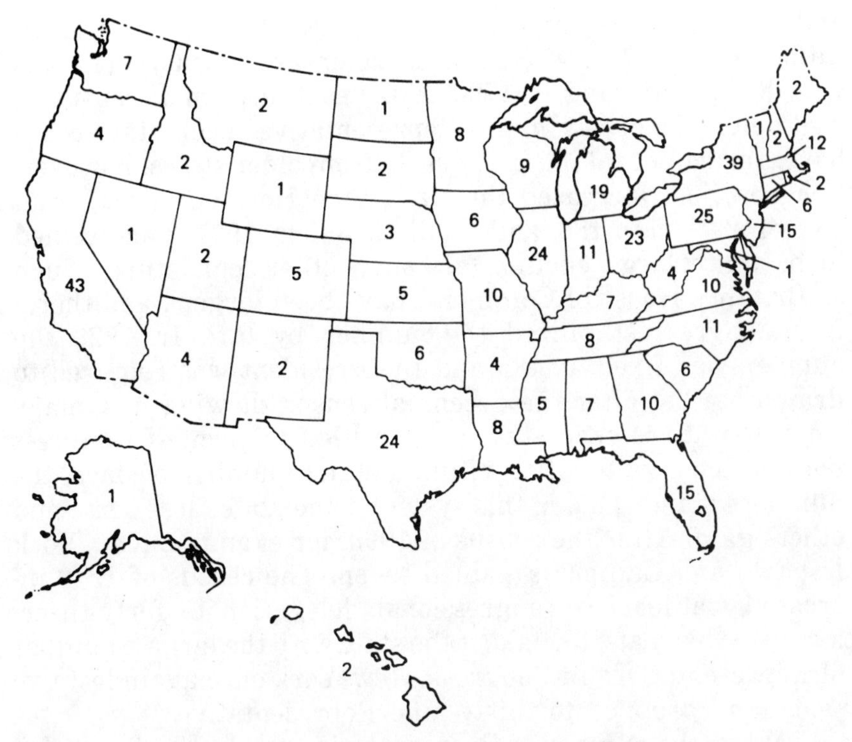

Representation in the House of Representatives according to the 1970 census.

Senate body re-elected every two years. Thus, the composition of the Senate remains somewhat more consistent than that of the House of Representatives, which is elected in its entirety every two years. House members must be at least twenty-five years old and citizens of the United States for seven years.

The Constitution sets no limits on the number of Representatives there may be. It only says that there should be no more than one Representative for every 30,000 people. Today, there is one for about every 465,000 people. This ratio was reached by chance, and by the development of our history. As our population grew, the number of Representatives was increased until the number was stabilized. The original House of Representatives had a membership of sixty-five seats. These were apportioned among the states according to population, with Virginia receiving ten, Massachusetts eight, New York and Maryland six, and the other states fewer. The Constitution requires that a census be taken every ten years. This was done, beginning in 1790. After each decennial census, it was determined how many Representatives each state could have. Instead of taking away seats from older states, however, Congress just increased the size of the House. It grew from 65 to 142, then to 186, and finally to 435 by 1911. This seemed to be quite large enough (although other legislatures, such as Britain's House of Commons, have been larger), and therefore Congress stabilized the number by law. In 1929 the number was fixed at 435 and the President was required to draw up a list after the decennial census showing how many Representatives each state was entitled to elect. If Congress does not change this list within a stated number of days, the numbers stand. Under this system some states lose seats and others gain. After the census of 1960, for example, New York lost two and California gained seven. The census of 1970 increased California's congressional delegation to forty-three, a gain of five seats, to make it the state with the largest number of Representatives in Congress. New York once again lost two seats, and dropped to thirty-nine Representatives.

When the number of Representatives each state is entitled to elect has been determined, then the question of how they are to be elected must be settled. Originally they were elected "at large"; all the candidates in a state campaigned for Congress and all the voters voted on each one of them. If there were ten seats up for election, the voter could choose ten candidates. This system had its drawbacks, however. If there were seven million voters in party *A* and only three million in party *B*, then all ten of party *A's* candidates could be elected and party *B* might have no representation, even though it had three million voters.

The system of electing Representatives-at-large was abandoned in the 1840s when Congress decided to create territorial districts. This task was assigned to the state legislature which usually drew up reapportionment plans every ten years. Although this system was more equitable than elections held at large, it could still be abused to the point where one party enjoyed greater representation in Congress than its numbers warranted.

REAPPORTIONMENT PROBLEMS

As an example of the way in which the reapportionment system may be abused, let us take a school situation. Imagine a school with eighty girls and seventy boys in the freshman class. They are divided into three classes of fifty students, each class being allowed to send one delegate to the freshman student council. If both the boys and girls were equally divided among the three classes, the girls would always outnumber the boys. Assuming the girls in each case would generally favor a girl representative on the council, the boys would theoretically be locked out. If the principal wanted to favor the boys, he would divide the three classes as follows:

Example No. 1

25 boys	30 boys	15 boys
20 girls	10 girls	50 girls
winner: boys	winner: boys	winner: girls

Thus, with two boys to one girl representative, we sense a possible unfairness in the results of the council meetings.

If the principal wanted to favor the girls completely, he could work out this arrangement:

Example No. 2

10 boys	30 boys	30 boys
14 girls	35 girls	31 girls
winner: girls	winner: girls	winner: girls

The boys would be frozen out of the student council completely.

Is there a fair way to reapportion the class? Yes, an equitable apportionment of the class might be something like this:

Example No. 3

24 boys	20 boys	26 boys
26 girls	30 girls	24 girls

This way, the boys will get one seat on the student council, the girls will get one easily by a ten-vote margin, and in the third class the division will favor the girls by two votes. Most likely, the girls will always get two seats on the council, but at least the distribution will be as fair as possible.

Note that in all but the last example, there are two unfair conditions. First, the classes (which represent election districts) vary in size so that their representatives each speak for different numbers of people. Second, the boys and girls (representing two major parties) are moved around to suit the interests of the principal.

In the first two examples given, we say that the classes were "gerrymandered" to help one side or the other. This word goes back into American history of the early nineteenth century. When the state legislature of Massachusetts worked out an apportionment plan, it followed the advice of Governor Elbridge Gerry, who suggested it draw up districts to favor the dominant political party. The legislature did so and produced one district shaped like a salamander. Some astute wit renamed it a "gerrymander" and the name came to be applied to any district drawn up to favor the party in power.

REAPPORTIONMENT AND THE STATE LEGISLATURES

The state legislatures were the keys to whether or not congressional seats would be fairly reapportioned every ten years. Before we can consider the question of congressional districts, however, we must determine how the state legislatures are elected.

Until recently, state legislative districts were poorly drawn. In one state, for example, a legislator represented 36 people, while another represented 35,000. In another state, one legislator represented about 90,000 persons, while one of his colleagues spoke for more than 900,000. The difference was not always this great in all the states, of course, but the fact that it could exist any place was considered gravely unfair.

There were three principal reasons for this condition. First, many citizens believed that there should be at least one representative for each county, no matter how small in population it might be. This concept became part of many state constitutions at a time when there were few counties and plenty of legislators to go around. Second, the number of legislators set by the state constitutions remained fairly stable while the number of counties grew until, under the principle of allowing one representative for each county, there were few legislative seats left over to provide more populous counties with greater numbers of representatives. Finally, where it was possible to reapportion electoral districts to promote more fairness in representation, state legislatures often failed to act. By 1960, some states had not reapportioned their state legislative districts for half a century and one had done nothing about its districts for a century and a half. Thus, all the shifts of population which had taken place over the years were ignored and one person's vote counted for more than that of another in the state legislature.

Since the weight of legislative strength usually rested in rural areas, this meant that persons living in cities and suburbs were underrepresented in the state legislatures. The result of this was that legislatures were more inclined to listen to the opinions of rural voters than urban ones.

When legislatures of this type sat down every ten years to draw up congressional districts, they often discriminated against city dwellers by gerrymandering the districts to the advantage of the party and the geographical area which dominated the state. In a state with sixteen million people, for example, half of whom lived in cities and the other half in rural areas, there might be nineteen Representatives from the cities and twenty-two from the rural areas.

The unfairness of congressional districts was not as great when compared with state legislative districts, but it was still inequitable. One Representative might speak for eight times as many people as another, but some state legislators often spoke for fifty times the number of people their colleagues did.

REAPPORTIONMENT AND THE SUPREME COURT

Over the years, efforts were made to challenge districting practices in the courts. One case, *Colegrove* v. *Green*, in 1946, involved the state of Illinois. In that state, one member of Congress represented 112,000 people while another spoke for 914,000. This was clearly an unusual case of discrimination in congressional districting, but the Supreme Court ruled that the matter was a political one and not an issue for the courts.

This position was reversed in 1962 by the decision in *Baker* v. *Carr.* In that case, a majority of the Supreme Court (six to two) ruled that it had the right to examine districting of seats for the state legislature of Tennessee. Tennessee had not been redistricted for sixty years and great inequities existed there. The Court based this assumption of power on the fact that Tennessee's districts were so unfairly drawn that they denied citizens the equal protection of the laws guaranteed in the Fourteenth Amendment.

This opened the door to many other lawsuits. In 1964, two years after the *Baker* v. *Carr* decision, six more decisions were handed down by the Court. These declared the legislative districts of six states unconstitutional. The best known of these decisions was *Reynolds* v. *Sims.* In these decisions, the Court went a little further into the subject than it had in 1962. It stated:

1. Each person's vote should be as nearly as possible equal to that of the next (this doctrine is called "one man, one vote");
2. If a state should decide to copy the federal government by having one house represent the people and another the counties, it could not do so, even if the people of the state approved the plan.

Chief Justice Warren spoke for the majority on the entire issue by saying that legislators should "represent people, not trees or acres" since they are elected "by voters, not farms or cities or economic interests."

Several other justices dissented from the majority on all these decisions. Writing on *Baker* v. *Carr,* Justice Frankfurter lamented the fact that the Supreme Court had reversed so many previous decisions by this action. It repudiated its former role by "asserting destructively novel judicial power." Another member of the Court, Justice Harlan, said of the 1964 decisions that the Fourteenth Amendment was not intended to be used in cases of this sort. He criticized the idea of using the Court as a cure for "every major social ill."

A great deal of debate was engendered throughout the country over the issues raised by these far-reaching decisions. Congress generally disapproved the Court's action but was divided over what course of action to take. The House of Representatives approved a bill to prevent the Court from taking any part in the apportionment problem, but the Senate would not accept this. Constitutional amendments were proposed, too, but no action was taken on them.

Note that the 1962 and 1964 decisions mentioned above referred to the districting for state legislatures, not to congressional districts. The Court did take a position on congressional districts in 1964 in the case of *Wesberry* v. *Sanders*. This involved the congressional districts of Georgia which, the Court ruled, were unconstitutionally drawn. One district consisted of over 800,000 persons while another had less than 300,000. This, the Court said, was wrong, since Article I of the Constitution stated that Representatives be choosen by the people and this meant "that as nearly as is practicable one man's vote in a congressional election is to be worth as much as another's."

Dissenting from this, Justice Harlan declared that all of Georgia's Representatives were elected by the people and that it was not up to the Court to decide whether or not all persons in the state had votes of equal weight. He based his argument on the Constitution and the writings of the Founding Fathers. As Justice Harlan saw it, the case involved more than giving equal weight to each vote. It was a struggle over the states' position within the federal system and the Court's place in the system of separation of powers.

The results of the reapportionment struggle were many. In the first place, the rural dominance which had existed in state legislatures and in the federal Congress began to pass, and urban and suburban representation increased. Second, the national geographical division of the House of Representatives began to shift. If the nation were divided into two loose categories, "sunbelt" and "snowbelt," it would have to be said that the latter predominated for many years. And a slim majority of seats were still held by the snowbelt states on the eve of the 1980s. In the 1970s, nine states lost representation and five gained. Most of the states losing seats were snowbelt, and all of the states gaining were sunbelt. It is reasonable to assume, based on preliminary forecasts by the Bureau of the Census, that this trend will continue during the 1980s. The third result of the reapportionment controversy was the emergence of a Supreme Court greatly expanded in its powers. Holding the equal protection clause of the Fourteenth Amendment as if it were a tape measure, the federal court system has been able to set aside election results, dictate district changes, and set standards for reapportionment which have placed it squarely in the center of the electoral process.

HOUSE AND SENATE LEADERS

No matter where they come from, whether city, suburb, or rural region, persons wishing to serve their country in political life usually associate themselves with the political party whose principles they generally agree with. If they are talented, dedicated, and loyal, the party will support their ambitions. It will nominate them for office, provide money and workers for their campaigns and continue to give them support as long as they remain reasonably loyal to party principles.

Once elected, new Representatives find themselves plunged into a little world of 435 citizens. In this world they soon learn that all 435 persons are not equal, since the House of Representatives is a highly organized body with many levels of importance. A new Representative, when compared with an experienced colleague, is like a kindergarten child to a twelfth grader. Both are students but they are by no means equal in influence, prestige, or knowledge.

Before the session of the Congress to which they have been elected begins, the new Representatives join the members of their political party in a caucus or party meeting. There they determine whom they shall nominate as Speaker of the House. They also select their majority leader, decide which Representatives will go on what committees, and select certain lesser officers of the House. Meanwhile, the Representatives belonging to the other political party are doing the same thing.

When the House meets, it votes on the choices for Speaker of the House. Of course, the candidate chosen by the majority party wins this very powerful position.

The Speaker is the most powerful member of the House. At one time in our history, he could prevent any legislation that did not have his approval from being enacted. This was so

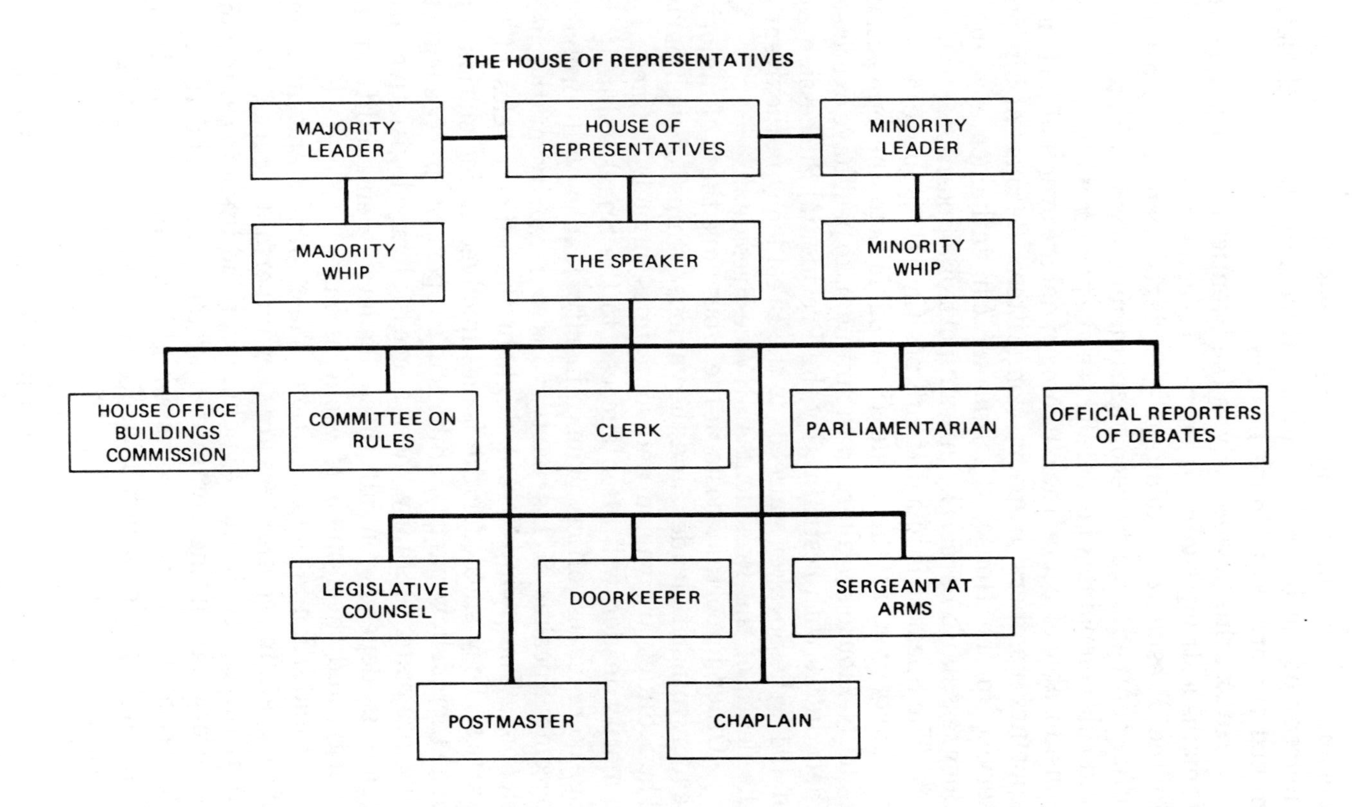
THE HOUSE OF REPRESENTATIVES
MAJORITY LEADER
HOUSE OF REPRESENTATIVES
MINORITY LEADER
MAJORITY WHIP
THE SPEAKER
MINORITY WHIP
HOUSE OFFICE BUILDINGS COMMISSION
COMMITTEE ON RULES
CLERK
PARLIAMENTARIAN
OFFICIAL REPORTERS OF DEBATES
LEGISLATIVE COUNSEL
DOORKEEPER
SERGEANT AT ARMS
POSTMASTER
CHAPLAIN

because he appointed all committees and was himself a member of the Rules Committee, the committee which determined the order of House business.

He lost this power early in the twentieth century, but still remains a strong figure. He is rated second in importance only to the President in dealing with legislation. As presiding officer of the House, he recognizes members who wish to speak, and rules on points of order. These are powers which may have considerable effect on the outcome of debate over a bill. He also appoints members to special committees. Because of his long service in the House, the Speaker can influence a younger Congressman's career by his support or opposition.

The Speaker is in a difficult position. He is supposed to aid his party, yet at the same time be fair to the opposition. Usually, House Speakers in the immediate past have exercised their duties with restraint. By the Presidental Succession Act of 1947, the Speaker succeeds to the Presidency in the event of the death of the President and Vice-President.

Other important posts in the House are those of majority leader, minority leader, and the various "whips" of each party. Their duties are varied and sometimes vaguely defined. The majority leader will often succeed to the Speakership if the Speaker leaves office. The minority leader will probably become Speaker if his party wins a majority at the next election. The "whips" rank high in the inner circles of the parties. They speak for the issues involved in legislation and urge their fellow party members to support the party's legislative program. Actually, how successful any legislative program is depends on all these leaders: their ability, their energy, and their spirit of cooperation.

In addition to these positions, the chairmen and members of the standing committees are very important figures. We will study these posts in the next chapter, in addition to examining the workings of the committee system itself. The House of Representatives, therefore, is a highly organized body. It has thousands of rules which have evolved over the years to aid the legislative process.

Because of its smaller size, the Senate does not need so many rules. Being composed of people elected for six years, it has a greater spirit of independence. The Senate does have its leaders, however. First of these is the President of the Senate,

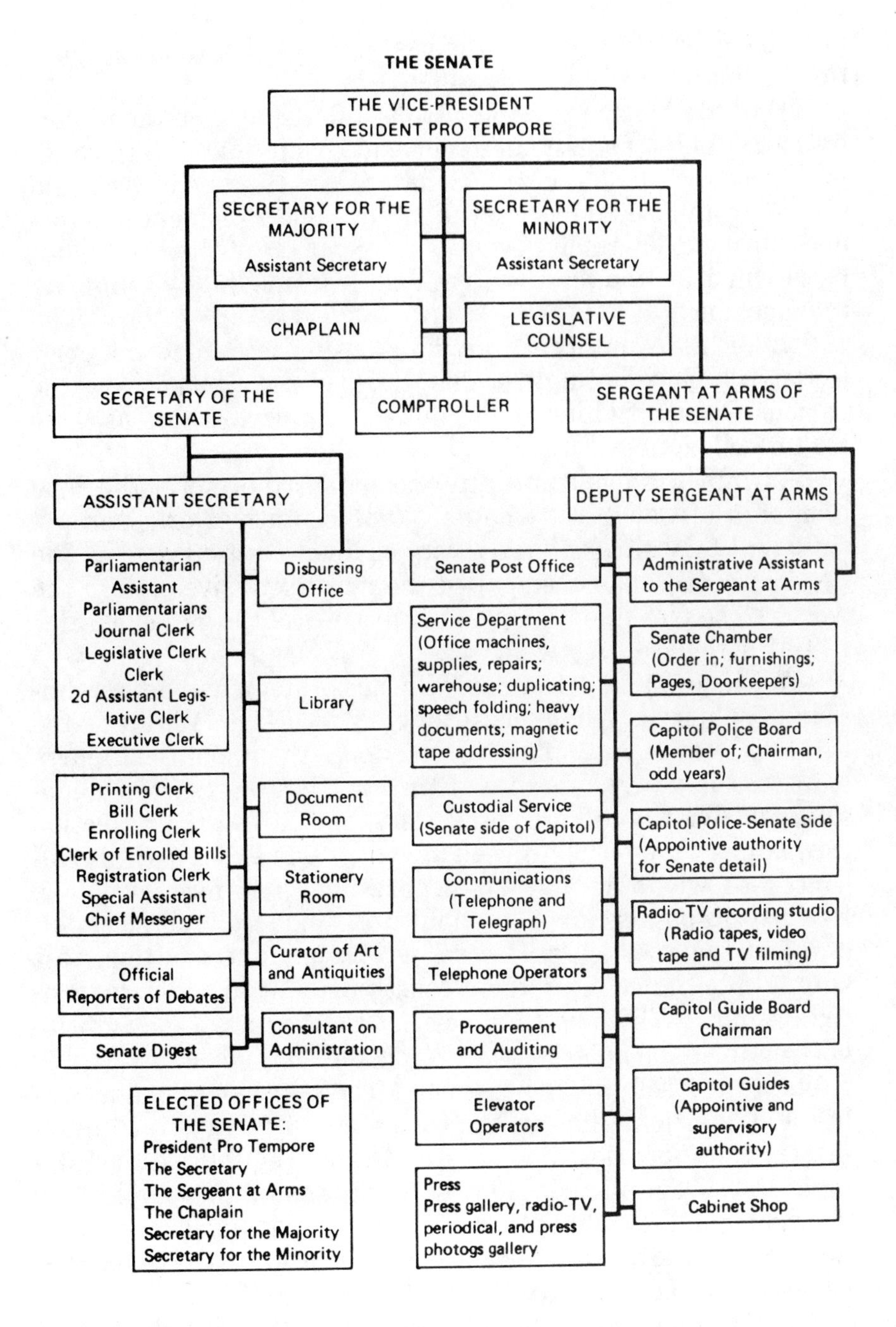
THE SENATE
THE VICE-PRESIDENT
PRESIDENT PRO TEMPORE
SECRETARY FOR THE MAJORITY
Assistant Secretary
SECRETARY FOR THE MINORITY
Assistant Secretary
CHAPLAIN
LEGISLATIVE COUNSEL
SECRETARY OF THE SENATE
COMPTROLLER
SERGEANT AT ARMS OF THE SENATE
ASSISTANT SECRETARY
DEPUTY SERGEANT AT ARMS
Parliamentarian
Assistant Parliamentarians
Journal Clerk
Legislative Clerk
Clerk
2d Assistant Legislative Clerk
Executive Clerk
Disbursing Office
Library
Printing Clerk
Bill Clerk
Enrolling Clerk
Clerk of Enrolled Bills
Registration Clerk
Special Assistant
Chief Messenger
Document Room
Stationery Room
Curator of Art and Antiquities
Official Reporters of Debates
Consultant on Administration
Senate Digest
ELECTED OFFICES OF THE SENATE:
President Pro Tempore
The Secretary
The Sergeant at Arms
The Chaplain
Secretary for the Majority
Secretary for the Minority
Senate Post Office
Service Department (Office machines, supplies, repairs; warehouse; duplicating; speech folding; heavy documents; magnetic tape addressing)
Custodial Service (Senate side of Capitol)
Communications (Telephone and Telegraph)
Telephone Operators
Procurement and Auditing
Elevator Operators
Press
Press gallery, radio-TV, periodical, and press photogs gallery
Administrative Assistant to the Sergeant at Arms
Senate Chamber (Order in; furnishings; Pages, Doorkeepers)
Capitol Police Board (Member of; Chairman, odd years)
Capitol Police-Senate Side (Appointive authority for Senate detail)
Radio-TV recording studio (Radio tapes, video tape and TV filming)
Capitol Guide Board Chairman
Capitol Guides (Appointive and supervisory authority)
Cabinet Shop

who is actually the Vice-President of the United States. He presides over the Senate, even casting a vote in the event of a tie. In his absence, the President *pro tempore* (for the time being) of the Senate presides. He is a Senator from the majority party and is usually an experienced veteran of long standing. One President *pro tem,* Senator Carl Hayden of Arizona, served in the Senate for seven terms. The President *pro tem* does not have as much power as the Speaker of the House, but he is third in line for the Presidency, immediately following the Speaker.

Like his counterpart in the House, the Senate majority leader is a powerful figure. The leader of the minority and the various Senate "whips" have duties similar to those of their House colleagues.

Within a short time after arriving, therefore, the new members of Congress, whether Representatives or Senators, find that they have entered a very exclusive organization. (The Senate, in fact, has been called the most exclusive club in the world.) The freshmen must learn the rules of the game in order to fulfill their duties well.

With so many different influences, they are understandably bewildered. Whom shall they try to please? Will it be the Speaker (or Senate majority leader), their political party leaders, the voters who put them in office, or their own consciences? We would hope, of course, that during their election campaigns they set forth their ideas clearly enough so that all concerned would know their general views on foreign policy, welfare proposals, labor, agriculture, finances, and so on.

But the question still persists. Are members of Congress simply mouthpieces for their constituents or are they legislative leaders? Which should they be? Do they have the right to vote against the interests of the people of their states or districts if they feel this is necessary? There are no easy answers to these questions since at the core of all of them is the fundamental question: how democratic or how republican should a democratic republic be? How much say should the people have and how much should their representatives have? The answers lie not in books but in the praise and protest, the votes and voices of American citizens.

As this chapter shows, a good Constitution is only a starting point in achieving good government. What is more important in the daily routine of government is how the Constitution is interpreted and applied. In this chapter, for example, we have seen how a more equitable system of representation in Congress was arrived at through action by the federal courts. In addition, we have watched Congress evolve a series of rules and precedents which have made it the vital legislative body it is today. Thus once again, the flexibility of the Constitution is demonstrated. The Constitution pointed the way, but the leaders who later rose to power carried us to our present point.

AFTER-CHAPTER REVIEW

REVIEW QUESTIONS

1. Define the following names, terms, or ideas.

"fence-mending"
censure
Seventeenth Amendment
election at large
President *pro tempore*
sunbelt
gerrymandering
Speaker of the House
reapportionment
"one man, one vote"
snowbelt

2. Vocabulary building.

colleague
constituent
decennial
astute
polygamist

3. Cases.

Colegrove v. *Green*
Wesberry v. *Sanders*
Baker v. *Carr*
Reynolds v. *Sims*

4. Review of the text.

a. List the qualifications for Senator and Representative.
b. Name and explain the duties of members of Congress.
c. Describe the average member of the House of Representatives.
d. Make a list of the privileges, financial rewards, and protections which members of Congress possess.

e. Describe the process by which Congress may discipline its own members.
f. Explain election at large and election by districts. Give the advantages and shortcomings of each method.
g. Name the most important officers of the House and Senate and explain their powers and duties.

DISCUSSION AND PROJECTS

1. Questions for discussion.

   a. Discuss the nature and problems of the United States Congress.
   b. Discuss the reapportionment of the 1960s. What were its effects? What was the national reaction to it?
   c. Using the daily newspaper or a weekly magazine as a guide, find out what Congress did last week.
   d. Write your Congressman (or delegate one member of the class to do so) to discover why he or she feels he is qualified to be your representative.
   e. Using the *World Almanac* or some other source as a guide, find out the names of those who hold the major offices of the House and Senate, how many members of Congress come from your state, and what their party affiliations are.

2. Debate topics.

   a. Resolved: Congress is anachronistic!
   b. Resolved: The present two-year term is too short a time to permit a House member to accomplish anything. The term of office should be lengthened.
   c. Resolved: Needed: a Senate chosen for life!

3. Opinion poll.

   Is Congress the "sick" branch of the federal government?

BIBLIOGRAPHY

Aikman, Lonnelle. *We, the People: The Story of the United States Capitol, Its Past and Its Promise.* Washington: United States Capitol Historical Association / National Geographic Society, 1970.

Baker, Gordon E. *The Reapportionment Revolution.* New York: Random House, 1966.

Bolling, Richard. *Power in the House.* New York: G. P. Putnam's Sons, Capricorn Books, 1974.

Diamond, Robert A., ed. *Origin and Development of Congress.* Washington: Congressional Quarterly, 1976.

Kline, Fred. "Library of Congress: The Nation's Bookcase," *National Geographic,* November 1975.

Mansfield, Harvey C., Jr. *Congress against the President.* New York: Proceedings of the Academy of Political Science, 1975.

"Mounting Discontent with First 'Billion-Dollar Congress,'" *U.S. News & World Report,* 7 March 1977.

Naughton, James M. "The Lost Innocence of Congressman AuCoin," *New York Times Magazine,* 31 August 1975.

Parris, Judith H. "Congress in the American Presidential System," *Current History,* June 1974.

Ross, Irwin. "'Tip' O'Neill—Speaker of the House," *Reader's Digest,* November 1977.

Also useful in studying Congress are the various publications available from Congressional Quarterly, Inc., 1414 22nd Street, NW, Washington, D.C. 20037. This company publishes a *Weekly Report,* a semi-annual *CQ Guide to Current American Government,* and a number of pamphlets and books such as that by Diamond listed above.

UPI

Television lights blaze down on the Select Senate Committee on Presidential Campaign Activities as the committee, chaired by Senator Sam Ervin, Jr., of North Carolina, prepares to open its investigation into the Watergate matter. The committee held its hearings in the historic Senate Caucus Room, where several other famous public hearings have been conducted.

5

Congress: What It Does

The thousands of laws passed by Congress during its history have been based to a great extent upon eighteen powers listed in Article I, Section 8, of the Constitution. Some of these powers are narrow and specific; others, such as the "necessary and proper" clause, are quite broad. In this chapter, we will examine these powers and explain their importance. We will also study the workings of Congress more fully, particularly the work of committees and the method of passing laws.

The powers of Congress will be considered under four main headings: financial, commercial, national security, and general powers.

FINANCIAL POWERS

Congressional power over financial matters is vast. It includes determining how more than $500 billion a year will be raised and how it will be spent. The House of Representatives has the constitutional power to originate revenue bills and, traditionally, to initiate spending (appropriations) bills. This power includes determining rates of taxation on business and personal income, customs duties paid by foreign exporters who send their goods to the United States, and excise taxes placed upon goods (whiskey, cigarettes, and other luxuries) sold in the United States.

Congress may also borrow money to meet emergencies or to balance the budget. This is done by the sale of bonds and other certificates of indebtedness to citizens, banks, corporations, and state and local governments. The present debt of the United States is more than $700 billion.

Still another financial power of Congress is its right to create a mint to coin money and to print paper money which shall be legal tender. Congress, of course, determines the conditions under which this is done. Since this power must belong exclusively to Congress, the Constitution provides the legislature with the power to punish counterfeiters.

The rights to tax, borrow and spend are more important than they seem to be at first. Congress also can use them for regulatory purposes. It can reduce the sale of alcoholic beverages, for example, by putting high taxes on these items. Thus, the taxing power can have a social effect. Congress has used its power over customs duties, too, to protect American businesses from foreign competition.

COMMERCIAL POWERS

On a par with its financial powers are the commercial powers of Congress. They stem from the following clause in Article I, Section 8: "To regulate commerce with foreign nations and among the several states." Early in our history, in a decision called *Gibbons* v. *Ogden,* the Supreme Court ruled that this power should be broadly interpreted. The case involved a monopoly granted to Robert Fulton to operate steamboats on the Hudson River. Fulton's firm permitted Ogden to engage in the business under the charter received from New York State. When another steamboat operator named Gibbons secured permission from the federal government, Ogden asked the New York courts to forbid it.

The case reached the Supreme Court, and John Marshall ruled that Congress alone has power over commerce between the states and that New York had no right to grant a monopoly. His decision meant that all foreign and interstate exchanges were within the regulatory eye of Congress. The term "commerce," therefore, extends to all forms of transportation—rail, water, road, and air—and to *everything* which moves in foreign or interstate commerce, including human beings. The commerce clause is the basis for federal kidnapping legislation, and several recent Supreme Court decisions upholding

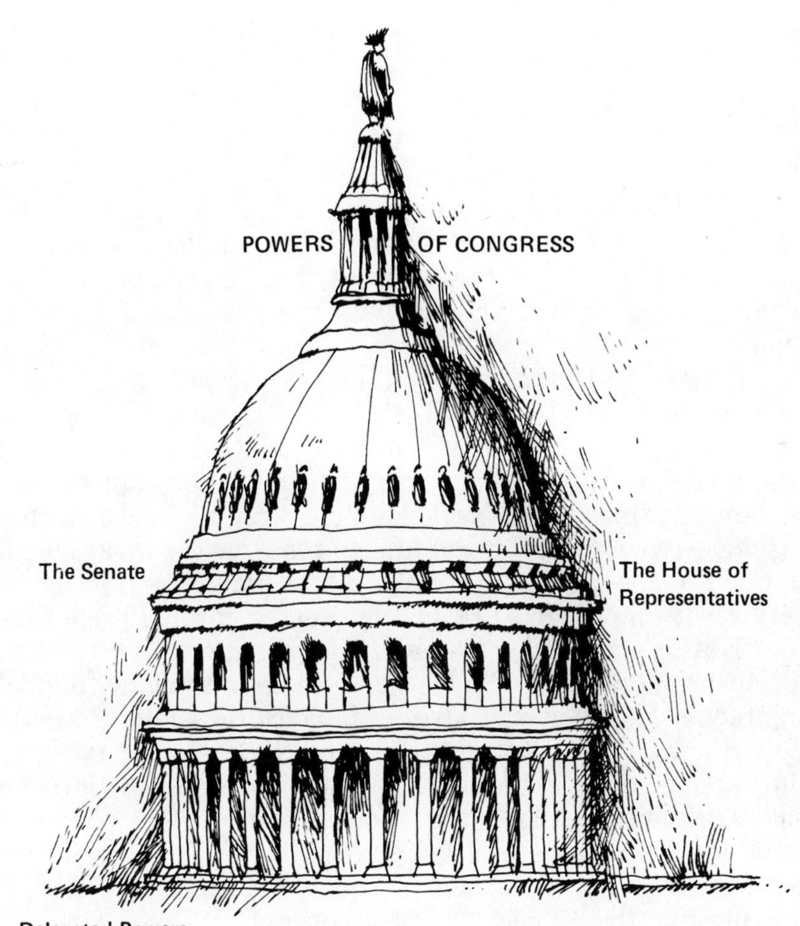

Delegated Powers

Collect taxes to pay for the cost of running the federal government
Regulate industry and trade among the states
Regulate trade with foreign nations
Raise armed forces for national defense
Declare war and make peace
Establish post offices and roads
Print and coin money
Rule on naturalization and immigration
Govern the District of Columbia
Admit new states to the Union
Borrow money
Establish a court system

Implied Powers

To make the proper and necessary laws to administer the delegated powers
To provide for the general welfare of the nation

civil rights legislation have also been based on it. We will return to this subject in later chapters.

NATIONAL SECURITY

The third category of congressional power covers all matters connected with defense, whether external or internal. These "war powers" grant Congress the right to declare war and make peace. Congress therefore has the responsibility of creating armies and navies and making provision for paying, supplying, and governing them.

Congress also has the power over the *militia*, a term it defined in 1916 as "all able-bodied men over eighteen and under forty-five." What we call the National Guard is the organized militia, military units trained and equipped for instant readiness. The National Guard may be used in three instances: to enforce federal law, to repel enemy invasion, and to quell domestic disorders. When the Guard is not in federal service, it may be used by state governors to maintain order. The National Guard represents one of America's oldest traditions: the tradition of the citizen-soldier. While distinguishing themselves in war, Guardsmen have also served the nation both during the Civil Rights crises of the 1950s and 1960s and during such natural disasters as the blizzards, landslides, and floods of the 1970s. After the shooting deaths of four persons on the Kent State University campus by Ohio Guardsmen in 1970, however, the use of the Guard in dealing with civil disorders has become the subject of much controversy.

Under the war powers, Congress has created the Selective Service System, passed laws controlling aliens, punished espionage, limited freedom of speech, and even regulated transportation and food consumption. On the basis of the war powers Congress supported President Franklin Roosevelt's imprisonment of Japanese and Japanese-Americans during World War II, when more than one hundred thousand persons were detained by American military authority. The action was taken because some of those imprisoned were believed to be disloyal to the United States. The Supreme Court declared this a constitutional use of war powers in the 1944 case of *Korematsu* v. *United States*. Not all the justices agreed, however. One of them stated he did not think it was necessary to take such drastic measures even in view of the emergency caused by Japan's attack on Pearl Harbor.[1]

GENERAL POWERS

The general powers of Congress cover a multitude of purposes. The Constitution empowers the Congress to create courts inferior to the Supreme Court and to establish the salaries, number of justices, and jurisdiction of these courts as well as of the Supreme Court. Congress also was charged with the responsibility of creating the District of Columbia when Maryland and Virginia ceded land for this purpose along the Potomac. The Maryland grant was chosen as the site for the present capital, which was first occupied during John Adams's administration in 1800. After years of fairly tight control over the city, Congress in recent years has allowed it more self-government. Residents of the district were permitted to vote in presidential elections after the adoption of the Twenty-third Amendment in 1961. And, as a result of a reform law passed in 1970, the district has a nonvoting delegate to the House of Representatives.

Congressional control over impeachment is its broadest disciplinary power. Any federal official of the executive or judicial branches may be impeached, that is, accused of wrong-doing.[2] This action is limited to the offenses of treason, bribery, "or other high Crimes and Misdemeanors." The House impeaches by majority vote and the case then goes to the Senate. If two-thirds of the Senators present agree, the impeached person is considered convicted of the impeachment or accusation. He or she can then be removed from office but may still have to face criminal charges for the misdeed, since the congressional process is not considered to be punishment. This drastic procedure rarely has been used in our history.

---

1. Many Japanese-Americans eventually served in the armed forces and distinguished themselves by their bravery and loyalty.
2. Members of Congress are subject to discipline by their respective houses and therefore are not impeachable.

Only twelve persons have been impeached by the House. Of these, only four have been convicted by the Senate. President Andrew Johnson was impeached in 1868, but the Senate was one vote short of convicting him.

In recent years, the impeachment process was once again employed on the presidential level. President Richard M. Nixon's efforts to conceal the involvement of his close associates in the burglarizing of Democratic headquarters at the Watergate building in Washington led to hearings by the House Judiciary Committee in 1974. The committee voted favorably on three articles of impeachment: obstruction of justice, misuse of the Internal Revenue Service and the FBI for political purposes, and refusal to release documents demanded by the Judiciary Committee. President Nixon avoided impeachment (and the conviction which might have followed in the Senate), by resigning in August, 1974.

Congress also has power over bankruptcy proceedings. Throughout history, societies have treated debtors in many different ways. Some were sold into slavery if they could not pay their bills, others were executed or imprisoned. In British and in early American history, imprisonment for debt was practiced. This was a rather futile way to solve the problem since debtors had to stay in jail until their debts were paid, and of course they could not hope to pay them while they were imprisoned. To ease the burden on persons or businesses which go hopelessly into debt, Congress has enacted bankruptcy legislation. A person in dire financial distress files a bankruptcy petition in federal court and, if his or her request is approved, a referee is appointed who sells any assets the debtor may have. Each creditor is paid a sum in proportion to the amount he or she is owed, and the debtor is then free to begin life again without carrying a hopeless burden.

The Constitution also confers on Congress the power to make uniform rules concerning naturalization, the process by which a person may become an American citizen. These regulations have varied greatly throughout our history. At one time, a person could not become a citizen unless he or she had resided in the United States for fourteen years (it is now five); and for many years, specific groups of people (such as Chinese) could not become citizens. On some occasions all the people of a

UPI

Peter Rodino, left, chairman of the House Judiciary Committee during the Nixon impeachment hearings in 1974, confers with Representative Lawrence Hogan during a session of the panel.

UPI

Senate Watergate Committee members and staff confer with Chairman Sam Ervin in July, 1973, during hearings investigating the involvement of President Nixon and his White House aides in the burglary of Democratic headquarters at the Watergate building. To Senator Ervin's left is Senator Howard Baker; directly to Ervin's right is Sam Dash, the committee's chief counsel.

certain area have been granted American citizenship at one time. When Texas was annexed, for example, all citizens of Texas became citizens of the United States.

The need for uniformity in weights and measures was also recognized in the Constitution. Can you imagine the confusion if everyone disagreed on how long a yard was, or how heavy a pound should be? To avoid this, Congress created the National Bureau of Standards under the Commerce Department. The bureau sets and maintains standards and also conducts scientific research. Congress has exercised its power under this clause to end confusion over daylight saving time. For years, the practice of putting clocks ahead one hour in springtime to allow for more daylight hours was a matter which local communities decided for themselves. Under a law of 1966, each state decided whether to accept or reject daylight saving time. Now time may vary from state to state within a given time zone, but at least it is uniform within each state. For years, people have urged that the whole nation go on permanent daylight saving time, and Congress has the power to pass a law requiring this. A more recent example of this power is Congress's decision that the nation will adopt the metric system in the near future and will phase out the old system of inches and pounds.

Congress is directed by the Constitution to grant patents and copyrights protecting the products of inventors and authors. A patent is an exclusive monopoly on an invention for a period of seventeen years. It allows inventors to profit from the products of their brains but does not give them a perpetual monopoly. Written works are copyrighted for the author's lifetime plus fifty years, according to a law which went into effect in 1978. The Patent Office is one of the busiest places in the city of Washington. It keeps records of millions of foreign and American patents. Every day it receives hundreds of applications, each of which must be researched to see if the invention suggested is patentable. The research can go on for years before a patent is issued. The Copyright Office protects written works such as songs, books, and speeches, as well as films and paintings. The United States has patent and copyright agreements with some, but not all, nations.

The postal system also comes under congressional powers. This is a broad power, although it may not seem so at first. The Postal Service is not obliged to carry everything a person wishes to send. For example, subversive and certain other types of literature may not be sent through the Postal Service. Recently a New Yorker was sentenced to prison for violating federal obscenity laws which forbid the sending of obscene materials through the mails.

Since the Postal Service uses public transportation, such as railroads and airplanes, any disruption in its service can violate regulations. When strikers in the 1890s stopped trains with mail cars on them, the strike leaders were punished for interfering with the mails.

The four categories of congressional power we have discussed—financial, commercial, security, and general—make up the bulk of the authority of the legislature. Other powers of Congress appear outside of Article I, Section 8. For example, Congress gained unlimited taxing power by the Sixteenth Amendment. For a time, under the Eighteenth Amendment, it had the power to prohibit the making or selling of liquor.

The Constitution grants power to the Congress, which then is free to enact legislation carrying out its intentions. Thus, congressional powers are not automatically used, nor must Congress act on them. When Congress does decide to use its powers, however, it follows an involved set of procedures. This is the lawmaking process.

CONGRESSIONAL COMMITTEES

At the beginning of every session, Congress divides itself into committees. It would be impossible for Congress as a whole to consider every one of the thousands of bills and resolutions submitted for consideration at every session. Congress therefore specializes, and small parts of the whole consider bills under different categories.

In the House there are twenty-two standing committees. Some are very large, as for example the Appropriations Committee of the House, while others, such as the House Committee on Standards of Official Conduct, are quite small. By an action of the Senate in 1977, committees were set at twenty-one, and members were permitted to serve on no more than three.

In both houses, the position of committee chairman is extremely important because the committee determines the fate of any bill, and the chairman determines the work of the committee. He or she tells the other committee members when to meet, what bills or resolutions to consider, and how to go about this. If a chairman is opposed to a particular measure, he

Party Make-up of Congress

	Democratic	Republican	Independent
92nd (1971–73):			
Senate	55	45	0
House of Representatives	255	177	0
93rd (1973–75):			
Senate	57	43	0
House of Representatives	242	192	1
94th (1975–77):			
Senate	62	38	0
House of Representatives	291	144	0
95th (1977–79):			
Senate	61	38	1
House of Representatives	288	147	0
96th (1979–81):			
Senate	58	41	1
House of Representatives	276	159	0

or she can usually "kill the bill," either single-handedly or with the support of the other committee members from the same political party.

This is so because each committee is organized along party lines. If sixty percent of the House is Democratic and forty percent is Republican, for example, then a ten-member committee would have six Democrats and four Republicans. The chairman, of course, would be a Democrat.

The entire committee system, from the chairman to the newest member, is based on two principles: seniority and election. Seniority puts a person by the chairman's "chair." Election seats him, if the members of his party think him worthy. Thus, the longer a person serves in Congress, the greater the opportunity for advancement, provided that the person performs well in the position.

Until recently, seniority was the sole means of determining service on a committee. Simply by staying alive and winning re-election countless times, a person earned a chairmanship. This produced what might be called a "gerontocracy," or government by the aged. While the average age of the American people was in the thirties, and of the Congress in the fifties, the average age of committee chairmen was considerably higher. In 1972, for example, the mean age was sixty-eight in the House and sixty-three in the Senate.

Committee chairmen receive many benefits, including the right to hire staff members, which gives them patronage power—that is, opportunities to help people who have done favors for the party in the past. And while it is forbidden to put one's own relatives or in-laws into congressional jobs, members of Congress often do favors by hiring some other member's relative. More important than this small power is the ability of chairmen to guide the course of committee work. Thus, a chairman can pursue a matter vigorously or feebly, depending on his or her attitude toward a bill.

There are procedures by which other committee members can circumvent an arbitrary decision by a chairman, but these involve a great deal of political in-fighting both in the committee and in the legislative body as a whole. While the procedures are less cumbersome than in earlier days, it is still difficult for "mavericks" to accomplish their ends. The rule in Congress is still "to get along, go along."

During the decade of the 1970s, vast changes were made to democratize the House of Representatives and its committee system. Among the significant steps were:

- Opening committee meetings to the public, with some exceptions, such as those pertaining to national security;
- Permitting the vote for the chairman to be taken in secret;
- Preventing a committee chairman from heading more than one subcommittee;
- Giving minority party committee members the right to hire staff to help in their committee work.

In addition to these changes, other reforms were undertaken, including the creation of committees to review the ethical conduct of members. To increase public involvement, radio and television coverage was allowed in both houses, with some modifications.

Above all, Congress became more aware of its oversight responsibility. For years, Congress acted as a law factory, grinding out thousands of laws every year without any real thought of the consequences in cost or inconvenience. The President was directed to do this, the courts were directed to do that, and the citizens were supposed to pay and obey. Sometimes these actions caused real hardships. Congress has now required that committees set up machinery to oversee the workings of the laws passed. Through the use of congressional oversight, the problems which arise may be corrected.

HOUSE PROCEDURE

In the House, all members are not equal. In fact, the House is divided into tiers of privilege, which might be drawn as follows:

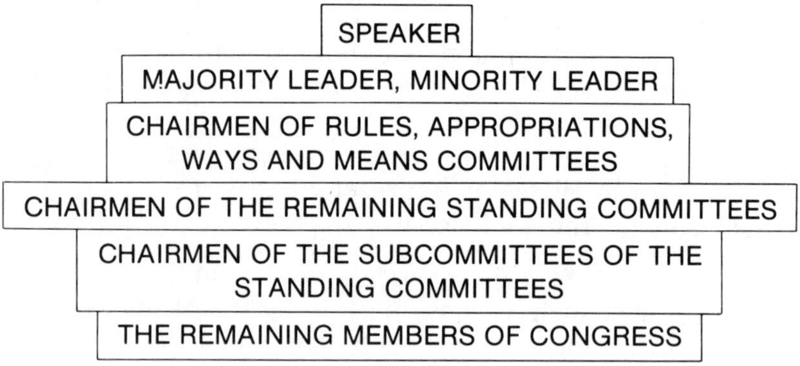

SPEAKER

MAJORITY LEADER, MINORITY LEADER

CHAIRMEN OF RULES, APPROPRIATIONS, WAYS AND MEANS COMMITTEES

CHAIRMEN OF THE REMAINING STANDING COMMITTEES

CHAIRMEN OF THE SUBCOMMITTEES OF THE STANDING COMMITTEES

THE REMAINING MEMBERS OF CONGRESS

The House Rules Committee stands out above all the rest. This committee determines when important bills will be debated, how much time will be allowed for them, and whether or not amendments may be made to a bill. This is called giving a bill a "rule" and places a kind of priority upon the proposed legislation so that it is considered before other less serious or controversial business.

House of Representatives

Senator Robert C. Byrd of West Virginia (left), was elected Senate majority leader in 1977. He has served in Congress since 1952. Thomas P. O'Neill, Jr. (right), a Democrat from Massachusetts, became Speaker of the House of Representatives in 1977, succeeding Carl Albert of Oklahoma.

Should the fifteen members of the Rules Committee decide to slow down any bill which a majority of them does not approve, they may refuse to give it a rule. In this way, the Rules Committee, which is supposed to be concerned with scheduling a measure for debate, can actually exercise a veto power over bills already approved by other House standing committees. Among the reforms adopted by the House in the 1970s, however, was one giving the Speaker greater power over the operation of the Rules Committee.

Congress operates by what seem to be and often are very roundabout, cumbersome procedures which block rather than expedite the legislative process. But these regulations illustrate another part of the rules of the game of government. Most citizens do not realize how complex these rules are. When they learn about them for the first time they must feel, as you probably do now, that they are nonsensical, time-consuming details. But life, in government as anywhere else, is the sum of its details. Committees, including the Rules Committee, are absolutely necessary to the functioning of the House of Representatives. They must have regulations providing for the orderly process of making laws. These regulations must be followed or chaos will result. Even so simple a game as baseball has hundreds of rules which players and spectators alike must know and observe in order to enjoy it.

In addition to standing committees, there are several other types of committees which should be considered. Subcommittees of the standing committees engage in specific investigations. They are appointed by the chairmen of the standing committees. Joint committees, which include representatives of both houses, are another type; they sometimes are temporary and at other times permanent. The conference committee is a temporary joint committee which serves the purpose of ironing out differences between Senate and House versions of bills.

A BILL BECOMES LAW

Now that you have some knowledge of the committee system, let us pass on to the process by which bills become laws. As you know, each Congress runs for two years, in two separate sessions. Congress begins its life in January of every year and operates until sometime between October and December. According to the Constitution, Congress must meet once each year. It may meet more often if called into special session, as we will see when we study the powers of the President.

Any one of the 535 members of Congress may introduce bills or resolutions. Bills are either *public,* that is, of importance to the whole country, or *private,* that is, affecting one person or one group. Resolutions are either *simple,* when only one House resolves or declares itself on a subject; *concurrent,* when both houses agree; or *joint,* when both houses agree on a matter and pass it on to the President for action by him. Here are some examples of these five types of measures considered by Congress:

1. Public bill—general legislation such as a tax reform bill;
2. Private bill—a measure to permit a certain individual to

come into the United States even though the immigration quota for his or her country has been filled;

3. Simple resolution—expresses the general views of one house on a particular subject. For example, sometimes the Senate resolves that the United States should or should not approve the admission of a nation to the United Nations;
4. Concurrent resolution—used to create joint committees of the House and Senate to determine when Congress should adjourn;
5. Joint resolution—used to declare war and to annex territories (as when Texas and Hawaii were annexed).

Simple and concurrent resolutions differ from the other types of measures in that they do not have the force of law and are not subject to presidential approval.

Whatever form it takes, the bill or resolution is placed in a "hopper" on the Speaker's table in the House or put on a clerk's desk in the Senate. A member of Congress is the only person who may introduce legislation, but this does not mean that only the ideas of members of Congress can be written into potential acts of Congress. In fact, ideas for legislation come from many sources:

- The President has the constitutional duty to propose measures. Thus, you often read of the "adminstration's program." Presidents are often judged on how successful they were in having legislative ideas adopted. Presidents Johnson and Eisenhower were quite successful in their attempts to work with Congress, while Presidents Carter and Ford met with frequent opposition.
- Members of Congress themselves may have projects they are very concerned with. Sometimes they become so associated with a project or cause that their names become almost synonymous with it.
- Reports of investigations by congressional committees often lead to new laws. For example, congressional probing into labor union troubles led to passage of the Landrum-Griffin Act to correct abuses of power by some union leaders.
- Lobbyists have an important effect on legislation, both in securing passage or repeal of certain bills, and in prevent-

ing passage of laws thought to be detrimental to their interests.

- Pressure groups which gain popular support can bring about the introduction of legislation.
- Individuals also are capable of influencing Congressmen to introduce laws. One patriotic American from New York waged a one-man campaign some years ago to have American gifts to needy people overseas clearly labeled. This "Mark American" program was designed to show where the gift was from and to prevent other nations from taking credit for it.

HOW BILLS ARE PASSED IN THE HOUSE

A bill must pass both House and Senate. Because the House is larger, the procedure is more complex there. Let us first consider House action on a bill.

Once introduced, a bill is numbered and referred to the appropriate committee. When its turn arrives, the bill is considered by the committee. It is here that most bills die. If it survives this big test, the measure usually is assigned to a subcommittee of the standing committee. The subcommittee begins to investigate by holding hearings on the bill. At these hearings, governmental officials, experts on the subject involved, representatives of pressure groups, and the general public can testify. The hearings may be public (open) or secret (closed-door), depending on the nature of the subject and the wish of the committee. The subcommittee also has attorneys and investigators available, when necessary, to gather information.

Most of the time, committee investigations cover matters of vital interest to part or all of the country. Cabinet members annually spend hundreds of hours testifying on the needs of their departments. This is serious business and is followed carefully by members of Congress and the public. Occasionally, however, there are light moments. Some years ago, a House subcommittee member announced that he had been asked to consider approving one grant to permit scientists in Australia to study the perspiration tendencies of aborigines, another to study the smells of ocean fish, and a third to determine the movements of mentally ill persons in Norway!

After a favorable subcommittee report, the bill goes to the full committee. The committee either passes it as it stands, passes it with amendments, defeats it, or replaces it with the committee's own version of the bill. When it leaves the committee, the bill is placed on a "calendar," which is a list or schedule showing the order in which the bill will be considered. The *Union* calendar deals with money bills—either revenue (how money is to be raised) or appropriations (how it is to be spent). The *House* calendar is for all other public bills. A *Private* calendar is set up for private bills and a *Consent* calendar for bills which are not opposed by members of the House.

If the Rules Committee has given the bill a rule, as it does with important legislation, the bill will be taken up before other bills on the various calendars. If not, it will be taken in its turn.

When the bill reaches the floor of the House, the Representatives get down to business. For some bills, particularly money bills, the House votes to become one great committee, called the Committee of the Whole. This needs only 100 members, not a quorum (one more than half of the membership, or 218), and the rules which usually govern the House are suspended. Even the Speaker leaves the chair and another member presides. The bill is read, each member is allowed five minutes to talk on it, and amendments are offered and voted on.

A member of the House may call at any time for a vote on the bill. This is referred to technically as moving the "previous question." If the House approves this proposal, a vote is taken on the bill itself. There are several methods of voting in Congress. The Speaker simply may ask for a voice vote, yes or no. A bill is in this way passed or defeated without any member being recorded specifically for or against it (in Latin, this is called *viva voce*). If one-fifth of the members present desire it, the vote of each person is recorded and published. In this more formal roll-call vote, members of Congress used to spend a great deal of time merely responding with their votes as their

U.S. Capitol Historical Society

The U.S. House of Representatives.

names were called. Since the average House roll call took about thirty minutes, congressional studies revealed that the House spent more than fifteen minutes out of every hour it was in session in answering one type of roll call or another. To speed up the process, the Ninety-third Congress (1973-1975) introduced a computerized system of electronic voting for the House of Representatives. When a roll-call vote is required, the Congress member uses a special card to register his or her vote at various outlets in the House chamber of the Capitol. The new system has reduced the thirty-minute time to about fifteen minutes.

Members of Congress need not vote. If they are unable to be in the chamber when a vote is to be taken, they may indicate in the *Congressional Record* how they stand on the bill. Or they may "pair" with other members of Congress on a bill. This is a procedure by which two persons who have opposite views agree that if one of them is away, the other will announce that their votes are canceling each other and will not vote.

U.S. Capitol Historical Society

The U.S. Senate

HOW BILLS ARE PASSED IN THE SENATE

There are more similarities than differences in the ways bills are acted on by the Senate and House. Most of the differences involve fewer rules for the smaller Senate. With only a hundred members, it may do things somewhat differently from the House. Senate members have assigned desks, for example, while House members do not. And Senators may debate at greater length on bills than House members. Occasionally, Senators engage in a filibuster, a practice based on securing recognition from the presiding officer and then not yielding the floor to anyone except allies in order to prevent the Senate from voting on a matter. This is similar to "freezing the ball" in basketball.

During a filibuster, Senators talk and read endlessly, and by no means limit themselves to the subject of the bill they are filibustering. They read poetry, prose, or even telephone directories to their colleagues. The whole point of a filibuster

UPI

The subway station under the Capitol. The subway travels from the Capitol to the old and new Senate office buildings.

is to focus attention upon a matter in hopes that the public will demand that the Senate reconsider it, or to tie up other business so badly that a compromise will be reached and the Senate can get back to work.

The method of cloture, or the choking off of debate, is used as a last resort. In 1917, the Senate adopted Rule Twenty-two, permitting the whole body to cut off debate. Over the last six decades, there have been changes in the method but, basically, it is as follows. To end a filibuster, sixteen Senators can petition for a cloture motion. This is followed within two days by a vote on the motion. If three-fifths of the Senate's entire membership (usually sixty, unless there are vacancies) approve the motion, the filibuster is ended, and debate is limited to one hour for each Senator.

Cloture votes are not guaranteed to succeed, by any means. In the past two decades, less than thirty percent have succeeded. This is due to the feeling of many Senators that the right to filibuster must be upheld, regardless of what they

UPI

Tongsun Park, a South Korean rice dealer, left, reviews documents during his testimony before the House Ethics Committee in April, 1978. Park was being questioned about the alleged payment of bribes to U.S. Congressmen and White House aides to boost U.S. military and other aid to South Korea.

may think about the particular bill involved.

Another difference which separates the Senate from the House is the constitutional power of the Senate to approve presidential appointments and treaties. These powers will be considered in a later chapter.

LOBBYING

The House and the Senate are similar in that they are both subject to pressures from lobbyists. Lobbying is as old as the nation and may be defined as a deliberate effort on the part of individuals or groups to influence legislation. Benjamin Franklin was a lobbyist at one time, speaking for the welfare of the American states to members of the British Parliament. Formal lobbying differs from ordinary efforts of group pressure in that the lobbyist is usually a full-time paid representative of a group seeking to influence legislation.

A lobbyist is often a lawyer, public relations person, journalist, or even a former member of Congress. Under the basic law governing lobbying, the Regulation of Lobbying Act of 1946, a lobbyist must register with the appropriate official of the House or Senate and must give regular reports on his or her expenses, salary, and employers. Many lobbyists represent only one organization, others speak for several, and a few represent a dozen or more.

Some of the most active and powerful groups to use lobbying techniques in Washington are well-known organizations such as the AMA (American Medical Association), the American Legion, the American Farm Bureau Federation, and the AFL–CIO (American Federation of Labor–Congress of Industrial Organizations). Others include ecology groups, temperance groups, railroad employees, and public utility companies. These and other lobbies annually spend millions of dollars to protect their interests.

Foreign nations, too, are active in lobbying Congress. The Arab and Israeli governments, for example, spend large amounts of money to present their views and to sway public and congressional opinion in their direction. Recent scandals concerning South Korean lobbying efforts have focused attention on possible abuses of this practice.

What do professional lobbyists do? They talk to members of Congress, offering arguments in support of their cause. They mail out literature, hoping to influence legislators in this way. The overwhelming majority of lobbyists are intelligent and honorable persons who respect members of Congress and make no attempts to threaten or bribe them to gain votes. They use facts to gain their ends, and they will often know more about the effects of a particular law on an industry or group than will the members of Congress. Despite the basic honesty of lobbyists, Congress must nevertheless keep a clear eye upon them, since they do plead for special causes. By frequent investigation, severe penalties for bribery, and public exposure of those who abuse the privilege, lobbying has been kept under control. Congress must also police its members carefully to prevent breaches of conflict-of-interest laws.

The workings of Congress are complex, but an understanding of them is vital to the citizen. As can be seen, the Constitution did not provide for all contingencies which might arise (filibustering, lobbying, etc.). Congess has had to make additional rules as the country grew. That the Constitution allowed for such growth is another illustration of its flexibility and another reason for its long life.

AFTER-CHAPTER REVIEW

REVIEW QUESTIONS

1. Define the following names, terms, or ideas.

excise tax
customs duties
patent
copyright
standing committee
joint committee
viva voce
filibuster
conference committee
vote pairing
Committee of the Whole
"previous question"
calendars
cloture
naturalization

2. Vocabulary building.

misdemeanor
impeachment
obscenity
ecology
bankruptcy
temperance

3. Cases.

Gibbons v. *Ogden*
Korematsu v. *United States*

4. Review of the text.

a. Make a list of all the legislative powers found in Article I, Section 8.
b. Distinguish between revenue and appropriations bills.
c. Describe the "war powers."
d. Explain the impeachment process in general and as it was partially employed in 1974.

e. How does the committee system work? Why does it favor one-party states and safe districts?
f. What are the powers and duties of committee chairmen? How does the Rules Committee chairman differ from other committee chairmen?
g. Name and explain the types of bills and resolutions which come before Congress. Can you give an example of each?
h. List and explain the major sources of legislation.
i. Describe the process by which a bill becomes law.
j. How do the Senate and the House differ in their powers and in their methods of procedure?

DISCUSSION AND PROJECTS

1. Questions for discussion.

a. Discuss the powers which Congress has under the "commerce clause." Include in your answer an elaboration of the *Gibbons* v. *Ogden* decision.
b. Read the chapter in John F. Kennedy's *Profiles in Courage* which deals with Andrew Johnson's impeachment. Discuss this entire affair.
c. What dangers are inherent in lobbying? Discuss the entire lobbying problem.

2. Debate topics.

a. Resolved: The seniority system must be abolished!
b. Resolved: Congressional rules must be changed to prevent a minority from paralyzing the work of the majority.

3. Opinion poll.

Should members of Congress be required to retire at age sixty-five?

BIBLIOGRAPHY

See Chapter 4 for related bibliography.

Bibby, John F., and Davidson, Roger H. *On Capitol Hill.* Hinsdale, Ill.: Dryden Press, 1972.

"*Congressional Record:* Saying One Thing, Publishing Another," *U.S. News & World Report,* 5 January 1976.

Dale, Edwin L., Jr., "Can Congress at Last Control the Money Tree," *New York Times Magazine,* 22 August 1976.

Diamond, Robert A., ed. *Powers of Congress.* Washington, D.C.: Congressional Quarterly, 1976.

Fenno, Richard F., Jr. *Congressmen in Committees.* Boston: Little, Brown, 1973.

"A Lesson from History—Trial of Andrew Jackson," *U.S. News & World Report,* 12 August 1974.

Rieselbach, Leroy N. *Congressional Reform in the Seventies.* Morristown, N.J.: General Learning Press, 1977.

UPI

The President's office, sometimes called the Oval Office, in the west wing of the White House. The west wing was added in the administration of Theodore Roosevelt, and contains offices for the President's staff, the Cabinet room, and press rooms.

6

The Presidency

To be President of the United States, one does not need special training. No college diploma, no previous job experience is needed. One needs only to have attained the age of thirty-five, to be a natural-born citizen, and to receive a majority of the votes cast by the Electoral College. The last is a hard requirement, since it can be met only after months and often years of campaigning to win the approval of the American voters, 81,681,938 of whom participated in the 1976 presidential election.

Just as the qualifications are vague, so the manner in which the president performs his duties is equally informal. There are no special working hours for the President, but he usually puts in twelve to fourteen hours a day. The schedule is lighter on weekends and vacations, but there is enough work to do to justify the observation that the President is the most overworked man in the world.

A President recently said of his office: "The Presidency has made every man who occupied it, no matter how small, bigger than he was and no matter how big, not big enough for its demands."[1] The late President Lyndon B. Johnson, who made this remark, was making a distinction between two important things—the Presidency and the President.

The *Presidency* is the institution empowered with duties such as executing laws and leading the country in war and

1. Quoted by Bill Moyers, *U.S. News & World Report*, 13 June 1966, p. 81.

peace. It is a continuing symbol of leadership under the will of the majority. The *President,* the man who occupies the office of the Presidency, is a temporary instrument charged with carrying out the responsibilities of that office. The American people have a special respect for their Presidency and resent any word or action which tends to degrade it.

This distinction is important because it shows that the office of the Presidency is bigger than any man who holds it. When he leaves, the Presidency remains. In many other countries such continuity has not existed. The dictator Adolf Hitler is an example of the union of office and man. His personal government did not survive his death.

PRESIDENTIAL BACKGROUNDS

Where do American Presidents come from and what occupations do they have before election to the nation's highest office? Most Presidents have come from fairly populous states, such as New York, Virginia, Ohio, and Massachusetts. In fact, these four states have accounted for about half of our chief executives. Geographically, the South leads in producing Presidents, having sent fifteen of her sons to the White House. The Northeast is a close second, while the West is underrepresented. Only six Presidents were born west of the Mississippi, but it is significant that these six are included among the last nine Presidents. Perhaps this shows a trend toward presidential leadership coming out of the West.

Most Presidents come to office with wide backgrounds in state or national government. Some have been governors, others Senators or Representatives, and still others have become famous through service in the Cabinet. Jefferson, Madison, Monroe, John Quincy Adams, and Van Buren all served as Secretaries of State. Some came to office from distinguished military careers, as was the case with Eisenhower, Grant, Taylor, and, of course, Washington.

Our Presidents generally have not come from the "first families" of America, socially or financially. Many of them, like Jackson, Van Buren, Lincoln, Garfield, and Andrew Johnson, had impoverished childhoods which they overcame by ambition and hard work. In recent years, American Presi-

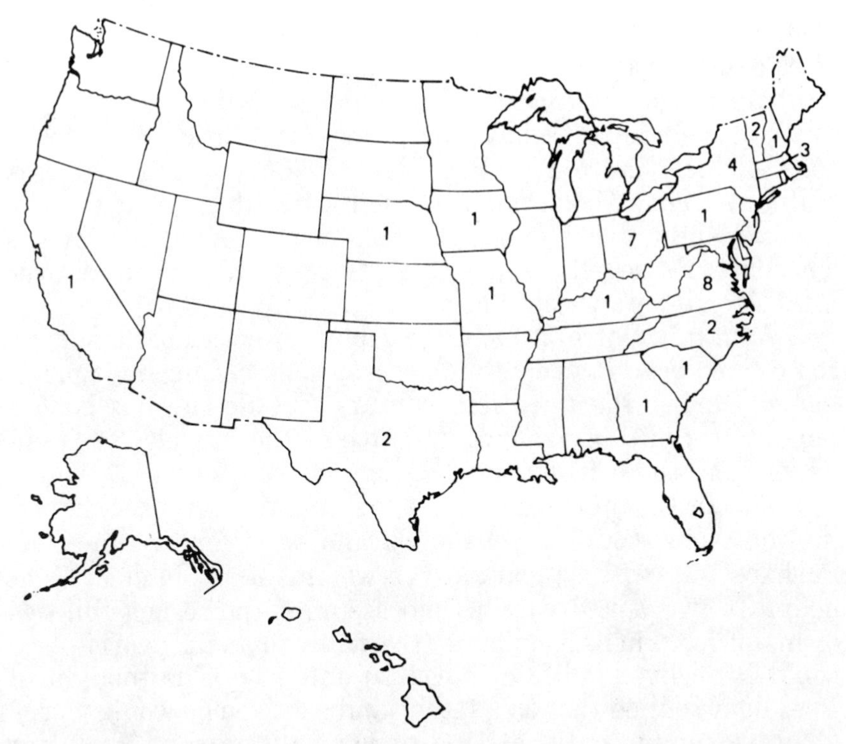

A map showing the states in which Presidents were born. Virginia and Ohio lead the list having produced fifteen of our thirty-eight Presidents.

dents have been fairly affluent men, although often they acquired their wealth by their own efforts.

One of the most common ways to become President has been to succeed to the office from the Vice-Presidency upon the death of the President. Eight of our thirty-eight Presidents have died in office (four by assassination), and in that manner have given the post to the "second man," as the Vice-President is sometimes called.[2] Eight Vice-Presidents were also successful candidates for the office in their own right: John Adams, Jefferson, Van Buren, Theodore Roosevelt,

2. There have only been thirty-eight Presidents but since Grover Cleveland's two terms were not consecutive, he is usually counted twice so that the number is given as thirty-nine.

Coolidge, Truman, Lyndon Johnson, and Nixon. And one Vice-President, Gerald R. Ford, succeeded to the office of the President upon the resignation of Richard M. Nixon.

Most Presidents have been in their fifties when they took office. The oldest President to be inaugurated was William Henry Harrison, who died a month later at the age of sixty-eight. The youngest man ever to hold office was Theodore Roosevelt, who was forty-two when he took over after McKinley's assassination.

A number of our Presidents have been school teachers, some have been lawyers, and several have been college presidents. During the twentieth century, the Senate has been a popular recruiting ground, and five of the last eleven Presidents have come from that body.

The Presidency is a nerve-wracking, dangerous, exhausting job. Why would anyone work and wish for this burden? Perhaps the most typical answer was made by John F. Kennedy. He was asked why he had assumed the responsibilities of his office when, as a man free from financial worries, he could have lived a life of pleasure and ease. The thoughtful President replied that as a father and a citizen he would worry about world and national conditions anyway and as President he was in a position to do something about them.

There are many rewards attached to being President, of course. The President receives $200,000 in salary, which according to the Constitution may not be raised or lowered during his term. In addition, he receives a $50,000 expense budget and a $40,000 travel allowance. A free 132-room home on eighteen landscaped acres is his on a four-year "lease" which he may only renew once. He receives stipends for office help and enjoys the services of cooks, chefs, maids, chauffeurs, and other personnel responsible for his needs. The Secret Service protects him and his family, and the armed forces provide him with jet planes, helicopters, and naval equipment. Actually, it is not the salary but the fringe benefits which make the job attractive!

These considerations, however, are not serious factors in inducing someone to run for office. Rather, the desire to "do something" about the state of the world and the nation is a more reasonable explanation. In addition, a person is guaran-

UPI

Jimmy Carter campaigning at the airport in Bedford, New Hampshire, on the final leg of his campaign for the presidency in 1976.

teed a place in history, the importance of which will be determined by his effectiveness in doing the job.

THE CAMPAIGN

To win the Presidency, one must overcome a series of obstacles which would make most people give up before they began. First there is the need to be in the public eye. The names Eisenhower and Grant were household words in their day because of the military prowess of these men, and there was little argument about the choice of our first chief executive. Other men, such as Governors Franklin D. Roosevelt and Woodrow Wilson, had plainly demonstrated their executive ability from the capitals of their states.

Not all presidential candidates are as well known as the above figures, however. Some potential choices, among them Harding and Polk, were loyal and popular party members rather than famous personalities. These men usually are referred to as "dark-horse" candidates, since they were not among the frontrunners of their parties when possible candidates were discussed.

The election of James Earl Carter, or Jimmy Carter as he prefers to be called, was one of the political "miracles" of this century. Almost unknown outside his state, even to the leaders of his party, in 1975 the former governor of Georgia began a nationwide campaign to sell his ideas and his leadership to the American people. And in 1976, he pulled off the political upset of our day, winning the Democratic nomination for the Presidency. Among the reasons for Carter's success was his willingness to enter primary elections across the country.

To show his party and the nation at large that he has vote-getting possibilities, the prospective candidate will enter primary elections in various states. These elections will be examined later in detail. The important thing to note here is that the primaries only measure the candidate's popularity with the party's membership in those states. In 1976, Jimmy Carter won nineteen out of the thirty-one primaries held. The real job of nominating a candidate is done at the national convention, a meeting of party delegates held the summer before the presidential election. This, too, will be discussed more fully in the chapter on the American political process.

Once nominated by a major party, the candidate begins his long and arduous campaign. His every move will be observed by millions, his words will be read, discussed, and dissected as avidly in Tokyo, Peking, Moscow, and London as in any American city. Although not yet elected, he is already an international figure, as is his opponent until the election returns are in.

A candidate must weigh every word he uses or he may find himself in deep trouble with the voters. He must also assume responsibility for the remarks of his associates. When presidential hopeful James G. Blaine failed to repudiate a bigoted statement made by a speaker with whom he shared the platform, he lost the support of many New York City voters, lost the state of New York, and lost the election.

ELECTING A PRESIDENT

Presidential elections are held on the first Tuesday after the first Monday in November every leap year. Voters cast their ballots for the President and Vice-President of the same party, the levers for these machines being locked together in states using voting machines. In reality, although the names of the candidates appear on the ballot, the voters are not voting directly for them but rather for delegates to the Electoral College, which officially chooses the President and Vice-President.

Each state is accorded a number of electoral votes equal to its Representatives and Senators in Congress. In 1976, California led with 45, New York had 41, and Pennsylvania, Texas, Illinois, Ohio, and Michigan each had more than 20. The candidate receiving the highest popular vote in a state wins all the electoral votes. There are 538 electoral votes (435 Representatives, 100 Senators, plus 3 for the District of Columbia). At least 270 are needed to elect. In 1968, the electoral vote was shared by Richard Nixon with 301, Hubert Humphrey with 191, and George Wallace with 46. In 1972, Nixon swept 521 electoral votes, while George McGovern won 17.[3] The election of 1976 was much closer, Carter receiving 297 and Gerald Ford 240, with one vote for Ronald Reagan.

The Electoral College system was introduced at the Philadelphia Convention of 1787 as a compromise between those who wanted a President elected by the Congress and those who sought a more popular voice in his selection. The Electoral College system allows for the selection to take place by vote of a small group (the electors), but these are first chosen by the people, at least at the present time.

On three occasions in American history it has happened that a man became President although his opponent received more popular votes than he. Hayes lost the popular vote to Tilden in 1876 by about 250,000 votes, but he received 185 electoral votes to 184 for Tilden. In 1888, Benjamin Harrison received 233 electoral votes to 168 for Cleveland, even though

3. Because a member of the Electoral College would not vote for President Nixon in 1972, the President received only 520 votes in the official tally.

Cleveland defeated him in the popular vote tally by 100,000 votes. And although Jackson won more popular votes than John Quincy Adams in 1824, the electoral vote was so badly split that no candidate received a majority and the election therefore went to the House of Representatives in accordance with the Constitution (see below). These are the only three cases, however, where the electoral vote did not coincide with the popular will.

More frequently in our history it has happened that a President has won less than fifty percent of the popular vote but more votes than his opponents. In this case, he is called a "minority" President. In 1960, Kennedy received 49.7 percent of the popular vote to 49.5 percent for Nixon, making Kennedy a minority President. Nixon himself became a minority President in his first election in 1968. Carter was a minority President in 1976, too. Although he defeated Ford by 1,681,417 votes, when Ford's total vote is added to that of minor candidates, Carter came to the Presidency with the votes of a shade under fifty percent of the American electorate. More than a third of our Presidents were elected by less than a majority of the popular votes, although they did receive the electoral-vote majority.

In the beginning, presidential candidates were chosen by caucus, a meeting of party leaders. Members of the Electoral College originally were elected by the state legislatures. Thus, the manner of choosing a President was indirect and less democratic than today.

Gradually, the people gained the right to choose the electors. Under the Electoral College system, electors meet in December of leap years in their state capitals to cast their votes, which are then forwarded to Congress.

Under the original Constitution, electors could vote for two men but could not specify which was their choice for President and Vice-President. It sometimes happened, therefore, that political enemies became President and Vice-President. This system collapsed in 1800 when Jefferson and Burr both received seventy-three electoral votes. The election went to the House of Representatives which, after several dozen ballots, chose Jefferson. Soon after this, the Twelfth Amendment was adopted, giving electors the power to list their choices for the first and second spots.

UPI

New York's Electoral College casting its votes for President-elect John F. Kennedy on December 19, 1960. The Senate Chamber of the State Capitol Building is being used for the balloting.

If a tie occurs in the Electoral College, or if no candidate wins a majority, the House chooses the President from the three who have the highest electoral votes. In 1824, no candidate had a majority, thus giving the House the chance to use this power in electing John Quincy Adams. At present, a quorum in the House is two-thirds of the states instead of a majority and each state has only one vote. The Senate exercises similar power with respect to the Vice-President.

Members of the Electoral College generally are not bound legally to vote for the person who receives the most votes in their states. A few state legislatures have required their electors to accept such a restriction, but most rely on the loyalty of electors to their party and on their sense of honor.

Of the thousands of votes cast over the years, the electors have been remarkably true to their word. In a few cases, however, electors have voted as they personally wished and not for the winning candidate. An elector from Oklahoma chose to cast his vote in 1960 for a different man, although Richard Nixon had won the state. And in 1972, a Virginian did the same, denying his vote to Nixon, who had received the highest number of votes in the state. The same thing happened to Gerald Ford, one of whose electors from Washington State voted for Ronald Reagan in 1976. The few examples of what are called "faithless" electors have never changed the outcome of an election. Still, many suggestions have been made to eliminate the indirect system and to establish the election of the President on the basis of direct popular vote.

DEATH OR DISABILITY OF THE PRESIDENT

Presidents are elected by the people in November and are officially selected by the Electoral College in December. What would happen if the President-elect were to die before his inauguration the following January? Or suppose it turned out that he was not qualified for office? These eventualities are provided for by the Twentieth or "Lame Duck" Amendment.[4] According to this amendment, the Vice-President-elect succeeds on the death of the President-elect. If neither qualifies, Congress will decide "who shall then act as President, or the manner in which one who is to act shall be selected and such a person shall act accordingly until a President or Vice-President shall have qualified."

During Washington's first term, Congress passed the Presidential Succession Act of 1792. This act provided for the succession of the President *pro tem* of the Senate, followed by

4. The "Lame Duck" Amendment is so called because it eliminates the session of Congress ridiculed as the "Lame Duck" session. Before the 1930s, the new Congress elected in November did not meet for thirteen months, a year from the following December. Instead, the old defeated Congress limped on like a lame duck until its term expired. The amendment also changed some of the dates originally set. Congress now convenes on January 3 and may stay in session until it wishes to adjourn. The President is sworn in at noon on January 20.

the Speaker of the House, if both President and Vice-President died. In 1886, the law was changed to allow for the succession of Cabinet officers in the order of the creation of their offices. The Secretary of State would be first, followed by the Secretary of the Treasury, and on down the line. This system was replaced by an act of 1947, still in effect, which reinserted the Speaker of the House and the President *pro tem* of the Senate between the Cabinet and the two executives.

No mention is made in these acts, however, of cases in which the President is temporarily incapacitated. This is a situation which has led to governmental crises in our country's history, although fortunately none have been too serious. When President Garfield was shot in 1881, he lingered for more than two months during which the government was leaderless. This did not adversely affect the country then, because we were only a bit player on the stage of nations. Some forty years later, President Wilson was stricken with an illness which prevented him from carrying out his full duties for weeks and left him permanently weakened. There was nothing the country could do but wait and hope that the President would recover.

In 1955, President Eisenhower had a stroke which left him powerless to run the country. Lacking any authorization to take over, all Vice-President Nixon could do was offer his sympathy and wait for medical reports. When Eisenhower recovered, he and Nixon discussed the problem at length and entered into an informal agreement about what to do if such a condition arose again.

Their agreement was carried on by their successors in office and became part of the basis for the Twenty-fifth Amendment, adopted in 1967. This amendment directs the President to communicate in writing to the Speaker and the President *pro tem* the fact that he cannot do his job. The Vice-President then takes over until the President informs the two officers in writing that he once again is assuming control of the Presidency.

If the President cannot communicate (if he has a paralytic illness, is in a coma, or has become mentally ill, for example), the Vice-President must secure permission of a majority of the Cabinet or some other body formed by Congress and then must tell the Speaker and the President *pro tem* that

Karl Schumacher, The White House

President Jimmy Carter confers with Vice-President Walter Mondale.

he is taking charge. He remains in office until the President assumes control again by writing to the two officers and stating that he is recovering his office. At that point, if the Vice-President and a majority of the advisers mentioned above do not feel that the President is capable, the Vice-President has four days in which he may write to the Speaker and the President *pro tem* on the matter. Congress then must assemble within forty-eight hours and decide, within twenty-one days, who shall discharge the duties. For the Vice-President to continue in the office as acting President, two-thirds of the Congress must agree by vote that the President is incapable of performing his duties.

This amendment may seem to be a very involved document. Indeed, it must be so, in order to protect the people from a potential dictatorship by the Vice-President on the one hand, and from a mentally unbalanced President on the other.

LIMITS ON RE-ELECTION AND REMOVAL FROM OFFICE

The President's term of office is four years, after which he may seek re-election for only one more full term. He is disqualified by the Twenty-second Amendment from holding office for more than two terms. In the event a Vice-President succeeds to the Presidency, he may hold the office (if elected, of course) for two terms if he steps in during the last two years of the former President's term or for one term if he succeeds in the first two years of the former President's term. President Lyndon B. Johnson, for example, was eligible for two terms since he took over in the second half of President Kennedy's term, but he chose to retire instead.

The President may be removed from office by Congress for "Treason, Bribery, or other high Crimes and Misdemeanors." This part of the Constitution has been used only once, against President Andrew Johnson in 1868. Disagreement over Reconstruction policies following the Civil War and a struggle between the legislative and executive branches for supremacy led to a House vote impeaching President Johnson. The term *impeach*, as we saw, means to "accuse" or "indict." The impeached President then was tried by the Senate which, because it was one vote short of the two-thirds necessary, failed to convict him of the charges against him. Had Johnson been convicted, he would have been deprived of his office as President. Richard Nixon's voluntary resignation saved him from the almost certain stigma of impeachment, as we saw earlier.

THE VICE-PRESIDENT

Andrew Johnson was one of eight Vice-Presidents who succeeded to the highest office on the death of the duly elected President. It would thus seem that the Vice-President is the second most important position in the nation, since the Vice-

UPI

Gerald Ford testifying before the Senate Rules Committee, which is examining his qualifications to be Vice-President. In December of 1973, both Houses of Congress voted to confirm Ford's nomination, as provided for by the second paragraph of the Twenty-fifth Amendment.

President is the only other man for whom all Americans may vote. In reality, this is not so. During most of our history the office has been held in considerable contempt. Instead of second prize, it usually was considered the booby prize.

Early in our history, before the emergence of two major political parties, men with widely differing views were often chosen as President and Vice-President. John Adams and his Vice-President, Thomas Jefferson, prove this, as do Andrew Jackson and his Vice-President, John C. Calhoun. Jackson and Calhoun were so unfriendly toward each other that Calhoun eventually resigned the Vice-Presidency.

In the fall of 1973, Spiro T. Agnew became the second man to resign the Vice-Presidency. His resignation did not result from political differences with the President but rather from serious personal problems—he had been found guilty of income tax evasion.

The second highest office sometimes has been looked upon as a way of removing a troublesome politician from active political life. It is said that Theodore Roosevelt was nominated on that basis. As it happened, he succeeded to the

Presidency less than a year after his inauguration as Vice-President.

Constitutionally, Vice-Presidents may not come from the same state as their Presidents; but even if this were not so, nominating conventions would never choose two men from the same state because it is felt that a geographically "balanced" ticket is necessary. Rarely are candidates even from the same section of the country. For instance, in the past the Democratic party has selected presidential candidates from all sections of the United States, but their running mates usually have come from the South.

The only constitutional duty of the Vice-President is to preside over the Senate. As president of the Senate, the Vice-President cannot be compared with the Speaker of the House in terms of power, although he does have some influence over legislation and the conduct of business, and may cast a vote whenever there is a tie. This tie-breaking power has been used often, with Richard Nixon casting it eight times during his two Vice-Presidential terms. In addition to his duties in the Senate, the Vice-President has picked up other chores over the years, some of which include taking part in Cabinet meetings and National Security Council meetings, helping to oversee the Naval Academy and the Smithsonian Institution, and taking an active part in the space program.

In recent years, Presidents have required their Vice-Presidents to tour the world as their representatives. Vice-Presidents Nixon, Rockefeller, Humphrey, and Mondale were very active in this manner, and achieved a great deal in fostering good will and understanding, as well as in making America's position better known to the world.

Another important feature of the office of the Vice-Presidency is its use in protecting and defending the President against critics. If the President is attacked by the opposition party, or condemned by a newspaper, television station, or radio program, he may allow the Vice-President to respond to the charges. In this way, the President protects the dignity of his office but also defends himself.

The Vice-President is elected by all the people, but he is responsible really to only one person. Whatever real power he has comes through "the boss." Proof of this dependence can be seen in a section of the Twenty-fifth Amendment not men-

Theodore Roosevelt, a President who acted vigorously and decisively, especially in the area of foreign policy. It is probably no accident that Roosevelt chose to be photographed with his hand on a globe turned to the Western Hemisphere.

Culver Pictures, Inc.

tioned before. When the office of Vice-President becomes vacant, the President may appoint a new one, subject to a majority vote of Congress. This congressional power has been exercised twice, once in the appointment of Gerald Ford and again, upon Nixon's resignation and Ford's ascension to the Presidency, in the appointment of Nelson Rockefeller.

THE POWERS OF THE PRESIDENT

The power of the Presidency was illustrated some years ago by an American scholar, who declared that the President had ten different jobs, half of these under the written Constitution and the other half growing out of his historical position in the twentieth century.[5] The constitutional duties are:

---

5. Clinton Rossiter, *The American Presidency*, 2nd ed. (New York: New American Library, 1960), pp. 14–36.

Chief of State

Chief Executive

Commander-in-Chief

Chief Diplomat

Chief Legislator.

The other duties, not as clearly defined as those above but still very important, were:

Head of His Political Party

Voice of the People

Protector of the Peace

Manager of Prosperity

World Leader.

Because of the enormous importance of his office, the President is a man of tremendous prestige, power, and influence. Only bold and innovative men have been chosen by the people to utilize the powers of the office and to solve the many problems of the country. Had timid and unambitious men been elected, the chief executive might be merely a figurehead today.

Scholars sometimes categorize Presidents as *weak* or *strong*, the weak President being one who carries out his constitutional duties but hesitates to exceed them, while the strong President is one who acts in a situation, even though the Constitution does not specifically direct him to. Theodore Roosevelt is offered as an example of a strong chief executive. He took many paths which others had been unwilling to walk. He was the first modern President to attempt intervention in a labor dispute which did not directly concern the federal government. William Howard Taft, however, was firmly convinced that the President should be the *executive*, that is, one who carries out or executes the will of Congress. He was consciously devoted to carrying out his duties and nothing more, while Teddy Roosevelt sometimes used the office to express his ideas on subjects such as divorce, over which the federal government had practically no authority. The terms weak and strong should not be viewed as terms of criticism, since they simply describe an individual's attitude toward his duties as

Edith Reichmann from Monkmeyer

Young people holding a "peace vigil" in front of the White House. Protests involving foreign policy frequently zero in on the White House, in acknowledgment of the President's broad powers in this area.

he reads the Constitution. They can be misleading words, however, and occasionally can be used for political purposes.

In actual fact, the office of the Presidency has expanded greatly since it was first created. In *The Federalist Papers*, written in the 1780s, Alexander Hamilton pointed out how the Presidential system differed from a monarchy:

- It is not hereditary;
- The President is subject to impeachment;
- He must secure senatorial consent for his appointments;
- He is subject to rejection or approval at the polls in four years;
- He may adjourn Congress on only one occasion, that is, when the houses cannot agree on the time of their adjournment;
- His veto is not an absolute veto but a *suspensive* one; that is, it does not kill a bill forever, since Congress may override it by a two-thirds vote of both houses.

Hamilton's writings were designed to assure the people that they would not be ruled by a less regal George III. Yet today,

American Presidents legally can wield far more power than George III ever dreamed of.

As commander-in-chief of the armed forces, the President may order troops into states to enforce the laws of the country, as Eisenhower did in Arkansas in the 1950s or as Nixon did during the postal strike of 1970. He may on his own authority send troops into foreign countries, as Truman did in Korea or as Lyndon Johnson did in the Dominican Republic. There are nearly two hundred instances in American history of Presidents using their powers as commander-in-chief for various purposes overseas, ranging from protecting American lives in China to intervening in the Russian Revolution with thousands of American troops. The question of Congress's part in all this has been raised in recent years. If the power to *declare* war rests with Congress and the power to *make* war resides in the Presidency, which of these powers is prior to the other? On the surface this may seem to be an easy question, but it is not. These powers do not divide the two branches of government so much as they make the President and Congress partners in any military endeavor. The fact that Congress has not declared war formally does not mean that a President is acting illegally when he commits troops to a certain course of action in a foreign country. The federal courts frequently have upheld the President's waging of an undeclared war on the basis of the fact that Congress has supported the action with financial and other legislative measures. A case decided in 1965, known as *United States v. Mitchell*, involved a man who would not report for military induction because Congress had not declared the Vietnam War. The Court held that "while Congress has not formally declared war with respect to the military action in Vietnam, nor did it in Korea, it has given its wholehearted approval to the action of the President by appropriations and other implementing help."[6]

In the last century, the President's authority was successfully defied by the states on many occasions. South

6. Eberhard P. Deutsch, "The President as Commander in Chief," *Journal of the American Bar Association*, January 1971, quoted in the *Congressional Record*, 27 January 1971, p. S351.

Franklin Delano Roosevelt speaking with a citizen. This photograph was taken while FDR was governor of New York. But even as President, FDR made a special effort to learn what ordinary Americans were thinking and feeling.

UPI

Carolina was joined by other states in nullifying federal legislation and, during the War of 1812, the governor of Massachusetts refused to permit the militia to aid in the defense of the country. It was not until 1827, in the case of *Martin* v. *Mott*, that the Supreme Court ruled that the President and not a governor could decide when an emergency existed which justified calling out the militia.

During the Civil War and the two World Wars, the Presidents involved used their "war powers" extensively. Lincoln suspended *habeas corpus*, the right under which a person may not be imprisoned without judicial permission. This was later approved by Congress. In World War I, Wilson received wide powers from Congress to enforce rationing, arrest subversives, and imprison anyone who impeded the war effort. During World War II, Franklin Roosevelt was empowered to imprison potential subversives, to place controls on prices, and to ration food, clothing, gasoline, tobacco, and many other items. Most of these controls were taken off after the wars, but during the period from the 1940s to the 1970s, even broader powers were granted by Congress to the President for emergency use, if needed.

The post-World War II Presidency became a very different one from any before that time, because powers that were intended to be temporary tended to become permanently associated with the office. Presidents acted, and when those actions were challenged by the Congress, the courts, or the people, there were always a batch of lawyers and a bunch of arguments to support the President's positions. People came to look to the White House for direction more and more.

Occasionally, the courts have challenged presidential actions, as in the case known as *ex parte Milligan*. In this case, a man was convicted by a military court in Indiana during the Civil War of trying to aid the Confederate cause. The Supreme Court reversed the decision, ruling in 1866 that the man had not been indicted or accused before a grand jury and that the military courts should not have taken over the case when civilian courts were available. Many years later, in 1952, the Supreme Court decided a case known as *Youngstown Sheet and Tube Co.* v. *Sawyer*. This case involved Truman's attempt to seize the steel industry during the Korean War and it was ruled that he had exceeded his powers in doing so.

This 1952 case was the most serious setback suffered by a President until the successful challenge Congress made to President Nixon in the War Powers Resolution of 1973. Passed in the Ninety-third Congress, the Congress which ultimately forced Nixon from office because of the Watergate wrongdoing, the resolution was vetoed by the President but repassed over his veto.

Under the resolution, the President may use armed force only in the following instances: "... after a declaration of war by Congress, in carrying out specific laws authorizing hostilities, or in the event of an attack on America, or its possesions, or its armed forces." When there is no declaration of war and the President introduces armed force into a situation, he must report to Congress within forty-eight hours. His report must include the circumstances surrounding his actions, indicate the amount of force being or to be used, and specify for how long a period of time the use of force is expected to remain necessary. Within sixty days of this report, the President must stop using the armed forces unless Congress has given him further authorization in some form or another, such as an extension of the time limit or an outright declaration of war. However, the President may continue the use of the armed forces for an additional thirty days if he states in writing that military necessity dictates it.[7] At any time during the sixty-day or extra thirty-day period, Congress may order a halt to the hostilities.

Despite these setbacks, the President, like the entire federal government, has grown greatly in power in the twentieth century. Aside from legal powers, the President may use his great prestige to secure his goals. An example of this was the 1962 "steel crisis," during which President Kennedy publicly condemned a rise in steel prices and threatened government action to prevent it. His announcement sent steel prices—and the stock market—down in a rapid but temporary dip.

The twentieth-century President has become the one man in America to whom all look for justice and protection, a "lobbyist for the people," as Wilson saw him. He promises a New Deal (Franklin D. Roosevelt) to "the forgotten man," or a Square Deal (Theodore Roosevelt), or a Fair Deal (Harry S. Truman), or a New American Revolution (Richard Nixon).

Communication has come a long way since Lincoln delivered his address at Gettysburg. The audience which listened to that stirring appeal was a mere handful compared to the millions who are reached daily by the White House through radio and televison. Today's President is brought much closer to the people by these means.

---

7. Clement Zablocki, "Permission for Committee on Foreign Affairs to File Conference Report on House Joint Resolution 542, War Powers Resolution of 1973," *Congressional Record,* 4 October 1973, pp. H8655-58.

During his tenure in office, Theodore Roosevelt described the Presidency as a "bully pulpit," and used it as if he were the moral leader of the nation as well as its chief magistrate. Since that time, other Presidents have expressed their sentiments in similar religious terms. President Carter, for example, has urged reform of those tax and Social Security laws which make it financially more advantageous for couples to live together without marrying, thus injecting himself into a moral issue.

The prestige of the office of President could best be seen in President Kennedy's term. His assassination in 1963 was the occasion for three official days of mourning, during which not just the nation but the world slowed down. It was as much a tribute to the office as to the man who graced it.

The American President sometimes has been called a "republican king," not because of the men who have held the office so much as because of the office itself. The Presidency is an important *symbol* to Americans, just as royal families are to those countries governed by monarchies. Americans have been fortunate indeed in their choice of chief executives. Very few have done harm to the office; almost all have added to its dignity by their respect for it.

AFTER-CHAPTER REVIEW

REVIEW QUESTIONS

1. Define the following names, terms, or ideas.

   "dark-horse" candidate
   "minority" President
   Presidential Succession Acts
   War Powers Resolution
   "Lame Duck" Amendment
   balanced ticket
   suspensive veto

2. Vocabulary building.

   repudiate caucus nullify

3. Cases.

   Martin v. *Mott*
   ex parte Milligan
   Youngstown Sheet and Tube Co. v. *Sawyer*
   United States v. *Mitchell*

4. Review of the text.

a. What are some of the characteristics of the American President—age, economic status, military service, place of birth, etc.?
b. How does a potential presidential candidate go about securing his (or her) party's support?
c. When do presidential elections (popular and Electoral College) take place? What part does the Electoral College play in the election of a President?
d. What was the Twelfth Amendment? Why was it needed?
e. What provisions have been made for permanent or temporary vacancies occurring within the Presidency?
f. What are the duties of the Vice-President?
g. Describe the relations of the President and Congress in recent years.

DISCUSSION AND PROJECTS

1. Questions for discussion.

a. Discuss the significance and the philosophy behind weak and strong presidential leadership.
b. The President has a perfect right to tell private enterprise what he thinks they should charge for their products. Discuss this statement.
c. How does the American President differ from a monarch according to *The Federalist Papers?* How is he similar?
d. In European history, whenever a king died, the people would cry, "The king is dead, long live the king!" What does this mean and how can we apply it to the concept we have of the *President* (the person in office) and the *Presidency* (the constitutional office itself)?

2. Debate topics.

a. Resolved: The Electoral College should be abolished.
b. Resolved: The office of the Presidency has too many powers and not enough limitations.

3. Opinion poll.

Is any one person sufficiently able to perform the duties of the Presidency now?

BIBLIOGRAPHY

Aikman, Lonnelle. *The Living White House.* Washington: White House Historical Association/National Geographic Society, 1975.

Barber, James D. *Choosing the President.* Englewood Cliffs, N.J.: Prentice-Hall, 1974.

Barber, James D. *The Presidential Character: Predicting Performance in the White House.* 2nd ed. Englewood Cliffs, N.J.: Prentice-Hall, 1977.

Corwin, Edward S. *Presidential Power and the Constitution.* Ithaca, N.Y.: Cornell University Press, 1976.

Flynn, James J. *Winning the Presidency.* Brooklyn, N.Y.: Theo Gans' Sons, 1976.

Hughes, Arthur J. *The American Presidency.* Encino, Calif: Glencoe, 1977.

Murphy, John F. *The Pinnacle: The Contemporary American Presidency.* Philadelphia: J.B. Lippincott, 1974.

Rossiter, Clinton. *The American Presidency.* New York: New American Library, 1960.

Rossiter, Clinton, ed. *The Federalist Papers.* New York: New American Library, 1961. Numbers 67-77.

Vinyard, Dale. *The Presidency.* New York: Charles Scribner's Sons, 1971.

"With Jimmy [Carter] from Dawn to Midnight," *Time,* 18 April 1977.

UPI

The Executive Office Building. This building, a short walk from the White House, contains many of the EOP agencies and other presidential advisers and assistants. The President also maintains an office here. The Executive Office Building was designed by A.D. Mullet, and built in 1871-1888. It formerly housed the Departments of State, War, and Navy.

7

The President and the Executive Branch

One of the greatest assests a President can have is flexibility. He must be able to switch from one job to another without letting any one of his duties blind him to the rest. He must be able to consult with congressional leaders on national legislation at 9 A.M., meet with a foreign diplomat at 9:30, and be ready to confer with his Cabinet at 10:00. In fact, legislative, diplomatic, and administrative duties consume most of his time. In this chapter, we will consider these three important duties and powers of the President.

THE PRESIDENT AND CONGRESS

The President's power over legislation is considerable. The Constitution directs him to inform Congress on the state of the Union "from time to time." This is the basis for his annual "State of the Union" message before the jointly assembled House and Senate. The message is listened to and later read carefully by people throughout the world, since it indicates future trends in American domestic and foreign policies. The Nixon administration made changes in the format of the annual message by dividing it into two parts, one for domestic matters and the other a kind of "State of the World" message describing policies and suggesting programs.

The President also has the right to recommend to Congress "such measures as he shall judge necessary and expedient." He frequently does this by sending messages "to the Hill" (slang for the Capitol, where Congress meets) urging

UPI

President Dwight D. Eisenhower is shown on January 7, 1960, delivering his State of the Union message to a joint session of Congress. Seated behind the President is Vice-President Richard Nixon.

passage of vital bills. Over the years, the Congress has come to rely more and more upon presidential leadership in proposing legislation. This tendency has grown to such an extent that some critics accuse Congress of giving up part of its own authority and responsibility.

Under several acts of Congress, the President also reports on the budget and the economic condition of the country. These technical reports on financial and economic trends play an important part in decisions Congress makes on budgetary and taxation matters. Here, again, the Congress relies on the executive branch for information and leadership.

While bills are under consideration, the President learns of their progress from his staff as well as from members of Congress. He may call influential lawmakers to ask their support for his programs or may even invite them to breakfast with him to discover their views in an informal way. The President has many means available to influence legislators. He can promise to campaign for a member of Congress or not to campaign, depending upon how the lawmaker supports the President's views. He will, on occasion, campaign against members of his own party if need be. All members of Congress know what effects these courses can have on their political futures. A letter from the President praising his or her work or an autographed photo can be very helpful in a lawmaker's bid for reelection.

The President also holds a great deal of patronage power, which allows him to appoint persons of his choice to judicial or executive positions. If he appoints someone suggested by a member of Congress, the President then will expect the legislator to support him in Congress.

These methods may be condemned as sharp practice or "deals." Sometimes they are, if they result in the appointment of inferior officers to government posts. But they also may be defended as part of the give-and-take of human relations. Politics can be defined as the art of compromise, and compromise does not mean the abandoning of principles but rather the working out of agreements which sufficiently satisfy all sides.

When a bill reaches his desk, the President may dispose of it in several ways, as we have already discussed. If he vetoes it, the veto may be overridden by Congress, although this happens to fewer than 4 vetoes out of every 100. President Franklin D. Roosevelt holds the record for vetoes with 631, only 9 of which were overturned during his twelve years in office. Grover Cleveland is next with 584 vetoes in eight years, of which only 7 were overridden. Andrew Johnson and Harry Truman were the least successful in dealing with Congress on this point, with 15 and 12 vetoes overridden, respectively. Truman's difficulties with Congress caused him to employ a little-used presidential practice which caused great controversy. This was the pocket veto, which he used while Congress was in recess but had not yet adjourned. As we saw, the pocket veto may be exercised by the President when Congress adjourns at the conclusion of its business. Then the President simply does not sign the bill and it dies within ten days. President Truman took advantage of this provision to declare a bill dead ten days after receiving it if Congress had taken a temporary recess. Later Presidents followed this practice, too, until President Nixon was challenged on it in the federal courts by Senator Edward Kennedy. The courts ruled that the practice was not called for by the Constitution. Under President Ford, the Attorney-General did not pursue the matter to the Supreme Court, but the Ford administration promised not to use the practice again. This set a powerful precedent for future Presidents.

If a situation arises which demands that Congress convene earlier than usual, the President may issue a call for a special session of Congress. Only about two dozen of these special sessions have been held and none have been in recent history. Either one or both houses may be called. The House has never been called alone, but the Senate has returned often to review treaties and appointments.

Occasionally, a President will threaten to call Congress back into session unless it acts on legislation he favors. He has the power to do this, but would be unwise to use it. A disgruntled Congress is not likely to give a President what he wants in special session if it has not done so in regular session.

THE PRESIDENT AND THE SENATE

The President's relationship with the Senate differs from his relationship with the House of Representatives for several reasons. First, the Senate alone approves treaties. Second, the Senate has the right to vote on presidential appointments. Third, the Senate has the privilege known as "senatorial courtesy," which it has advanced over the course of American history.

Treaty-making is a joint effort of the President and the Senate, although it is strictly up to the executive branch to negotiate with the foreign country involved. Treaties have covered many subjects, including settlement of boundary disputes, peace terms following a war, purchase of territory, agreements for mutual defense, and even control over migratory birds. This last instance is especially important because Congress's right to make treaties concerning migrating birds was challenged in the courts. In the case of *Missouri* v. *Holland* in 1920, the Supreme Court ruled that treaties are the supreme law of the land, just as are other acts of Congress.

Negotiations with another country over a certain issue are opened by the President. When these are completed, each

UPI (both)

The Secretary of State often presents the President's requests to Congress. Here, on the left, Secretary of State Henry Kissinger appears before the House International Relations Committee in April, 1974, to urge congressional approval of President Ford's request for military and humanitarian aid to South Vietnam. On the right, President Carter's Secretary of State, Cyrus Vance, reports to the Senate Government Affairs Committee on the effect of terrorism in the Middle East peace negotiations.

country then considers the treaty according to its own laws. In the case of the United States, the document is examined by the Senate Foreign Relations Committee, which may hold hearings on it, make amendments to it, and approve or disapprove it. When the treaty is reported to the full Senate, it must be ratified by a two-thirds majority of those present.

The President often makes agreements with foreign powers by a method called the "executive agreement." In fact, there have been more executive agreements than treaties in American diplomatic history. There have been eight thousand international pacts involving the United States, and executive agreements have outnumbered treaties nearly seven to one. Although they are supposed to cover only minor matters, executive agreements often have been used to bind the United States to policies of great importance. Naturally, the Senate does not agree with the excessive use of this power by the President; but since each branch is separate and equal, each has the right to place its own interpretations on its powers, subject to judicial review.

The President and the Senate must work together to appoint the thousands of executive and judicial posts throughout the federal government. In addition, the President must recommend and the Senate must approve the commissions of all armed forces officers. It is impossible, however, for the Senate to scrutinize the lives of all these persons to see if they qualify for government service. During President Eisenhower's eight years in office, he offered more than 40,000 persons as nominees *every year*. In one two-year period, President Nixon recommended more than 117,000 persons. Most of these were personnel of the armed forces, but there were also many diplomats, postal officials, judges, and Cabinet officers.

If serious objections are raised to the appointment of a nominee, the President very likely will withdraw the name, rather than suffer a defeat by the Senate's refusal to confirm the person. An example of this was the withdrawal by the President in 1977 of the name of a candidate for the post of Director of the CIA. Sometimes, rather than antagonizing the President by voting against his choice for a certain post, the Senate will direct its Judiciary Committee to study the appointment again, as it did in 1966 over the appointment of a federal judge whose qualifications did not seem to be outstanding. Later, the President withdrew his name. If Congress is out of session when a post becomes vacant, the President need not call a special session. Instead, he can make a "recess appointment," which lasts until the end of the next regular session of Congress. If no action is taken by then, the appointee loses his or her place.

When making appointments, the President must be mindful of the traditional practice called "senatorial courtesy," which requires him to consult with the Senators from his party before making appointments in their states. Should the President ignore this courtesy, a Senator may declare that the person is "personally obnoxious" to him and the Senate very likely will oppose the nomination. This is another example of the "unwritten constitution" and of the give-and-take of political life. Senatorial courtesy also refers to the privileged

HEW

Patricia Roberts Harris was sworn in as Secretary of Health, Education, and Welfare in 1979. She previously served as Secretary of Housing and Urban Development from January 23, 1977, to August 3, 1979.

treatment usually given to a former Senator when the President nominates him for an appointive office.

There is another side to senatorial confirmation which has caused conflict between the President and the Senate. If a President appoints an executive official, such as a Cabinet officer, and that person is approved by the Senate, may the President remove the official on his own, or must he obtain Senate approval for the removal? This question created controversy in the 1860s when Andrew Johnson removed his Secretary of War, a move contrary to Congress's Tenure of Office Act which prohibited the removal of senatorially confirmed officials without Senate permission. This law was later repealed and the right of the President to remove members of his "official family," that is, close advisers, is recognized universally in our day.

With respect to employees of the executive branch who are not so closely associated with the President, the use of the removal power has been defined by court decisions. In the 1926 case of *Myers* v. *United States*, the Supreme

Court ruled that the President could remove an official from a position as postmaster without Senate approval for the action. This decision was diluted somewhat in the case of *Humphrey's Executor* v. *United States* in 1935.[1] Here, a President had removed a member of the Federal Trade Commission, an agency created by Congress and having powers which are legislative, executive, and judicial. In creating the FTC, moreover, Congress had indicated the conditions under which a person could be removed and also had granted the commissioners a term of seven years. The President, the Court said, should not have removed the official because his duties were not only executive but also of a legislative and judicial nature. This decision gave considerable independence from presidential control to such regulatory agencies as the FTC. Because of this case, and owing to senatorial courtesy and the political considerations we have discussed earlier, the President is not a free agent in the use of his appointment power.

Nor is the President completely free in conducting foreign affairs. He has the power to recognize new governments and to receive ambassadors from them, but the Senate must confirm American officials who are sent as representatives of the United States. Both houses must consent to loans or other forms of aid to any country. The President usually has his way, although some have found it an uphill struggle.

In his use of his pardoning power, however, the President is able to act on his own. Under the Constitution, the President may pardon all persons accused or convicted of crimes. This, of course, applies only to crimes involving the federal government, not the states. The most celebrated recent use of this power was President Ford's blanket pardon of Richard Nixon in September, 1974. President Ford's pardon absolved former President Nixon from prosecution for any criminal act he might have committed during his entire Presidency. The pardon caused a great controversy throughout the nation but was a valid use of presidential power. It also illustrates the point that a pardon may be granted before any charges are brought and proven. The President also may grant re-

1. The official's name was William Humphrey. After Humphrey's death, the executor of his estate, Rathbun, completed the litigation.

prieves, which temporarily suspend a sentence or commute it to a lesser punishment. Finally, he may grant amnesties, or large-scale pardons for whole groups. His pardoning power cannot be used, however, in cases involving congressional impeachment.

ASSISTANTS TO THE PRESIDENT

About 2.8 million persons are needed to carry out the duties of the executive branch. They are divided among the following groups:

I. The Executive Office of the President (EOP). This consists of various bureaus or offices under the direct supervision of the president, including the Office of Management and Budget, the White House Office, the National Security Council, etc.;

II. The Cabinet departments, of which there are thirteen, ranging from the Department of State to the Department of Housing and Urban Development;

III. Various independent and semi-independent agencies such as the Federal Trade Commission, the Veterans' Administration, the Interstate Commerce Commission, and the Federal Communications Commission.

Running a government is a great deal like running a school. The principal has his or her immediate staff of secretaries and assistants; the school is divided into academic departments for teaching social studies, science, etc.; and there are specialized offices for guidance, library, and food services. The head of the institution has much less control over, let us say, a cafeteria employee than over his or her own office staff. The same holds true for the President on the federal level. He controls some offices directly (EOP), has power over others through his hand-picked (and removable) Cabinet members, and on others has very little influence. Some of these offices and their functions will be examined in the following pages.

It must be remembered that government work is a vital part of our national economy. More than 15 million people (out of about 92.5 million employed) are engaged in civilian work for the federal, state, and local governments.[2] This does not include military personnel, of whom there are more than 2.7 million. Meeting the payroll for federal civilian employees is quite a task, since the average salary of a federal worker is more than $15,874 a year. The largest employers of personnel in the federal service are the Defense Department, with a million civilian workers, and the Postal Service, with more than 650,000 employees. The remaining workers are scattered throughout other agencies and departments.

To regulate the expenses of these organizations, Congress created the General Accounting Office (GAO) in 1921. This "watchdog" agency is under the direction of the Comptroller General of the United States, whose duty it is to see that each individual agency makes proper use of the funds appropriated for it. The Comptroller General is appointed by the President and confirmed by the Senate, holds office for fifteen years, and may be removed only by joint resolution of Congress or by impeachment. If the GAO disapproves of a department's expenditures, the money may not be spent.

THE EXECUTIVE OFFICE OF THE PRESIDENT

Let us begin our study of the three major categories of employment in the federal executive branch with the EOP. This group covers the agencies directly answerable to the President and was created in 1939, during the administration of Franklin D. Roosevelt. However, President Roosevelt would hardly recognize the EOP today because of the frequent changes which subsequent Presidents, especially Nixon and Carter, have made in it. The White House Office, for instance, is made up of 462 employees, including the President's press secretary, physician, military and scientific aides, counselors, assistants, deputy assistants, special assistants, and secretarial personnel. Through these workers, the President maintains contact with Congress, his Cabinet officers, the press,

---

2. This 1976 figure breaks down as follows: 2.8 million persons are employed by the federal government; 6.3 million by state and local governments for education; and 1.4 by state governments and 4.9 by local governments for other services.

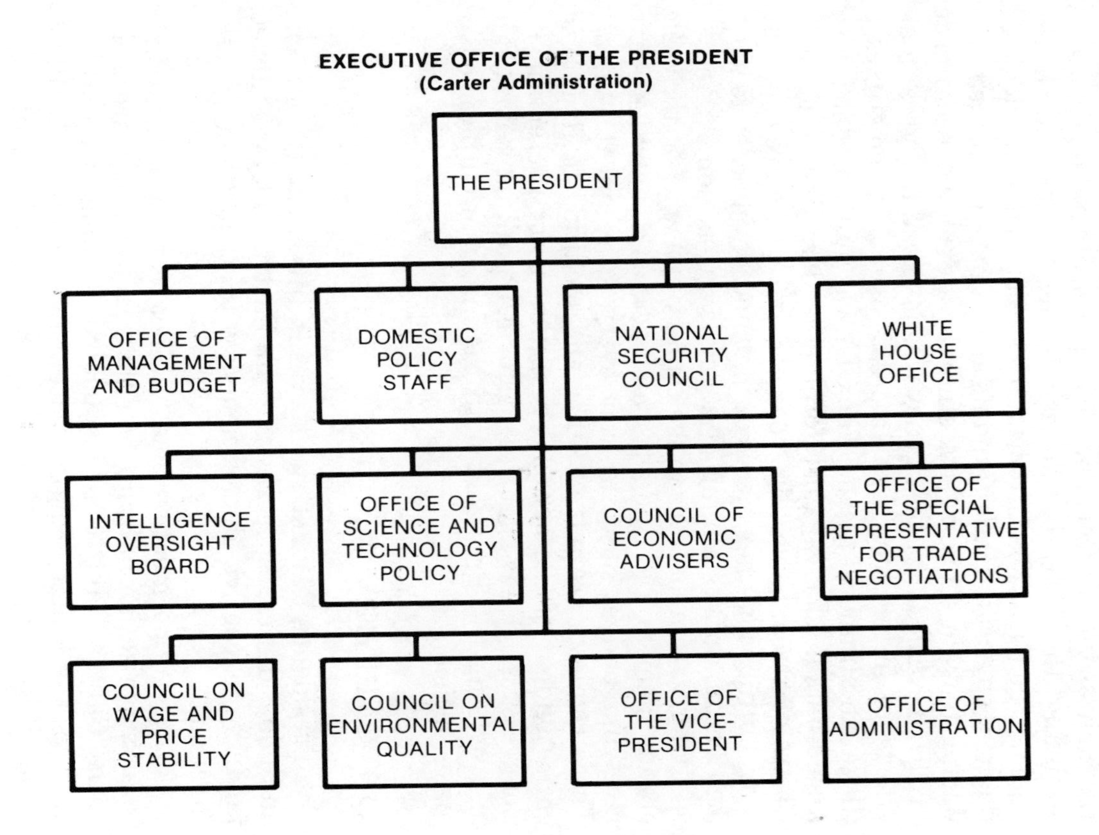
EXECUTIVE OFFICE OF THE PRESIDENT
(Carter Administration)
THE PRESIDENT
OFFICE OF MANAGEMENT AND BUDGET
DOMESTIC POLICY STAFF
NATIONAL SECURITY COUNCIL
WHITE HOUSE OFFICE
INTELLIGENCE OVERSIGHT BOARD
OFFICE OF SCIENCE AND TECHNOLOGY POLICY
COUNCIL OF ECONOMIC ADVISERS
OFFICE OF THE SPECIAL REPRESENTATIVE FOR TRADE NEGOTIATIONS
COUNCIL ON WAGE AND PRICE STABILITY
COUNCIL ON ENVIRONMENTAL QUALITY
OFFICE OF THE VICE-PRESIDENT
OFFICE OF ADMINISTRATION

and the American people. A letter written to the President will be answered through this office.

The National Security Council, another EOP office, advises the President on all policies, foreign and domestic, particularly as they concern the whole picture of national security. Assisting the NSC in its task is the Central Intelligence Agency, or CIA. The CIA usually is pictured as a "cloak and dagger" spy organization, and its agents have performed many daring feats of espionage. A study by a Senate subcommittee in 1975 revealed that the agency was involved in a great many efforts to foster American interests overseas, sometimes by illegal and immoral means. The CIA was implicated in several assassination plots against foreign leaders, including Fidel Castro of Cuba. Generally, however, its agents are concerned with putting together pieces of information in order to arrive at a better understanding of a particular nation's plans.

Of great importance to the country as a whole is the Office of Management and Budget, which acts as a central office for receiving budget requests from every governmental agency. These requests are put together and modified to fit into the entire budget of the national government for presentation to Congress. All EOP agencies perform the all-important duty of providing the President with the information he needs to make decisions.

THE CABINET

The President's Cabinet also serves in this capacity; but it has additional duties, especially the administration of the thirteen far-flung executive departments, with their many diverse functions.[3]

There is no mention of a Cabinet in the Constitution. It is an organization built up over the years as needs arose. The term "Cabinet" and the idea behind it comes from British history. The king of England began the practice of calling a group of his supporters from Parliament to meet with him in

3. The Post Office Department, formerly a Cabinet department, became an independent agency under the name U.S. Postal Service in 1970.

UPI

President Carter holding his first Cabinet meeting in the Cabinet Room of the White House on January 24, 1977. Shown (clockwise from bottom left) are Bert Lance, Director of the Office of Management and Budget; Patricia Harris, Secretary of Housing and Urban Development; Bob Bergland, Secretary of Agriculture; W. Michael Blumenthal, Secretary of the Treasury; Griffin Bell, Attorney General; Ray Marshall, Secretary of Labor; Andrew Young, Ambassador to the United Nations; Joseph Califano, Secretary of Health, Education, and Welfare; Cyrus Vance, Secretary of State; President Carter; Harold Brown, Secretary of Defense; Juanita Kreps, Secretary of Commerce; Brock Adams, Secretary of Transportation; and James Schlesinger, advisor for energy and later Secretary of the new Department of Energy. Cecil Andrus, Secretary of the Interior, was not present when the photograph was taken. Lance subsequently resigned. In July of 1979, in a major shakeup of the Cabinet, Carter replaced Califano, Blumenthal, Schlesinger, Adams, Bell, and later Young.

a cabinet or room. Gradually, Cabinet ministers came to be chosen from the majority party in Parliament and over the years the power to select them grew to reside in Parliament itself and not in the king. Because they ministered to the king, they were called "ministers" and the chief among them became known as the "prime minister." Each minister took care of a division of the government (financial, home affairs, or imperial functions) while still remaining a legislator in Parliament.

The American system grew away from this idea in a very important way. Rather than coming from the legislative branch, the Cabinet is a creation of the executive branch. The President is obliged neither to consult the Cabinet unless he wishes to, nor to follow its advice if he does consult it. A well-known story concerning Lincoln's relationship with his Cabinet illustrates this. When all of his Cabinet members had voted to oppose an ideal he believed in, Lincoln raised his own hand in support of the suggestion and said, in words similar to these, "The 'ayes' have it."

Not all Presidents have acted this way, however. President Eisenhower placed great faith in the judgment of the men he chose. President Washington wisely invited both Alexander Hamilton and Thomas Jefferson into his Cabinet, and these men, whose views differed so widely, gave the first President the benefit of two separate opinions.

Some Presidents have relied more on one or two Cabinet members than on the entire body or have even placed confidence in men outside their Cabinets. Such a group usually is called a "kitchen cabinet," a phrase supposedly stemming from President Jackson's informal meetings with a few friends to discuss problems. In modern times, FDR relied greatly on the judgment of Harry Hopkins, a friend and administrator; Eisenhower sought the advice of his Secretary of State, John Foster Dulles; while Kennedy listened carefully to his Attorney-General (and brother), Robert Kennedy. None of these men relied solely upon their closest advisers. Rather, they used them as friendly private walls, against which they could bounce their ideas.

Regardless of how carefully he or she may be listened to, however, a Cabinet member is more than an adviser. He or she administers a complex bureau employing from 17,000 to about a million persons (Labor Department to Department of Defense). The Secretary of Defense, with the above-mentioned million civilian workers and more than 2.7 million military personnel, has charge of a population about equal to that of the whole United States in 1790.

Each department is a world in itself, divided into bureaus which conduct business, supervise operations, maintain contact with the public, and conduct training programs for their employees. Let us use the Department of Health and Human Services and the Department of Education as examples of Cabinet development.

In 1953 the Department of Health, Education, and Welfare was formed to take over supervision of some agencies already in existence and to provide expanded federal services in other areas. While employment in other Cabinet departments grew slowly in the 1960s and 1970s, HEW grew from 61,641 persons in 1960 to 106,705 in 1972 and to 156,775 in 1977. It thus became the fourth largest governmental unit (after Defense, the Postal Service, and the Veterans' Administration). And, as Congress legislated new programs for the department's jurisdiction, it was given more funds to spend and more duties to carry out.

At the end of 1979, the department was reorganized. A thirteenth Cabinet-level agency, the Department of Education, was created from the dozens of education programs in HEW, as well as from programs run by other departments and agencies. The new department, which is larger than the Departments of Energy, the Interior, Commerce, Justice, and State, studies the progress of education in the country, points out nationwide problems, provides loans and grants to the states for educational improvement, and makes it easier for college students to borrow money to complete their educations.

The Department of Health and Human Services was the new name given to HEW following the creation of the new Department of Education. Like the other departments, HHS is under the direction of a secretary who is assisted by an undersecretary, a number of assistant secretaries, directors, commissioners, assistant commissioners, and a host of other titled supervisors. The department includes several large divisions, such as the Social Security Administration and the Food and Drug Administration, as well as bureaus, institutes, and offices devoted to vocational rehabilitation, medical education and research, the problems of aging, juvenile delinquency, and a wide range of additional responsibilities.

The Commerce Department is another agency with a multitude of duties. It, too, has a secretary, undersecretary, assistant secretaries, etc. Created as a separate department

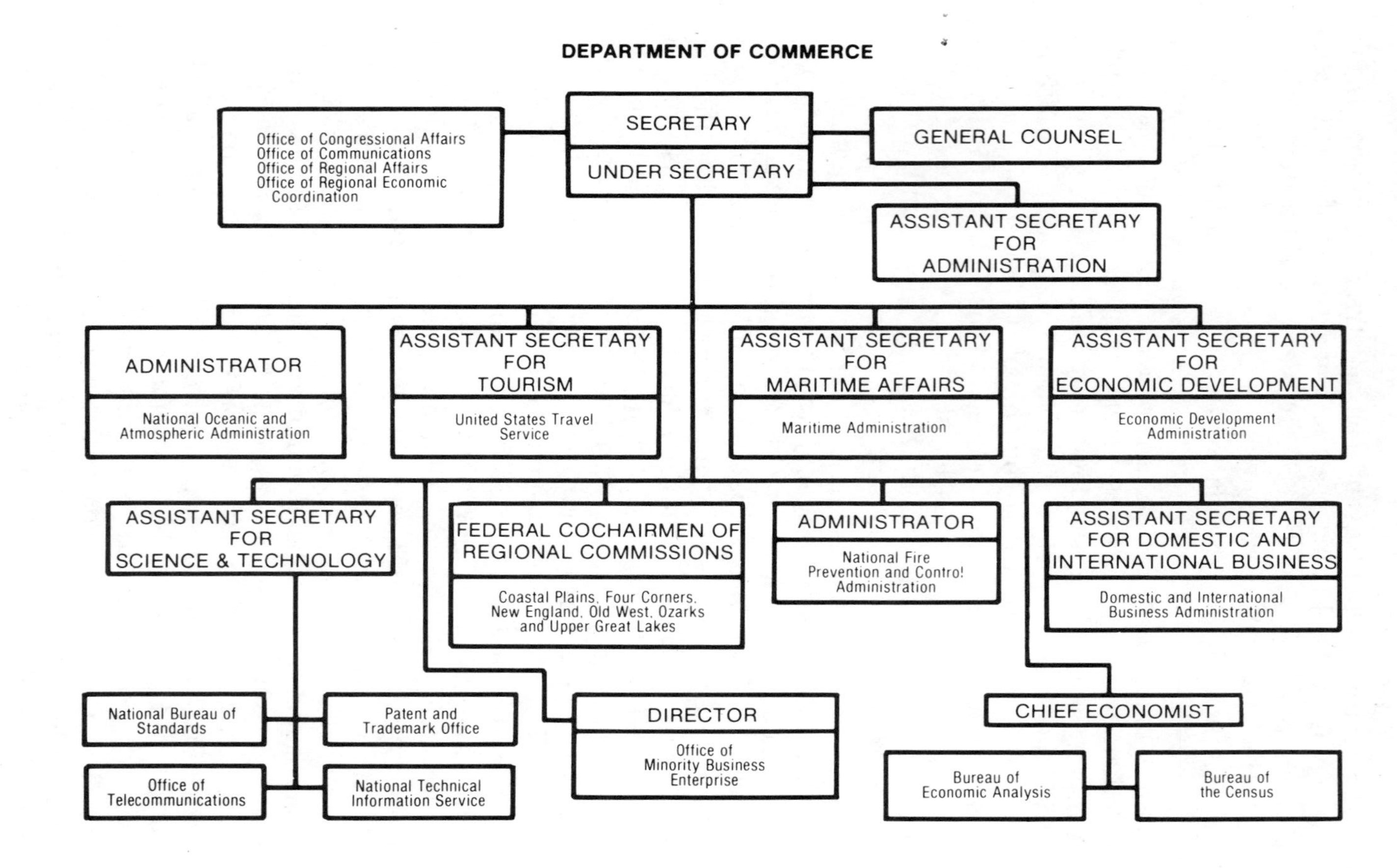
DEPARTMENT OF COMMERCE
SECRETARY
UNDER SECRETARY
Office of Congressional Affairs
Office of Communications
Office of Regional Affairs
Office of Regional Economic Coordination
GENERAL COUNSEL
ASSISTANT SECRETARY FOR ADMINISTRATION
ADMINISTRATOR
National Oceanic and Atmospheric Administration
ASSISTANT SECRETARY FOR TOURISM
United States Travel Service
ASSISTANT SECRETARY FOR MARITIME AFFAIRS
Maritime Administration
ASSISTANT SECRETARY FOR ECONOMIC DEVELOPMENT
Economic Development Administration
ASSISTANT SECRETARY FOR SCIENCE & TECHNOLOGY
FEDERAL COCHAIRMEN OF REGIONAL COMMISSIONS
Coastal Plains, Four Corners, New England, Old West, Ozarks and Upper Great Lakes
ADMINISTRATOR
National Fire Prevention and Control Administration
ASSISTANT SECRETARY FOR DOMESTIC AND INTERNATIONAL BUSINESS
Domestic and International Business Administration
National Bureau of Standards
Patent and Trademark Office
Office of Telecommunications
National Technical Information Service
DIRECTOR
Office of Minority Business Enterprise
CHIEF ECONOMIST
Bureau of Economic Analysis
Bureau of the Census

in 1913, it promotes foreign and domestic commerce and manufacturing in the United States. Almost anything relating to American economic life comes within the jurisdiction of the Commerce Department. Its "travel agency," known as the United States Travel Service, for example, encourages foreigners to travel in this country since this is an important source of revenue. Commerce also includes the National Oceanic and Atmospheric Administration (which administers the National Weather Service), the Patent and Trademark Office, and the Bureau of the Census. This last bureau has not confined itself to the one ten-year census called for by the Constitution. It gathers statistics on agriculture every five years and at other intervals assembles data on commercial activities such as manufacturing and transportation. Beginning in 1985, the Census Bureau will take a complete census every five years instead of the ten-year head count which has been taken since 1790.

The Treasury Department, another multi-purpose organization, supervises national financial matters. Some of the agencies under the direction of the Secretary of the Treasury are the U.S. Customs Service, the U.S. Secret Service, and the Bureau of Engraving and Printing.

A newer Cabinet department is the Department of Energy (DOE), formed in 1977 to coordinate and regulate all aspects of the nation's energy requirements. With approximately 20,000 employees and a budget above $10 billion, the DOE is responsible for solar, atomic, and geothermal energy as well as for the traditional fossil fuels and hydroelectric power.

A Cabinet officer has a difficult task. He or she is responsible to one person—the President—and serves at his pleasure. But it is also important to keep tens of thousands of employees happy, and to satisfy the public's needs as well. When presidential policies carried out by the Cabinet member fail or are challenged, the Secretary takes the criticism, not "the boss." Cabinet members are expected to shield the President and take the blame. This may account for the fact that the Cabinet is not a good place to look for presidential candidates any more. In the early history of the nation, Jefferson, Madison, Monroe, John Quincy Adams, and Van Buren all served as Secretary of State before holding the highest office. In the twentieth century, only two men (Taft and Hoover) had Cabinet experience before being elected to the Presidency.

Secretaries do not handle all aspects of their departments, of course. In actual practice, bureau chiefs and other high-ranking officers below the Cabinet level do not go to the secretary for every decision. They are experienced men and women who can follow general guidelines and take care of details on their own. They are expected to follow general policies laid down by the President through the Cabinet, but they sometimes are slow in putting into practice policies they disapprove.

INDEPENDENT AGENCIES

Even more independent than officials in the twelve executive departments are the chiefs and other officers of non-Cabinet agencies and commissions. Under various acts of Congress, agencies like the Interstate Commerce Commission (ICC), Federal Trade Commission (FTC), Federal Communications Commission (FCC), and the Securities and Exchange Commission (SEC) operate almost independently of the President. These four are among the leaders of the federal agencies and, within their sphere of operations, have very broad powers. An examination of the ICC, our oldest regulatory agency, will illustrate the power of these agencies.

The ICC was created in 1887 after years of public agitation over the way railroads sometimes charged different rates for different customers and engaged in other discriminatory practices. Over the years, its authority has been expanded to regulate motor vehicles which engage in interstate commerce, as well as pipelines, ferries, barges, and other water carriers.

An eleven-member commission appointed by the President and confirmed by the Senate heads the ICC. The commissioners' terms run for seven years and they have the right to elect their own chairman. The ICC, therefore, is quite immune from presidential control, particularly in the light of the case of *Humphrey's Executor* v. *United States*, as we saw earlier in the chapter. The Commission makes regulations and decides on matters brought before it, thus making it both legislative and judicial in its duties. It is called quasi-legislative (or similar to a lawmaking body) and quasi-judicial (or similar to a court). Of course, if a railroad or other carrier thinks a decision is unjust, appeal may be made to the federal courts.

Suppose a railroad has been losing money on one of its branches. It might wish to correct this situation by raising rates, discontinuing passenger service, or borrowing money to buy new machinery with which to operate more efficiently. Since the railroad may not act without ICC approval in any of these cases, the commission has a direct effect upon the fortunes of railroad operators and their stockholders.

In addition, several thousand ICC inspectors keep a constant watch on railroads, trucking companies, bus firms, etc., to make sure employees and equipment conform to ICC specifications. Drivers must meet high standards of performance and safety devices must be in good repair.

Agencies, bureaus, commissions, and the like have grown up in the federal government in much the way a home is furnished. As the need arises, new couches, tables, and television sets are added. All have different functions, cost varying amounts of money, and satisfy different needs in the family. It is the same with the growth of federal agencies. As radio became widespread, the FCC was created to regulate it as well as telephone and telegraph companies. When television was introduced, the FCC assumed regulation of this medium. When serious space research was undertaken, NASA (National Aeronautics and Space Administration) was born. If there had been no wars, there would be no need for the VA (Veterans' Administration). And if these agencies did not exist, we would not have a Civil Service Commission to provide personnel for them.

Most federal employees do not work in Washington, D.C. They are spread out across the land. The country is divided into ten Standard Federal Regions in order to provide closer contact with the state and local governments and with the people. In each of these regions, Federal Regional Councils operate to coördinate the activities of governmental agencies. One city has been selected in each of the regions to serve as the Federal Regional Council office site. In Standard Federal Region Number IX, which takes in California, Nevada,

Arizona, and Hawaii, the central city is San Francisco.

The main purpose of the federal administrative machinery is to carry out the will of Congress, the President, and the courts in serving the people best. Although federal administrators have often interpreted this will in their own way, they are ultimately responsible to the three constitutional branches of government.

Most of the work of the federal bureaucracy consists of regulating the vast economic and social unit we call the United States. To do this, tens of thousands of regulations are necessary. These are available in the *Code of Federal Regulations*, a government document published every year. For day-to-day regulations, the *Federal Register* is used. This is a daily publication listing requirements for every aspect of American life and governing manufacturing, commerce, health, and environmental matters. When the *Federal Register* finished its first year of publication in the 1940s, it consisted of 2,500 pages. By 1970, this had grown to 20,000 pages for that one year. And by the end of the decade of the 1970s, that number had tripled. Many Americans felt that they were being strangled by red tape.

One federal agency, the Occupational Safety and Health Administration (OSHA), was criticized for its minute directions governing the smallest details in a way far beyond normal considerations for safety. Instead of simply requiring sturdy ladders, for example, this agency decreed specifications in a dozen or so confusing pages.

STAFFING A GOVERNMENT

How does one go about staffing a government? What is the best method? Should the incoming President invite in all his loyal party workers, fire the old workers, and replace them with friends? Or should workers be recruited for their jobs on the basis of competitive tests, without regard for party affiliation?

The first system was tried for almost a century. When a new President took office, hundreds and sometimes thousands of government employees were fired and new officials were appointed. This applied not only to highly placed policy-makers but also to the lowest positions in government. It was known as the "spoils system," from a remark made by one of President Jackson's associates that "to the victor belong the spoils." In other words, loyal party workers deserve rewards. There was also some justification for this view on the basis of the "rotation in office" theory. Jackson observed that men who remained in office too long became complacent and inefficient, tending to think they were indispensable. He believed that offices should be rotated to permit the addition of fresh ideas and to allow more citizens to serve their country.

The spoils system was not very successful in administering the federal government efficiently. After the Civil War, therefore, a movement toward the *merit system* began. Under this method, applicants for some federal offices would be screened by testing instead of being chosen on the basis of party loyalty. The merit system was resisted at first by many persons, including those who felt their jobs might be endangered by it. But the assassination of President Garfield by a man who had failed to get a federal job helped weaken the opposition, and in 1883 an act was passed which created the Civil Service Commission. The Pendleton Act, as it is known, provides for a three-person bipartisan commission, one member being selected by the President as chairman.

The Civil Service Commission conducts tests, draws up registers or lists of qualified candidates for jobs, and makes certain that laws restricting the political activities of civil servants are obeyed. It also strives to improve the service by encouraging able persons to seek and remain in government service. Career information is distributed to schools and post offices and is announced on television, radio, and in newspapers. As much as possible, salaries of civil servants are kept on a par with those of workers holding similar jobs in private industry.

The original act gave the President the power to classify certain jobs within the government as under the merit system. President Arthur classified about ten percent of federal employees, and later Presidents increased it to about ninety percent. A worker classified under the merit system may not be removed for political reasons, or dismissed for any reason other than disloyalty, incompetence, or defects of character (such as excessive use of alcohol or keeping questionable company). Even under these circumstances, the worker must be granted a hearing and possesses many guarantees that justice will be done.

The merit system has eliminated job insecurity and has brought more efficiency into many levels of government, but it has raised problems of its own. A question often asked is: how do you control it? When a civil servant's job is protected, how eager will he or she be to carry out policies ordered by the President or his appointees, who have only a short tenure in office? All modern Presidents have complained of bureaucratic intertia and have discovered that the way to get around the opposition of bureaucrats to a specific program is to start a whole new agency for the sole purpose of carrying out the idea. This in turn causes new problems in the form of increased expense and additional bureaucrats.

In 1978, President Carter asked that reforms be enacted by Congress to make the federal bureaucracy more receptive to change. The result of this request was a reform bill signed in 1978 replacing the Civil Service Commission with an Office of Personnel Management under a Director appointed by the President and a Merit Systems Protection Board to supervise the Federal government's employment system. Federal employees were granted the right to join or not join unions as they saw fit, and to bargain collectively with their agencies in a limited way.

Still another problem is the attitude of bureaucrats toward the public they serve. Many cases of the thoughtless, unfeeling, and downright vicious actions of civil servants have been recorded, but there is not much the average citizen can do about them. Bureaucrats have their own ways of doing things and it is difficult to budge them from their routine paths. Bureaucratic language, sometimes called "gobbledygook," is in a class by itself as a means of communication. Here is a recent example, a definition of an exit:

> Exit is that portion of a means of egress which is separated from all other spaces of the building or structure by construction or equipment as required in this subpart to provide a protected way of travel to the exit discharge.

The growth of a large bureaucracy in America is very recent, having taken place in the last forty years. It is significant that all other industrialized nations have developed large bureaucracies, too. The citizens of these countries are as concerned as we over the best way to use a bureaucracy without falling under its control. The problems created by it are new and therefore call for new solutions. Unless answers are forthcoming, the American bureaucracy may create a class of petty dictators, each supreme in his own sphere.

The President may command in many areas, but his power is by no means unlimited. He, too, falls under the system of checks and balances. His is a rewarding position for a person with the proper temperament and necessary dedication. Yet it is at times a lonely post, filled with frustrations. Very difficult problems must find final solution at his desk, for where else can he pass them?

AFTER-CHAPTER REVIEW

REVIEW QUESTIONS

1. Define the following names, terms, or ideas.

special session	CIA
recess appointment	"kitchen cabinet"
senatorial courtesy	HEW
ICC	"rotation in office"
FTC	Pendleton Act
EOP	GAO
Federal Register	OSHA
Standard Federal Region	*Code of Federal Regulations*

2. Vocabulary building.

patronage	commute
pardon	reprieve
quasi-	amnesty
gobbledygook	

3. Cases.

Missouri v. *Holland*	*Myers* v. *United States*
Humphrey's Executor v. *United States*	

4. Review of the text.

a. Name and explain the ways by which a President may influence legislation.
b. In what ways does the President's relationship with the Senate differ from his relationship with the House?
c. Describe the treaty-making process.
d. Review the courses of action the President may take in dealing with a person convicted of a federal crime.
e. Select one agency or bureau from each and discuss its make-up, powers, and duties: EOP, Cabinet, independent agencies.
f. Define the merit system and the spoils system. What are the advantages and disadvantages of each?

DISCUSSION AND PROJECTS

1. Questions for discussion.

a. Should presidential power over the executive branch be expanded, left as it is, or reduced?
b. We all agree that Congress should reduce the number of government employees by reducing the amount of money available for them. Where should we begin? What agencies or services should we dispense with?
c. Should the Senate's role in foreign relations be expanded or decreased?

2. Debate topics:

a. Resolved: The British Cabinet system, which gives Cabinet posts to members of the legislature, is better than the American system.
b. Resolved: Both the House and the Senate should have control over foreign affairs.

3. Opinion poll.

Should the federal government be reduced in size and responsibilities?

BIBLIOGRAPHY

See Chapter 6 for related bibliography.

"The American Presidency," *Current History,* June 1974. The entire issue of this excellent monthly is devoted to the Presidency.

Cronin, Thomas E. *The State of the Presidency.* Boston: Little, Brown, 1975.

Friedel, Frank. "Profiles of the Presidents," *National Geographic Magazine,* November 1964, January 1965, May 1965, October 1965, and January 1966. These articles also have been published in book form under the title *Our Country's Presidents.* Washington, D.C.: National Geographic Society, 1966.

"An Inside Look at Our Runaway Bureaucracy," *U.S. News & World Report,* 3 October 1977.

Koenig, Louis. *The Chief Executive.* 3rd ed. New York: Harcourt Brace Jovanovich, 1975.

Koenig, Louis. "We Will Need a Presidency of Substantial Power," *U.S. News & World Report,* 8 November 1976.

Methvin, Eugene H. "Why Can't Do-Nothing Bureaucrats Be Fired?" *Reader's Digest,* November 1977.

Miller, Arthur S. *Presidential Power in a Nutshell.* St. Paul, Minn.: West Publishing, 1977.

"Superbrain's Superproblem," *Time,* 4 April 1977. Discusses the creation of the Department of Energy under James Schlesinger.

"What's Right and What's Wrong with the Federal Worker," *U.S. News & World Report,* 3 October 1977.

UPI

A night view of the United States Supreme Court building, with its Grecian columns reflected in a nearby pool. This marble building, designed by Cass Gilbert in the form of a classic Greek temple, was built in 1935 on the summit of Capitol Hill and faces the Capitol.

8

The Federal Judiciary

The American people are very partial to lawsuits. Matters which are settled in other countries without reference to the courts are the subject of expensive and time-consuming legal battles in the United States. This country has more lawyers in proportion to population than any other nation, and the number is growing annually. There is plenty of employment for most people associated with the legal process.

Most litigation (that is, legal action) is conducted under state jurisdiction, either directly in the state courts or indirectly through subordinate courts of counties and municipalities. In recent years, however, the federal court system has become extremely active in litigation. The chief justice of the United States recently cited an increase of almost fifty percent in the period from 1957, when 92,000 cases were filed, to 1977–1978, when 172,000 were introduced in federal courts.[1]

During most of American history, the federal court system was limited because of our firm belief in the division of powers, a subject we studied in Chapter 3. It was generally considered that state courts should handle most legal problems which arose within a state and that the federal judiciary should rule only in matters such as:

1. Disputes between states;
2. Disputes between the federal government and a state;
3. Disputes between citizens of different states;
4. Disputes involving federal officials.

---

1. "How to Break Logjam in Courts," *U.S. News & World Report*, 19 December 1977, p. 22.

But times have changed, and federal court judges can never be sure what subjects they will be studying from one year to the next. Over the past few years, they have been asked:

1. May a state permit corporal punishment in its schools?
2. May a school refuse to register students who do not cut their beards or who let their hair grow too long?
3. Must a person join a union to keep his job even though his religious beliefs forbid it?
4. Is it lawful for children to say prayers in public schools?
5. Are state laws permitting pregnant women to have abortions constitutional?[2]

Questions like these crop up constantly in our complex society and the agency empowered with the final word on them is the Supreme Court. In a sense, the Supreme Court of the United States (SCOTUS) is like the "given" in a geometric theorem. In this branch of mathematics some parts of a question are given to the student, who uses them to solve the rest of the problem. Thus, the "given" in American government would read as follows:

> Given:
> A body of nine judges appointed for life and protected against removal from office for all but the most unusual activities. They are charged with the responsibility of deciding on the constitutionality of laws (and actions taken under laws) by public officials on all levels of government.

With this accepted by all as part of the problem, Americans hope to solve the serious question of how to live with each other in a peaceful, harmonious society.

THE FEDERAL COURT SYSTEM

The Supreme Court is not the entire federal judiciary, but only the highest court in it. This chapter will examine the entire

2. Answers to the above, based on recent Supreme Court decisions, are: 1. Yes; 2. Yes; 3. Yes; 4. No; 5. Yes.

federal court system, its duties and performance. You probably have heard the remark, "Don't make a federal case out of it." This is slang for not treating a matter too seriously. In a sense, it is an inaccurate compliment to the importance of the highest court system. The remark also implies the existence of a nonfederal court system. And this is true, since we have not just one court system in our republic, but fifty-one.

And these fifty state systems differ from the one federal judiciary not in their importance but in the fact that they cover different types of cases. Where they overlap, they do so from different viewpoints. To illustrate this, let us use murder as an example. Murder is not a federal crime and thus, had the murderer of President Kennedy lived, he would have been tried in the state of Texas under Texas law.[3] It would have been the job of Texas prosecutors to secure a conviction within the rules of Texas law. The decision then could have been appealed up to the highest Texas court.

If the murderer's conviction had been upheld in these courts, the next step would have been the federal courts. The case might have reached the Supreme Court, which would have examined the record to see if the defendant had been accorded all the rights guaranteed him under the Constitution. If there were no "federal question" involved, the Supreme Court might have refused to hear the case.

Well, you may ask, when is a matter one for the state courts and when is it one for the federal courts? The answer to this question has not been defined. We do know that in the past century the federal court system has grown tremendously in power and jurisdiction. This is due to:

1. Constitutional amendments, such as the Fourteenth, with its equal protection clause;
2. Acts of Congress, such as those covering civil rights, health, and safety passed during the 1960s and 1970s.
3. Supreme Court decisions, such as *Gitlow* v. *New York* (see Chapter 2) and other cases increasing federal court power.

3. In 1965, Congress made the murder of the President a federal crime subject to the death penalty. It also provided against kidnapping, assaulting, or murdering him or the Vice-President.

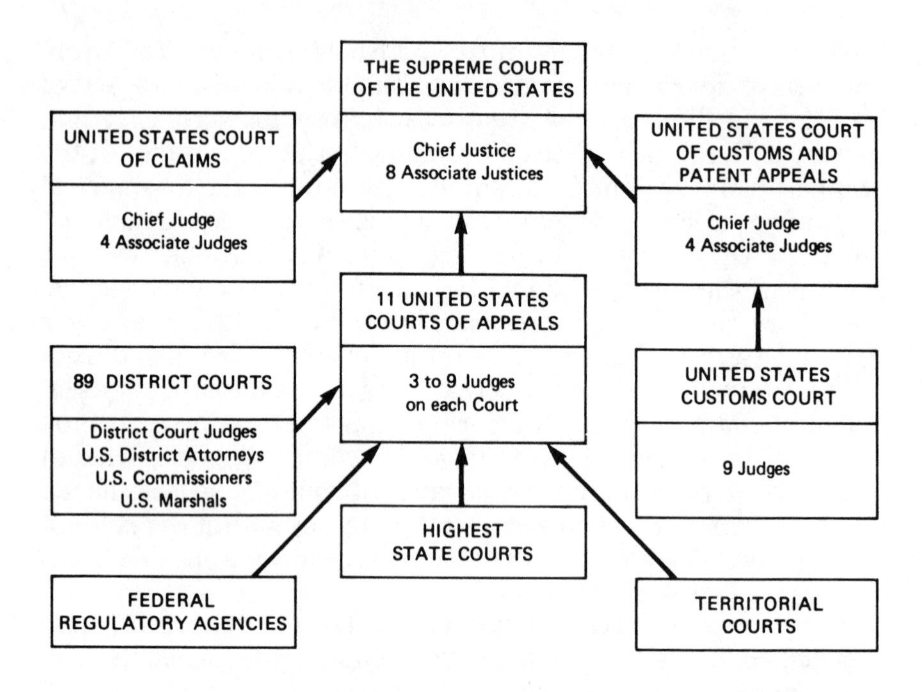

Is this increased federal court power good or bad? Another good question, but unfortunately the answer to this one must be vague, too. We know that when the federal government acts in a certain field, either through Congress, the courts, or the executive, the law of the land becomes more uniform. Whether this is an advantage or not, of course, depends on what kind of a law the federal government enforces. The important thing to note is that the Supreme Court in the past century has tended to assign a greater role to the federal court system than ever before.

THE SUPREME COURT

At the top of the federal court system is the Supreme Court, which since the 1860s has consisted of a chief justice and eight associate justices. They are appointed for life by the President with the consent of the Senate. The associate justices receive $72,000 a year and the chief justice $75,000. Most justices have been men of excellent education, and many had prior experience as judges in state court systems. Others have been former Cabinet members, legislators, or governors. William Howard

Taft was the only man to be both President and a member of the Supreme Court (he was chief justice). In earlier times, political figures were chosen, and their appointments were often based on friendship with the President. Lately, Presidents have selected judges of the lower federal courts whom they may know but who could not be called "cronies."

The Supreme Court has two kinds of jurisdiction; that is, it may hear cases which come to it by original suit or on appeal. *Original jurisdiction* is practiced when a case begins initially in the Supreme Court. This is a rare practice. More commonly the Court exercises its *appellate jurisdiction.* When a case is decided in the lower federal courts, the Supreme Court may choose to permit the unsatisfied contestants to appeal. In some instances, the Court will hear the case automatically, as when an act of Congress is declared unconstitutional. The usual way cases reach the Supreme Court, however, is through the process known as *writ of certiorari.* This is an order given to a lower court to send up all records on a particular case to the higher court. By this means, the Supreme Court may pick and choose its cases.

The Supreme Court hears only a tiny fraction of cases tried in the federal courts. Of the 172,000 cases filed in 1977–1978, only 4,700 were directed toward the Supreme Court. And the Court made short work of the overwhelming majority of these by rejecting appeals, refusing to review the decisions of lower courts, or making decisions without giving reasons. About 130 were selected for close argument and review.[4] These were chosen because they involved some very important matter. By ruling on one particular issue, members of the Court hope they will be setting a precedent, that is, laying down a general rule which will guide courts and legislators all over the country in similar instances. Sometimes the Supreme Court takes a case to upset an old precedent and to set a new one. In the 1890s the Supreme Court ruled that racial segregation could be practiced in schools as long as they were equal in facilities. But in 1954, in the case of *Brown* v. *Board of Education of Topeka,* the Court ruled that segregated schooling was

4. "How to Break Logjam in Courts," *U.S. News & World Report,* 19 December 1977, pp. 22, 24.

UPI

A mother and child on the steps of the Supreme Court Building. The mother is holding a newspaper that headlines the 1954 *Brown* v. *Board of Education of Topeka* decision.

unconstitutional. Many times the Supreme Court makes a law by what it does *not* do. Its refusal to review a decision by a lower court, for example, amounts to accepting the decision of the lower court on the matter.

Cases are either civil or criminal. A civil case is one in which some dispute arises between the United States and an individual, group, or state, or between one group or individual and another on a federal matter. A criminal case is one involving the commission of a federal crime. Let us take a tax matter as an example. If the Internal Revenue Service said an individual had taken too much money for charitable deductions from his income tax, the taxpayer either could pay the difference or go to court to decide the matter. This would be a civil suit. If the Internal Revenue Service thought the taxpayer had tried to defraud the government of revenue, then a criminal case could be started.

APPEALS AND DISTRICT COURTS

The case load on the federal court system is very heavy, with some cases dragging on for as long as four years. To ease the burden on the Supreme Court, Congress in 1891 created the Courts of Appeals. These courts hear cases appealed from lower courts and from decisions made by federal regulatory agencies. There are eleven Courts of Appeals, including one for the District of Columbia. Each court handles cases for several states. There are eighty-eight judges in this system, appointed for life and paid a salary of $57,500 a year. Districts range in size from three to fifteen judges. Cases usually are heard before at least three judges. The Courts of Appeals handle thousands of cases each year (19,000 in 1977 compared to 11,600 in 1970), taking much of the burden off the highest court. When appealed to from the Court of Appeals, the Supreme Court usually, but not always, denies the appeal—that is, refuses to rehear the case. This says that the higher court agrees with the decision of the lower.

The workhorses of the federal court system are the District Courts. There are more than three hundred District Court judges, and the country is divided into more than ninety judicial districts. Over ninety percent of all federal cases are heard and settled at this level, in spite of the thundering vow which all Americans occasionally make, "I'll take this case to the Supreme Court!" District court judges hear cases such as:

1. Illegal entry into the country in violation of immigration laws;
2. Other criminal offenses such as narcotics violations, auto theft, counterfeiting, forgery, etc.;
3. Civil suits involving parties from different states. If, for example, a New Yorker and a Californian engage in a dispute, the injured party may seek justice in either of the above states or, if the amount of money involved is over $10,000, in the federal courts.

TYPES OF LAW

The federal courts are courts of law, but that is a very broad term, since scholars and judges have discovered many kinds of law. In their simplest form, laws are just rules which people agree upon when living together in society. The courts of America, however, apply several different types of law to different cases:

- Statutory law—comes from a legislative source, for example, the U.S. Congress;
- Constitutional law—decisions are sometimes based on the Constitution itself;
- Common law—over the years, decisions by judges have become the basis for future judicial action. Hence, common law is sometimes called judge-made law. It uses precedents of the past to guide judges in present decisions;
- Equity law—designed to provide for cases not covered by common law. If, for example, a builder dug out part of your backyard to make it easier for him to put in a foundation for a house he was building, you could sue him under common law and would probably be paid damages. But if you knew in advance that he was going to do this, you might, under the law of equity, ask a judge for an injunction, an order forbidding the builder to dig up your yard. Thus, equity law protects you from potential damage while common law protects you from actual damage.

DECISION-MAKING IN THE SUPREME COURT

When a matter at law reaches the Supreme Court by one of the three methods described, the case is then heard. Sometime between October and June, the months when the Court sits, lawyers for each side will be allowed to present their sides. These lawyers first must be admitted to plead before the Supreme Court, since not all lawyers are permitted to do so. They follow a prescribed, formal method of procedure. A written brief presenting the facts in their case is filed, and each lawyer is accorded one hour to speak before the Court.

There must be six justices to make a quorum. After hearing a group of cases, the justices confer and express their views. When they reach a decision, one of the judges is assigned the task of writing the "majority" opinion. Sometimes other judges agree with the decision but for different reasons, so they write "concurring" opinions. Justices who disagree with the majority position write "dissenting" opinions. When the decisions are

Supreme Court Historical Society

The Justices of the Supreme Court, photographed in 1979. Seated left to right, they are Associate Justices Byron R. White, William J. Brennan, Jr., Chief Justice Warren E. Burger, Associate Justices Potter Stewart, Thurgood Marshall. Standing left to right are Associate Justices William H. Rehnquist, Harry A. Blackman, Lewis F. Powell, Jr., and John Paul Stevens.

made, they are announced by the Court and are published officially by the government and, of course, are commented on vigorously in newspapers and through other media.

It is always difficult to predict how the Supreme Court is going to decide a given case, since the men involved are learned individualists as free from popular or governmental control as any group could be.

The Supreme Court, in fact, is a completely independent branch of government. Although it is true that members are appointed by the President with Senate approval, once this is out of the way the justices are on their own. Short of a constitutional amendment, impeachment proceedings, or drastic congressional action, the Court is free. As one chief justice said, whatever restraint it exercises must come from itself. Suggestions have been made to change the method of selecting justices from allowing legal associations to pick candidates who would then be appointed by the President, to election by the people.

Election of judges takes place in many states today. In addition, some states permit their citizens to *recall* judges, that is, to draw up a petition signed by a certain percentage of the voters. This petition recalls the judge, who must then stand for re-election. Although it seems severe, this action is rarely taken in the eight states where recall is authorized.

SPECIAL COURTS

The Constitution specifically provides for only one court—the highest—but it authorizes Congress to create inferior courts whenever they are needed. Congress created the District and Appeals courts under this authority. In addition, Congress has created other courts designed to handle specialized areas. The Court of Claims was established by Congress in the 1850s to adjudicate claims against the federal government. Before this time, whenever a citizen made a claim against the government, Congress had to pass a special law to compensate him. The Customs Court, created in the 1920s, is charged with the work of settling disputes which arise over imports. If an importer disagrees with the decisions of a customs official, this is where the problem can be argued out. The Court of Customs and Patent Appeals also was founded early in this century. It hears appeals from the Customs Court and also handles patent and copyright problems. Other courts in the judicial system include the Tax Court, to which a citizen may take his or her tax problems; the Court of Military Appeals, which hears appeals from military court-martial cases; and territorial courts for such areas as the Virgin Islands, Guam, and other areas under federal control.

Not all of these courts were created under the authority of Article III of the Constitution. Some came into being under Article I, Section 8, which grants legislative powers to Congress. Congress has the power to make laws governing taxation and to create a tax court to settle disputes. It also decides whether a court is *constitutional* or *legislative*. One of the main differences between constitutional and legislative courts is that legislative court judges do not always serve for life. For example, a judge on a territorial court serves an eight-year term. The lesser courts have varying numbers of judges, the Customs Court having nine and the Court of Military Appeals three.

A visit to the downtown areas of most fairly large American cities might be confusing in that federal, state, and municipal buildings are grouped together in one location. The Supreme Court building in New York, for instance, does not house the chief justice. This is a state supreme court, not federal. In a later chapter, some of the state court systems will be described.

FEDERAL JUDGES

Where do federal judges come from, and on what basis are they chosen? Judges do not "graduate" to the federal courts from the state systems, although some have. Nor are justices of the lower federal courts necessarily promoted to the Supreme Court. Instead, Presidents pick judges in much the same way that they select Cabinet members. They try to secure people who share their views on government. And they usually stay within their party. President Eisenhower appointed more than 200 Republicans and only 13 Democrats, while President Kennedy selected more than 120 Democrats and only 11 Republicans.

Presidents do not always succeed in their choices, even though they are hand picked. Theodore Roosevelt found that Justice Oliver Wendell Holmes, whom he nominated, was completely individualistic in his decisions. Thomas Jefferson abolished judicial positions and even began a program of impeaching judges, but met with little success. Andrew Jackson ignored some Supreme Court decisions, saying on one occasion that Chief Justice John Marshall "has made his decision. Now let him enforce it." This illustrates the great weakness of the Supreme Court: it must rely upon the executive to enforce its decisions. In modern times, when a state, the federal executive, or even a large segment of a state's population disagrees with the Supreme Court, little can be done to carry out its decrees. In spite of the ban on prayer in public schools made by the Court in 1963, for example, many schools still continue to permit prayers and Bible reading.

Brown Brothers

Chief Justice Charles Evans Hughes administers the oath of office to newly elected President Franklin D. Roosevelt in 1932, one of the ceremonial duties accorded the leader of the Supreme Court.

Many efforts have been made to weaken or change the Supreme Court. In the 1930s, President Franklin Roosevelt found his New Deal program defeated by hostile Court decisions. Furthermore, no justices had retired or died in his first four-year term (President Taft had been able to appoint six members to the Court during his four years in office). Roosevelt tried to persuade Congress to increase the size of the Court to fifteen, but the Congress (even though Democratic) defeated the plan overwhelmingly. In his next four years in office, however, Roosevelt was able to appoint five justices to the Court.

You may wonder whether judges really are judicious or fair, since they seem to be appointed in such a partisan manner. No one can be completely objective, but judges try to be fair to both sides. They are older and, hopefully, wiser than the average citizen. (The average age of Supreme Court justices is a bit over sixty-five, and five members are in their early seventies.) Presidential appointment guarantees a wide range of views. The present Supreme Court is made up of the appointees of five Presidents. It thus represents a cross-section of views.

Our federal court system has its failings. Its jurisdiction overlaps that of the state court system; its judges are not always perfectly fair; and it is slow, cumbersome, and expensive. Yet it serves the same purpose for us in legal matters that the National Bureau of Standards in Washington does in measurements. This bureau has the responsibility for determining and maintaining uniform standards of weights and measures. Without its standards, each person might have his own interpretation of units of weights and measures. Similarly, the Supreme Court is the legal yardstick for us, determining what judicial standards should be applied. Let us hope that anyone who can think of a better system, a more effective "given" for our problem is invited to the next Constitutional Convention!

AFTER-CHAPTER REVIEW

REVIEW QUESTIONS

1. Define the following names, terms, or ideas.

original jurisdiction
appellate jurisdiction
writ of certiorari
statutory law
equity law
common law
recall
civil suit
criminal suit
constitutional law

2. Vocabulary building.

precedent injunction litigation equity adjudicate

3. Cases.

Brown v. *Board of Education of Topeka*

4. Review of the text.

a. List the major divisions of the federal court system, indicating the number of judges in each, their tenure, and their jurisdiction.

b. Discuss the major differences between the federal and state court systems.
c. Make a list of the ways by which federal court power has been increased.
d. Describe the relationship between the President and the Supreme Court, using specific examples of harmony and friction.

DISCUSSION AND PROJECTS

1. Questions for discussion.

a. Do the nine men who comprise the Supreme Court make up an oligarchy? If so, is this dangerous for the future of our form of government?
b. Discuss this French definition of law: "Law is the expression of the general will." Is this a useful definition? A dangerous one? Explain your answer.
c. Make a field trip to the central part of your town. Ask the personnel of the courts there what the powers and duties of their courts are. Write a report on this.

2. Debate topics.

a. Resolved: The nation's founders never intended the Supreme Court to have the power it now possesses.
b. Resolved: Federal judges should be elected or should not serve for life terms, or should be forced to retire at the age of seventy or seventy-five.

3. Opinion poll.

Has the Supreme Court become too powerful for its place in the American governmental system?

BIBLIOGRAPHY

Abraham, Henry J. *The Judiciary*. Boston: Allyn & Bacon, 1973.

Becker, Theodore L., and Feeley, Malcolm M. *The Impact of Supreme Court Decisions*. New York: Oxford University Press, 1973.

Flynn, James J. *Famous Justices of the Supreme Court*. New York: Dodd, Mead, 1968.

Harrell, Mary Ann. *Equal Justice under the Law*. Washington: Foundation of the Federal Bar Association / National Geographic Society, 1975.

Kidney, James A. "Are Judges Getting Too Powerful?" *U.S. News & World Report*, 16 January 1978.

"A Report Card on the Supreme Court," *U.S. News & World Report*, 7 March 1977.

Rossiter, Clinton, ed. *The Federalist Papers*. New York: New American Library, 1961. Numbers 78-83.

Schmidhauser, John R., and Berg, Larry L. *The Supreme Court and Congress*. New York: Free Press, 1972.

The people in this photograph, and especially the man carrying the sign, are exercising First Amendment rights guaranteed to all Americans, namely the right to assemble peaceably and ask the government to correct something they think is wrong. The man with the sign is also exercising his right to free speech. Although Americans sometimes take such rights for granted, in many countries in the world the man would be arrested by police and thrown into jail for just carrying such a sign.

9

Civil Rights and the Supreme Court

Most of this chapter and the next will deal with the Supreme Court. This may seem strange, since we just finished a chapter devoted to the federal court system. But the last chapter covered what the Supreme Court *is*; now we will be dealing with what it *does*. And one of its most important functions is to guarantee equal justice under the law to everyone; that is, to protect our civil rights.

Today, the words "civil rights" often are used in a confusing and narrow manner. We cannot think of them, in fact, without thinking of a civil rights movement, demonstration, or march. But what is called the "civil rights movement" today should not be confused with the term "civil rights." The civil rights movement is the organized (and very justifiable) effort by leaders of minority groups (such as blacks, Indians, and Spanish-speaking persons) to secure equal rights for that segment of the population they represent. Chapter 11 will discuss the Thirteenth, Fourteenth, and Fifteenth Amendments and their effects on racial discrimination. Civil rights, on the other hand, are the great liberties we all possess under the Constitution and the Bill of Rights.

In this chapter, we shall outline the liberties guaranteed to *all* of us by the First, Second, Third, and Fourth Amendments of the Bill of Rights. It always should be kept in mind that these amendments are subject to Supreme Court interpretation. Hence, the importance of the courts in this section of American life is shown.

THE FIRST AMENDMENT

The First Amendment is the core of the Bill of Rights and of our liberties in general:

> Congress shall make no law respecting an establishment of religion, or prohibiting the free exercise thereof; or abridging the freedom of speech, or of the press; or the right of the people peaceably to assemble, and to petition the Government for a redress of grievances.

These few words mean much; millions of words have been written about them and millions more may be expected in the future.

FREEDOM OF RELIGION

The "establishment of religion" clause was placed in the Bill of Rights to express the belief held in the eighteenth century that people should worship as they pleased. It denied to the federal government the power to set up a favorite church which would be supported by the taxes of all citizens, regardless of their religion. At the time of the adoption of the Constitution, many European nations and some of the American states had *state-churches*, that is, churches favored above all others. Even after the adoption of the Constitution, some states continued to pay salaries to ministers and to discriminate against members of other religions in such matters as officeholding. The restraint written into the First Amendment did not, of course, apply to state governments but only to the federal. You may remember from Chapter 2 that the Bill of Rights was not originated to protect the citizens from the state but rather to protect them from federal tyranny.

The religion clause, therefore, simply forbade Congress to set up a single church supported by the government. As time passed, however, it came to have much broader meanings. Thomas Jefferson stated that he thought it established a "wall of separation" between religion and the government (or between church and state, as it is referred to now). What does this "wall of separation" mean? If a Protestant church is burning down, may a public fire department put out the fire?

If a member of a religious order passes a teaching examination, may he or she wear a distinctive uniform in a public school? Do children have the right to say prayers in publicly supported schools? May bus service be provided for parochial school students? May textbooks be provided?

Other questions on the subject are even more involved. Does the state have the right to interfere with a person's religious practices? On the surface, the answer seems obvious, yet suppose a person's religion entails the handling of poisonous snakes. May the state intervene to safeguard health? Or suppose the Aztec religion were revived. Would the state have the right to prevent modern-day Aztec priests from practicing human sacrifice? A less extreme but actual recent case occurred in 1964, when a woman was admitted to a hospital with a bleeding ulcer. Since she was in need of blood, the hospital ordered a transfusion. The woman refused it because, as a Jehovah's Witness, she believed it violated her religion. The hospital obtained a court order from the Federal Court of Appeals in Washington and the woman's life was saved. The Supreme Court refused to hear an appeal from the lower court decision, thus indicating its agreement with it. A similar case occurred in 1977 when the Court agreed to a lower court decision involving a mental patient who received tranquilizers although their use violated her religious principles.

In another case involving religious practices, the Supreme Court in 1878 declared that one could not commit immoral acts under the cloak of religion. In the case of *Reynolds* v. *United States*, the Court held that a Mormon named Reynolds was convicted justly for practicing polygamy, even though his religion permitted a man to have more than one wife.

In a series of cases called the Flag Salute cases, Jehovah's Witnesses objected to saluting the United States flag. They claimed it was against their religion to worship any idol, and forbade their children to salute the flag in school. In 1940, the Supreme Court approved state laws punishing this refusal; but three years later, it reversed its decision and declared that local officials could not force children to salute. In 1977, the Court struck down a New Jersey law which required students who did not wish to recite the Pledge of Allegiance to stand up while their schoolmates were reciting it. However, the Court said, in forcing students to stand the state was not interfering in their religious freedom so much as in their freedom of speech—a freedom that will be discussed in the next section of this chapter.

One of the most important cases dealing with the First Amendment came in the 1920s, when an act was passed in Oregon which would have forced most Oregon school children to attend public schools, thereby ending the parochial school system in that state. In the case known as *Pierce* v. *Society of Sisters*, the Supreme Court declared that the law violated the Constitution and that parochial schools had a right to exist. It stated:

> The child is not the mere creature of the state; those who nurture him and direct his destiny have the right, coupled with the high duty, to recognize and prepare him for additional obligations.

The primacy of parents in the education of their children was further upheld by the Court in 1972, when it ruled seven to nothing that children of Amish parents were not required to attend high school if they did not wish to.

Another facet of the problem of religious training was explored in several cases dealing with "released time" programs, which permit public school students to receive religious instruction during the school day. In the *McCollum* case in the 1940s, the Court ruled that the released time program in Illinois violated the separation of church and state, since religious leaders came into the public schools and used regular classrooms to impart their teachings. In 1952, in the case of *Zorach* v. *Clauson*, the Supreme Court stated that New York City's released time program was constitutional, since students left the building to secure religious instruction.

In a case even more significant than the released time decision, the right of a parochial school child to receive aid from the state or local government was stated in *Everson* v. *Board of Education* in 1947. Here, the Court declared that New Jersey parochial school children could receive bus transportation paid for by public money. The important argument made here was that the state was not aiding a religious *school* so much as it was helping a *citizen* who happened to attend such a school. The same kind of assistance was given to veterans of

Children receiving instruction in a parochial school. Although the doctrine of separation of church and state has led to many complicated practical issues, the broad outcome of this doctrine has been that people are free to worship as they choose and to set up schools in which the principles of their faith are taught.

World War II and of later conflicts. Under the GI Bill of Rights, students could attend any school they wished and could receive support from the federal government.

Most recently, several important judicial steps have been taken to define the relationship between church and state still further. In 1962, the Regents Prayer case (*Engel* v. *Vitale*) was decided. Officials of New York State, with the help of ministers, rabbis, and priests, had composed an interdenominational prayer for public school students to recite each morning. Although the prayer was entirely voluntary, several parents challenged its use in the school district their children attended, and the high Court declared that public officials had no business composing prayers.

A year later, the Court went still further and eliminated Bible reading and the recitation of the Lord's Prayer from public schools. This action raised a storm of protest and a demand for a constitutional amendment to permit public prayer. The Supreme Court argued, however, that the First Amendment requires federal and state governments to "maintain strict neutrality." Opponents of this view declared that the Court was not asking for neutrality, but was vigorously favoring antireligious sentiments. The Court strongly urged that all young people be taught about the Bible from a literary and historical point of view and urged the study of all religions. These ideas failed to satisfy hostile critics, who pointed out that studying cooking is far different from eating.

Supporters of the antiprayer decisions pointed out that the decisions could be changed by constitutional amendment, if Congress wished it. However, congressional supporters of a prayer amendment have never been able to muster the necessary two-thirds vote to begin the amending process.

The financial problems of church-related schools grew more serious during the 1960s and 1970s and forced many of them to merge or to close. Seeking to help save this system, state and national legislatures voted various forms of aid. A New York State program to lend textbooks on nonreligious subjects was declared constitutional in 1968 *(Board of Education* v. *Allen)* because this aided the pupil and not the school. Recent efforts to pay money directly to schools for teaching secular subjects and for keeping records have not been upheld, although the Supreme Court did permit federal aid to go to church-run colleges for building programs, as long as the buildings did not serve religious purposes (*Tilton* v. *Richardson*, 1971). To provide non-classroom services to parochial school children, state legislatures have voted funds for guidance counseling, testing materials, remedial programs, and similar assistance with approval of the Supreme Court (*Wolman* v. *Walter*, 1977).

FREEDOM OF SPEECH AND OF THE PRESS

Another broad guarantee accorded citizens under the First Amendment is that of freedom of speech and of the press. It covers a wide range of topics, including television, motion pictures, and radio, as well as speaking and writing. As we have learned, no right is unlimited; it always brings with it a corresponding duty. Thus, the right to free speech brings with it the duty to exercise restraint and to pay the consequences for failing to do so. As one judge put it, freedom of speech does "not protect a man in falsely shouting 'fire' in a theatre and causing a panic."

How free may we be in speech and writing? May we drive down a main street at two o'clock in the morning, insulting people over a loudspeaker? May we make remarks or produce motion pictures which hold up someone else's religion to ridicule? May we write pamphlets urging our servicemen to refuse military service during time of war? Or may we call upon our fellow citizens to overthrow the government?

Another question of grave importance concerns the nature of speech itself. Is speech only words, or can it take the form of action? We all know how to *look* insolent or disobedient. In fact, an old expression is "Don't look at me in that tone of voice!" Actions that speak louder than words are known as "symbolic speech." Thus, the Supreme Court has ruled that Congress may not put a limit on certain campaign contributions by private citizens because that would limit their freedom to express themselves under the speech provision of the First Amendment. And the refusal of the student just mentioned to stand for the Pledge of Allegiance is another form of symbolic speech.

But speech usually means words, either spoken or written. And the use of words, as the great English scholar Samuel Johnson once said, falls between thought and action. If we *think*, "I would like to rob that house," there is nothing any government can do to stop us in our thought. If we *act* to rob the house, the government can do plenty. But if we *say* or *write* something indicating our desire to commit robbery or urging others to do so, it is difficult to decide what to do with us. Some scholars say that nothing should be done to a person for what he says or writes. They would ignore the street-corner speaker who encourages his listeners to riot or to loot. Others declare that if his statements show a *tendency* toward bringing about unlawful acts, the speaker should be prosecuted. There is also a third position, which is known as the "clear and present danger" doctrine.

Jean-Claude LeJeune

Two women applauding the speaker at a rally held to gather support for the idea that young men who refused to fight in the Vietnam War should be given amnesty, or forgiveness. Partly as a result of public opinion on the issue, President Ford announced a limited program of amnesty for draft resisters and deserters in 1974; President Carter broadened the program in 1977.

The "clear and present danger" doctrine was expressed in the 1919 case of *Schenck* v. *United States*. During World War I, a Socialist had urged American servicemen to refuse to fight, and had pleaded with other Americans to resist the draft and the war effort. The radical's actions violated the Espionage Act of 1917 and the federal government sent him to jail. The Supreme Court approved this decision on the grounds that Congress had the right to prohibit speaking and writing if there was a "clear and present danger" that the remarks would bring about the intended results.

The danger of worldwide Communist subversion has caused considerable concern for most Americans. Since the Communists ruthlessly established their dictatorship in Russia in 1917, they never have stopped trying to overthrow non-Communist governments around the world. In 1934, for example, the Communist party of the United States published a "manifesto" in which it reminded the "American working masses" that the solution to their problems was "by the path of revolution." The manifesto urged the creation of a "socialist society of the United States" which would "mark the end of world capitalism."[1]

1. Quoted in Allen Guttmann and Benjamin Munn Ziegler, eds. *Communism, The Courts and the Constitution* (Boston: D.C. Heath, 1964), pp. 13–14.

Alarmed by this and by other examples of totalitarian agitation in America, Congress passed the Smith Act of 1940. This act made it illegal to teach or advocate the overthrow of the United States government "by force or violence." Since politicians advocate the overthrow of the existing government at every federal election, this last phrase is very necessary. The means they wish to employ—the secret ballot—places them worlds apart from subversives. The Smith Act was upheld by the Supreme Court after a long trial which ended in 1951. The case is known as *Dennis* v. *United States*, and involved the conviction of eleven top leaders of the Communist party.

During the late 1940s and early 1950s, two important events occurred which showed the extent of subversion existing in the free world. A scientist named Klaus Fuchs was convicted in Britain of conveying atomic secrets to the Soviet Union. At about the same time, two American spies, Ethel and Julius Rosenberg, were charged with the same crime. The actions of these spies placed the Soviet Union ahead in its race to become a nuclear power. The Rosenbergs were convicted of espionage and were executed.

Other acts to limit the Communist menace were passed in 1950 and 1954. The first was the McCarren Act, which called for the registration of Communist "front" organizations with the Attorney-General's office. It also denied subversives the right to secure passports from the Department of State. In 1954, the Communist Control Act was passed, outlawing the Communist party. The argument offered for this was that the party was not a political group but a conspiracy.

The Smith Act and its two companion laws did not fare well in the Supreme Court during the late 1950s and into the 1960s. In a number of cases, the Court reduced the effectiveness of the laws by declaring, for example, that it was a violation of an individual's rights to force him to register as an officer of a Communist organization, since he or she would then be incriminating himself, that is, admitting he or she was guilty of belonging to a conspiracy. The Court also said that the action of Congress in denying passports to Communists was unconstitutional.

In addition to the problem of Communism in the field of freedom of speech and of the press, several other questions

UPI

Two *Washington Post* reporters in their office. Bob Woodward (left) and Carl Bernstein (right) were largely responsible for breaking the Watergate story. Their investigative reporting, made possible by the First Amendment right guaranteeing freedom of the press, led ultimately to creation of a Senate committee, the establishment of a special prosecutor, and a number of indictments against high government officials. In many countries in the world, these two men would have been shot or imprisoned rather than praised for their exposure of governmental wrongdoing.

arise. For example, we know that a person may not slander or libel another individual. But what if a whole group is subject to libel? In a case tried some years ago, the Court stated that an Illinois man who distributed literature condemning a whole group of people was convicted rightly of "group libel." It also ruled that a public official could not collect damages from a newspaper which carried advertisements he considered libelous (*New York Times* v. *Sullivan*, 1964). This last decision is viewed as a protection of the right of the people and the press to criticize their governmental leaders, a right that has existed in America since the famous early heroes in the struggle for freedom of the press.

In a six-to-three decision in 1971, the Supreme Court upheld the right of several newspapers to publish documents classified by the federal government as secret, on the basis of the right of the people to be informed (*New York Times Co.* v. *United States*). In 1972, however, the Court ruled that freedom of the press did not exempt a reporter from revealing the sources of his or her news for grand jury use.

Another controversial area under freedom of the press is that of censorship. American postal authorities have long contended that they should not have to carry obscene books, pamphlets, or magazines in the mails. The problem centered over just what should be declared "immoral" in the field of writing or pictures. Congress has passed some twenty laws governing this subject since the 1840s. In the 1957 case of *Roth* v. *United States*, the Supreme Court said that a person could not claim protection for obscene writing under the First Amendment. A similar decision was made in 1966 in the case of a New York magazine publisher, but this decision was based not so much on the magazines as on the way they were advertised.

But these decisions did not really answer the question, "How do we decide whether or not a book or magazine—or movie or play or painting or song or television program—is obscene?" In the late 1960s and early 1970s, the Supreme Court was more lenient on the subject of obscenity than any previous Court. State laws and Post Office regulations were set aside (held unconstitutional) in many cases which earlier Supreme Courts had held to be valid. The yardstick used was whether or not the article in question had any "redeeming social value" or was just plain smut. If even the smallest merit remained, the Court upheld the right of the distributor to exhibit or sell it. In a 1973 decision, however, the Court placed less emphasis on "redeeming social value" and suggested that local communities develop their own definitions of obscenity. The Court held in the case known as *Miller* v. *California* that it would not set standards because it was "neither realistic nor constitutionally sound to read the First Amendment as requiring that the people of Maine or Mississippi accept public depiction of conduct found tolerable in Las Vegas, or New York City." Quoting an older decision, the majority said the yardstick should be "the average person, applying contemporary community standards." A decision made by the Court in 1974 reiterated this standard, but warned communities that they did not have absolute power to ban works they considered pornographic (*Jenkins* v. *Georgia*).

There is danger in letting courts of any kind anywhere set standards of decency, but as long as some persons exceed the protected rights of freedom of speech, the line must be drawn. Chief Justice Burger made the point in the *Miller* decision that to "equate the free and robust exchange of ideas and political debate with commercial exploitation of obscene material demeans the grand conception of the First Amendment and its high purposes in the historic struggle for freedom."

Censorship may involve issues other than obscenity, of course. Some years ago, New York officials refused to permit a movie to be shown because they said it was sacrilegious; that is, it offended the religious beliefs of a large group. In 1952, this case (known as *Burstyn* v. *Wilson*) was decided by the Supreme Court in favor of the movie's backer. The Court said that governments could not censor on the grounds of sacrilege, since it was almost impossible to define this term in a country with so many different thoughts on religion.

In other cases involving the right to freedom of speech, the Court has ruled that, while freedom of speech is a very broad right, it can be restricted when necessary to protect society. Local governments must permit speakers to express their views, but they have the right to require the speaker to acquire a permit and they can regulate the use of public address systems. In each case of this sort, however, the Court has taken into consideration the conditions surrounding the event. As one justice said, "The character of every act depends on the circumstances in which it is done."

THE RIGHT TO ASSEMBLE AND TO PETITION

In addition to freedom of religion, speech, and the press, the First Amendment also guarantees the right of the people to assemble peaceably and to petition the government "for a redress of grievances." The right of people to assemble in private buildings such as homes or rented halls is practically unlimited. Yet, in states where gambling is forbidden, even private homes are not sacred. The same is true if persons gather for

Jean-Claude LeJeune

American Nazis holding a public rally. These citizens are exercising their First Amendment rights of freedom of speech, assembly, and petition, thereby testing the American belief that we must, as Justice Oliver Wendell Holmes said, protect "freedom for the thought we hate" as well as freedom for the thoughts we agree with.

conspiratorial purposes such as to plan a robbery. On the streets or in public buildings, local governments have much more power. But they must exercise their power without discrimination. They may not permit one group to assemble and deny permission to another simply because they agree with one group and disagree with the other. If the American Nazi party is permitted to assemble in a public park for a rally, for example, opposing groups, including Communist-sympathizers, must be accorded the same privilege. If there is danger that such a rally may lead to riots, however, the local government may take steps (within reason) to prevent this by prohibiting the meeting.

The right of petition is sacred to English-speaking peoples. In the Declaration of Independence, Jefferson wrote as one of the grievances against George III: "we have petitioned for redress in the most humble terms; our repeated petitions have been answered only by repeated injury." Thus, in Eng-

Jean-Claude LeJeune

A woman gathering signatures for a petition calling for the impeachment of President Nixon. In America, anyone can get up a petition for practically anything because this is a free country. The only requirement is that petitions or initiatives which have the effect of binding state legislatures usually must be signed by registered voters.

land and in America, citizens hold this right to be very important and do not want to see it ignored. In England during the 1840s, a reform group presented a petition with millions of signatures to the British Parliament. The petition had to be delivered in three carriages. In America, petitions have not been that large, although those with tens of thousands of signatures are not unusual.

When citizens petition Congress to pass or repeal a certain law, it does not bind members of Congress to do so. Since they are elected officials, they would be foolish to ignore or to ridicule such a direct request of the people, but there is no legal way to compel them to act on any measure. The right of petition, which can be expressed by a single individual in a letter to a member of Congress or to any other public official, is very powerful, even though it is not similar to the "initiative." The initiative, written into some state constitutions, is different from petition in that it *binds* the legislature to consider a proposal provided a certain percentage of the voters petition for it. Recently, a member of Congress introduced a proposed constitutional amendment to give the American people the right to propose legislation.

Elected leaders want to know what the people are thinking. They spend a fortune on opinion polls just to find this out. A respectful, brief, and thoughtful letter can often tell them more than anything they can read in the newspapers or in opinion polls.

In the late 1960s and early 1970s, different groups of people used their First Amendment rights in new and sometimes untested ways to call attention to their aims. Government buildings were occupied, universities were disrupted, flags and draft cards were burned, and streets and highways were blocked by demonstrating groups. The courts of the nation moved cautiously but surely to settle the controversies arising over the acts committed and the reactions of law enforcement authorities. Acting calmly and with restraint, the courts tried to balance the slender scale between liberty on one side and the need for order on the other. Above all, the most noteworthy observation to arise out of the decade of demonstrations of all kinds was that both the demonstrators and the general public—often far apart in their ideas and methods—were united in their reliance upon the courts to sort out the rights and wrongs of each case.

THE SECOND AMENDMENT

The Second Amendment to the Bill of Rights is brief and specific:

> A well-regulated militia being necessary to the security of a free state, the right of the people to keep and bear arms shall not be infringed.

This guarantee, like others in the Bill of Rights, is a limited right. It means more than the citizens' right to possess firearms. It protects their right and duty to serve in the armed forces. In older societies, some groups of people could not serve their country, since military service was limited to an elite class. Because of this, the higher class felt it alone could govern the country, without giving other classes a voice. By serving in the armed forces, or at least by possessing the right to do this, the citizens protect their right to participate in governing themselves.

The Second Amendment also prevents the national government from absolutely prohibiting the ownership of firearms by citizens. The federal government has, however, passed laws to exercise some control over the interstate commerce in guns. Such weapons as sawed-off shotguns may not be sold, nor is it legal for persons to engage in interstate commerce in guns if they have serious criminal records. Other than that, the federal government has not been very active in this area. This explains the ease with which President Kennedy's assassin obtained a mail-order rifle for a few dollars. The assassination of Senator Robert Kennedy in 1968 was offered by supporters of gun controls as further proof of the need for strong federal action. On the other hand, opponents of gun-control laws argued that guns, like autos, were only lethal when improperly used by people.

Some state governments have stricter laws governing firearms and other deadly weapons than the federal government. In almost all states, licensing is regulated carefully and the carrying of concealed weapons such as knives or pistols is limited severely.

THE THIRD AMENDMENT

The Third Amendment to the Constitution deals with the quartering of troops, that is, the power of a government to force a homeowner to provide lodging and food to military personnel. It reads:

> No soldier shall, in time of peace, be quartered in any house without the consent of the owner, nor in time of war, but in a manner to be prescribed by law.

Quartering of troops without permission from homeowners was common before the Revolutionary War and had been condemned by Jefferson in the Declaration of Independence. It was more than just a violation of a person's right to privacy. It was a form of coercion which had been practiced by rulers in Europe to terrorize their subjects. It had been used, for example, in France by the Catholic rulers to force Protestants to convert to the Catholic religion. In America, several Quartering Acts had been imposed upon the American people in the eighteenth century, the most severe being one passed in 1774, which aroused a great deal of resentment.

THE FOURTH AMENDMENT

The last amendment we will consider in this chapter is the Fourth. It is related to the Third, in that both protect the principle that a "man's home is his castle."

> The right of the people to be secure in their persons, houses, papers, and effects, against unreasonable searches and seizures, shall not be violated, and no warrants shall issue but upon probable cause, supported by oath or affirmation, and particularly describing the place to be searched, and the person or things to be seized.

Note the exceptional care with which this amendment is drawn up. The right of privacy must not be so absolute that it can be used to protect criminals; nor must it be so weak that it cannot protect law-abiding citizens. Each word is selected carefully with this difficult reconciliation in mind.

Under totalitarian governments, no guarantees of individual privacy are observed. Many persons live in fear of a knock on their doors which could mean that they or their loved ones might never be seen again. In the United States and other free nations, this fear does not exist, thanks to the Fourth Amendment and the strictness of courts in upholding it.

The key words in this amendment are *warrant, unreasonable, probable,* and *particularly*. The word *warrant* means "justification," and in the legal sense it refers to a document issued by a magistrate (some judicial official) indicating the name, address, and possible offense committed. The person asking for the warrant (a police officer, for example) must convince the magistrate that an offense probably has been com-

Mimi Forsyth from Monkmeyer

A policeman gives a motorist a traffic ticket. A traffic ticket is a summons to appear in court, where a person may choose to plead guilty or not guilty to the violation charged. (A man who was found guilty of turning right on a red light—which is legal in some states but not in others—took his $10 case all the way to the Supreme Court. The Court refused to hear it, however.) If one does not respond to the summons, a bench or court warrant is automatically issued for one's arrest. A Supreme Court decision indicates that if one is arrested on such a warrant, the police may conduct a thorough search of one's car and person and use any evidence found.

mitted. To do this, he must present some evidence and he must be willing to take an oath (or if he does not believe in oath-taking, he must affirm or pledge his word) that conditions may be as he describes them. The document may not be vague; it must *particularly* cite the offense and the offender.

There are, of course, instances when authorities may act without a warrant, but they must be able to show that there was no time to secure one. Otherwise the person arrested must be freed. Similarly, if, in searching a home for one thing which was described in a warrant, the officers find other evidence of criminal activity, they may not be able to secure convictions for the other unnamed offenses.

Persons on the street may be searched by a superficial patting if a responsible and expert officer suspects that wrong-doing may exist. This practice, based on "stop and frisk" laws, was declared constitutional in 1968. In a 1973 decision, the Court declared that a police officer who arrests a person for a traffic violation may search that person thoroughly if he feels it is necessary. Anything found in the person's possession may be used as evidence against him. In 1977, the court ruled that a police officer may order a motorist to leave his or her car even to be cited for a simple traffic ticket.

If the authorities seize evidence without a warrant or with an improper one, the courts simply refuse to let that evidence be used against the accused person when his case is tried. In the 1914 case of *Weeks* v. *United States*, the Supreme Court ruled that evidence illegally obtained by federal officers could not be used in federal courts. The name applied to this prohibition is the "exclusionary rule." It is also known as the "Weeks Doctrine." Later, the Court ruled that illegally obtained evidence could be used in federal cases as long as federal officers were not involved in getting it. Thus, local authorities were able to search a person's home improperly and later turn the evidence over to the federal authorities. In several cases more recently, however, the Supreme Court has changed that ruling.

When the Weeks Doctrine was developed, it did not apply to state cases. States used their own methods in guaranteeing individual freedom through their own bills of rights. In 1961, though, in *Mapp* v. *Ohio*, the Supreme Court extended the federal rule on illegally obtained evidence to state courts. In 1963, in the case of *Ker* v. *California*, the Supreme Court held that state and local officials must follow the same strict standards regarding searches and seizures as federal officers.

An interesting case dealing with the Fourth Amendment is *Frank* v. *Maryland* (1959), in which Baltimore health officials tried to obtain entrance to the home of a person named Frank because they thought the house was rat-infested. They had no warrant and Frank would not let them in. He was fined. The Supreme Court stated that in such a case the inspectors had the right to demand entrance to a person's home provided they came during the day, even though they had no warrant. They could not, however, force their way in. This decision was reversed in 1967 when the Supreme Court ruled that inspectors must secure warrants before entering private homes. The warrants may be issued for entire areas of a municipality, however, and need not specify individuals (*See* v. *Seattle* and *Camara* v. *San Francisco*).

Los Angeles Police Department

Evidence to be used against citizens must be obtained by observing strict legal safeguards. The use of trained dogs, such as this one, to sniff out marijuana and other drugs, is considered to be within the legal boundaries allowed by the courts.

Police authorities must be very circumspect in their regard for the rights of all persons, even those who seem most obviously to have broken the law. But, if they may not enter a person's home without observing the strictest legal safeguards, how about listening from outside? Is it lawful to tap a person's phone or "bug" his home? This knotty problem illustrates the way government has become more involved since Jefferson's day. (Not that Jefferson was unconcerned about people listening in to conversations; he invented the dumb-waiter to make sure that he could talk to his associates without fear of disloyal servants overhearing him.) On the issue of wire tapping, the Supreme Court was at first somewhat lenient. In *Olmstead* v. *United States* in 1928, it ruled that evidence obtained against a bootlegger by tapping his telephones was legal and could be used in court. This broad permission was restricted in later years to allow for the invasion of a person's privacy through electronic devices only after a court order had been issued. This order is to be given only after the court has been satisfied that a good reason exists for it.

The first four amendments to the Constitution are only part of our protection against unjust governmental interference in our lives. By interpreting them in a liberal manner, the Supreme Court has shown its understanding of one of the great principles of American government, that a good government protects the liberties of its citizens without endangering their security.

AFTER-CHAPTER REVIEW

REVIEW QUESTIONS

1. Define the following names, terms, or ideas.

"establishment of religion" clause
"clear and present danger" doctrine
Communist Control Act
Weeks Doctrine (exclusionary rule)
initiative
Klaus Fuchs
Smith Act
McCarren Act
Espionage Act
right of assembly
"symbolic speech"
Ethel and Julius Rosenberg

2. Vocabulary building.

"front organization"
"released time"
incriminate
censorship

3. Cases.

Reynolds v. *United States*
Flag Salute cases
Board of Education v. *Allen*
Pierce v. *Society of Sisters*
Zorach v. *Clauson*
McCollum case
Everson v. *Board of Education*
Wolman v. *Walter*
Engel v. *Vitale*
Schenck v. *United States*
New York Times v. *Sullivan*
New York Times Co. v. *United States*
Roth v. *United States*
Burstyn v. *Wilson*
Mapp v. *Ohio*

Weeks v. *United States* *Ker* v. *California*
Olmstead v. *United States* *Frank* v. *Maryland*

4. Review of the text.

   a. Describe the relationship between church and state in the United States. What were the most important cases in our history concerning this relationship and what was the significance of each?
   b. Explain freedom of speech in all its aspects and describe the status of this right throughout our history.
   c. List and explain the major decisions regarding Communist subversion in the United States.
   d. How does the U.S. Postal Service exercise control over national life?
   e. List all the rights guaranteed by the first four amendments to the Constitution and describe them in your own words.

DISCUSSION AND PROJECTS

1. Questions for discussion.

   a. Write an essay on the following subject: The Supreme Court is biased against (or for) religion.
   b. Discuss the term "civil rights." What does it mean to you?
   c. Discuss the following question: Do we need a very strict law regulating firearms?

2. Debate topics.

   a. Resolved: Prayer should be permitted in our public schools.
   b. Resolved: I can say anything I want!

3. Opinion poll.

   Do you think the Supreme Court has been at fault in protecting personal property even at the expense of effective law enforcement?

BIBLIOGRAPHY

See Chapters 8 and 10 for related bibliography.

Corwin, Edward S. *The Constitution and What It Means Today.* Princeton, N.J.: Princeton University Press, 1973.

"Criminal Justice in America," *Current History,* June 1976.

"In Supreme Court: Fresh Battle over Individual Rights," *U.S. News & World Report,* 3 October 1977.

Martz, Carlton S. *Freedom of Expression: Speech, Petition, and Assembly.* Encino, Calif.: Glencoe, 1977.

Mitchell, John G. "God, Guns and Guts Made America Free: The National Rifle Association and the Constitutional Right to Bear Arms," *American Heritage,* February/March 1978.

Moynihan, Daniel P. "Government and the Ruin of Private Education." *Harper's,* April 1978.

Rosenblatt, Albert M., and Rosenblatt, Julia Carlson. "A Legal House of Cards," *Harper's,* July 1977. Discusses the exclusionary rule.

Worten, Stanley N., ed. *Freedom of Speech and Press.* Rochelle Park, N.Y.: Hayden, 1975.

Daniel Brody from EPA

A community center and legal aid office in Cambridge, Massachusetts. Many community legal assistance programs, which are designed to provide legal help to people who are too poor to hire private attorneys, are funded by state and federal grants. Legal aid lawyers have many times successfully brought suit on behalf of their clients against the same government which is paying their salaries. This indicates the commitment our political system has to the idea that one of the main purposes of government is to seek justice for all.

10

Civil Rights: Guarantees Against Oppression

The first four amendments to the Constitution are only part of the shield of liberty constructed for us in the early days of the "great republic" (as President Kennedy called our country). Three other amendments in the Bill of Rights offer more guarantees against oppression. These are the Fifth, Sixth, and Eighth Amendments. The Ninth Amendment provides for any rights that might have been overlooked. When we add to these the rights woven into the body of the Constitution, such as those in Article I, Section 9, we find a considerable body of protection.

In outline form, here are the parts of the Constitution that we will study in this chapter:

Fifth Amendment—due process, freedom from self-incrimination;

Sixth Amendment—guarantee of fair trial;

Eighth Amendment—protection against unfair punishment;

Ninth Amendment—further popular protection;

Other Constitutional guarantees (Article I, Section 9).

THE FIFTH AMENDMENT

The Fifth Amendment, a broad guarantee of many freedoms for us, is closely linked to the Fourth. The Fourth, as we have seen, deals with arrests and the gathering of evidence. The Fifth takes us from there toward a trial. It reads:

> No person shall be held to answer for a capital, or otherwise infamous crime, unless on a presentment or indictment of a grand jury, except in cases arising in the land or naval forces, or in the militia, when in actual service in time of war or public danger; nor shall any person be subject for the same offense to be twice put in jeopardy of life or limb; nor shall be compelled in any criminal case to be a witness against himself, nor be deprived of life, liberty, or property, without due process of law; nor shall private property be taken for public use without just compensation.

JURIES

Juries are of two types: small or *petit* juries consisting of twelve jurors who hear a case tried and decide it, and larger or *grand* juries made up of as many as twenty-three persons, who listen to the testimony of witnesses and decide whether enough evidence exists to bring the matter to trial. Indictment by a grand jury does not mean a person is guilty of a crime. It merely means that the jurors think there is sufficient reason to hold a trial.

The grand jury must be used on the federal level, but this does not apply to the states unless the system is part of a state's judicial procedure. Many states still use grand juries, but several dozen have substituted other procedures. In some states, the attorney for the people files what is called an "information" to the court which will hear the case. This paper sets forth his or her reasons for believing that the accused person should be prosecuted.

Qualifications for service on juries vary among the states, but the federal government established a uniform rule for federal trial juries by determining that any literate citizen, male or female, over the age of eighteen and without a felony conviction could serve after a residence of one year in the judicial district. Thus, a person accused of a "capital or otherwise infamous crime" (in other words, one for which he could be executed or imprisoned) is protected against injustice by the close scrutiny of many of his fellow citizens.

When a person is under military jurisdiction, he is governed by a legal system known as the Uniform Code of Military Justice. This code sets forth special rules to be followed in cases arising out of crimes committed within the armed forces. Servicemen convicted of crimes under the military code have the opportunity to appeal to the Court of Military Appeals.

DOUBLE JEOPARDY

A citizen who has been tried and acquitted (found not guilty) in a criminal case may not be tried for the same offense again. This is his or her protection against "double jeopardy," that is, endangering his or her life or freedom twice. Double jeopardy does not work against a person, however, once he or she has been convicted. If he or she wants to appeal the decision, the person has the right to waive (set aside) this right in the hope of winning his or her freedom or at least a lesser sentence. The double jeopardy guarantee is limited by the fact that both federal and state courts have control over the prosecution of many crimes. In the case of *Bartkus* v. *Illinois*, which was finally settled in 1959, a bank robber was found not guilty in a federal court but later was convicted in an Illinois court for the same offense. He received life imprisonment and appealed to the Supreme Court, stating that he had been put in jeopardy twice. The Supreme Court let the Illinois decision stand.

In addition, if a person has committed many offenses in the course of an illegal action, he or she may be tried for each offense. A man who enters a store, kills the owner, steals postal money orders, and throws his mask away on the sidewalk may be tried for everything from murder to littering. His case may be heard in the courts of the state and in the federal courts.

SELF-INCRIMINATION

Important as the double jeopardy provision is, it is not the heart of the Fifth Amendment. The most important guarantee it offers is the protection against "self-incrimination." This clause means that people are not expected to be witnesses against themselves. They do not have to give testimony to help the court convict them. Our laws state that the government must prove a person guilty; the person is not obliged to prove himself or herself guilty or not guilty. Accused persons may, if they wish, take the witness stand and incriminate themselves. They even may permit their signed confessions to be used against them. But the government may not force them to do these things.

If a person refuses to take the stand, observers might think to themselves, "If he is innocent, what is he trying to hide? Why doesn't he just get up there and tell the truth?" This type of thinking is naive, since a skillful attorney (as your knowledge of movie and television lawyers will tell you) often can make a seemingly good case against the most innocent. Let us say, for example, you were required to answer only "yes" or "no" to the question, "Have you stopped cheating on your exams?" Either answer would give a bad impression. Of course, this is a trick question and probably would not be admitted in court. Still, from his long courtroom experience, a clever lawyer can make almost anyone look bad. On occasion, prosecuting attorneys have tried to influence a jury by hinting that refusal to testify meant that the accused had something to hide. In a recent case, the Supreme Court ruled that such remarks violate the Fifth Amendment.

In 1964, the Supreme Court ruled that the Fifth Amendment guarantee against self-incrimination extended to state cases. In the case of *Malloy* v. *Hogan*, a convicted gambler was ordered to testify in a Connecticut investigation. He refused on the grounds that this would incriminate him. He was imprisoned for contempt of court, and the higher courts of Connecticut agreed with this action. The Supreme Court, however, ruled that the gambler had been denied his rights under the Fifth Amendment.

This brings to mind other questions about self-incrimination. Suppose a person refuses to testify before a congressional investigating committee? After all, this is not a court and the amendment reads that a person may not be "compelled in *any criminal case*." Congress, therefore, has ordered persons to testify. The argument against this is that, although the committee is not a court, what is said before it may be used later against the witness in a trial. The person thereby is giving

Hinton from Monkmeyer

A client conferring with his lawyer. Engraved on the wall of this Criminal Courts Building, just above the lawyer's head, is the line: "Where Law Ends There Tyranny Begins."

evidence indirectly against himself or herself. The Supreme Court has ruled that the self-incrimination guarantee also applies to investigating bodies.

This protection is beneficial to the citizen, but it might severely restrict congressional efforts to gather important information. To get around it, the Immunity Act was passed in 1954. This act permits committees to force witnesses to testify under certain conditions, even though what they say will be incriminating. If they incriminate themselves, they are given immunity from prosecution. Failure to testify in these cases can lead to contempt charges and result in imprisonment.

How far can the self-incrimination privilege be carried? Does it go beyond legislative committees? May a person applying for a job with a company that forbids the employment of Communists refuse to answer questions about his or her Communist party affiliations? May an individual applying for a license to practice law refuse to answer such questions? The Supreme Court has ruled that states may protect their citizens and their legal professions in cases like this, but also has indicated that this power must be exercised prudently and with restraint.

Over the years, the use of confessions in criminal cases has played an important part in gaining convictions against criminals. It would seem that a person who has confessed to a crime would automatically be found guilty. But a confession is only part of the evidence needed to convict an accused person. If it can be shown that the person was in any way coerced into making a statement, the confession is useless. In the 1964 case of *Escobedo* v. *Illinois*, the Supreme Court stated that a person must be told of his right to have a lawyer while being questioned by police. If he is denied his right to see a lawyer or if he is not told of it, his statement may not be used as evidence. The meaning of this decision was further emphasized in 1966, with the *Miranda* v. *Arizona* case. The decision in this case gave the accused the following even more significant safeguards: he must be told of his right to legal counsel; if he waives this right at first, he later may change his mind; and if the police see that he is reluctant to answer questions, they must stop interrogating him. Probably you have heard the *Miranda* rights recited many times on television ("You have the right to remain silent ..." and so on). These two decisions caused great controversy. Many people felt that the Court's expansion of the Fifth Amendment would lead to an increase in lawlessness, while others felt that it was necessary to safeguard persons from police coercion.

The *Miranda* decision came in for especially heavy criticism. When it was handed down by the Court, led at that time by Chief Justice Earl Warren, many political leaders, law enforcement officials, and plain citizens thought the ruling too permissive. They demanded that it be tightened up. After the election of 1968, Warren retired and was replaced by Chief Justice Warren Burger, an appointee of Richard Nixon. During his five years as President, Nixon appointed three more justices. The "Nixon four" generally have held that the *Miranda* decision is a valid interpretation of the Constitution but that it should be expanded. In cases decided in 1975 and 1977, the Court has followed in that direction. *Oregon* v. *Mathiason* is the name of the 1977 case, in which *Miranda* protections were not read to a suspect who came of his own free will to a police station to answer questions about a crime for which he was not yet under arrest.

One final matter relating to self-incrimination must be considered. This protection extends beyond the accused person to his or her spouse, doctor, lawyer, and other individuals who occupy a special relationship to him. Thus, in the 1958 case of *Hawkins* v. *United States*, the Supreme Court ruled that a wife's incriminating testimony against her husband may not be used in court.

DUE PROCESS AND EMINENT DOMAIN

The last two sections of the Fifth Amendment provide protection against the violation of "due process" and the arbitrary confiscation of property. The "due process" clause is found in both the Fifth and the Fourteenth Amendments. It means that *all* the protections listed in the Bill of Rights and in the body of the Constitution must be extended to the accused person in a criminal action. Due process is taken to mean the way justice is dispensed, and so it is sometimes called "procedural" due process. It appears twice in the Constitution because it applies to federal courts in the Fifth Amendment and to state courts in the Fourteenth.

The framers of the Bill of Rights were anxious to protect private property from unfair governmental seizure, but they also respected the right of "eminent domain." This governmental power refers to the taking of private property for public use. If the state where you live is building a highway near your home, and if this highway can go either across your property or through a factory employing hundreds of people, it would be in the public interest to choose the route through your property. The state (or federal authorities, depending upon the circumstances) must give you a just compensation for your loss. If any question arises over the price or over the need for acquisition, it is settled in the courts.

THE SIXTH AMENDMENT

The Sixth Amendment continues to elaborate on the guarantees provided for citizens accused of crimes. It reads:

> In all criminal prosecutions, the accused shall enjoy the right to a speedy and public trial, by an impartial jury of the state and district wherein the crime shall have been committed, which district shall have been previously ascertained by law, and to be informed of the nature and cause of the accusation; to be confronted with the witnesses against him; to have compulsory process for obtaining witnesses in his favor, and to have the assistance of counsel for his defense.

This amendment seems to be specific, yet many questions arise. How speedy must a trial be? How public should it be? What is meant by an impartial jury? If an accused person cannot afford a lawyer, must the federal or state government provide counsel for him?

Trial by jury is one of the cornerstones of our legal system. An accused person usually has the right to waive this protection if he wishes. If he demands trial by jury he will be tried before twelve jurors who must reach a unanimous decision in order to convict him. If they fail to agree, a "hung" jury results and the case may be retried without violating the double jeopardy guarantee. Trial by jury in state cases is guaranteed by state constitutions, but sometimes the rules in state trials differ from those in federal courts. In some states, for instance, smaller juries are used in certain criminal cases and a less than unanimous vote sometimes is all that is needed for conviction.

The right to a speedy trial protects a person from being left indefinitely under a charge which, even if he theoretically is considered innocent until proven guilty, could cause him much hardship. Imagine how unfair it would be if the President in power could have his opponent in an election accused of a crime in September and not brought to trial until after the November elections. Yet, a trial conducted too quickly also can violate due process.

The right to a public trial protects the accused from being tried in secret, as is the case in Russia, where a person may be tried without even being present. On the other hand, the decision in one case was thrown out by the Supreme Court because the trial was *too* public. In the 1965 case of

Estes v. *Texas*, a majority of the Court ruled that televising the trial created too much public interest, thus violating the due process clause of the Fourteenth Amendment. The case became a kind of real-life serial for television viewers and the very presence of so many cameras and technicians had a harmful effect upon all the parties in the trial.

At the beginning of a trial, the jury must be impartial. If a white person has been the victim of a crime supposedly committed by a black, is an all-white jury impartial enough to settle the case without prejudice? In some instances, the Court has answered "no," as in the 1935 case of *Norris* v. *Alabama*. In this celebrated case, Chief Justice Hughes ruled that the conviction of Clarence Norris was unfair since blacks had been excluded deliberately from service on Alabama juries, even though there were many black citizens qualified for jury duty.

A trial should be held in the area in which the supposed crime was committed, unless doing so would be detrimental to the accused person. If so, the accused may apply for a "change of venue," a judicial order which will allow the case to be tried elsewhere. A well-known case was the Richard Speck multiple murder trial in 1967, which was tried in Peoria, Illinois, rather than in Chicago where the murders were committed. However, the government may not deliberately seek out an area where there is a better-than-average chance of getting a conviction. Due process also is violated if the person is not made aware of the charges against him. There have been cases where bewildered or mentally ill persons have been convicted of very grave crimes after being told they were to be tried on lesser charges.

Another Sixth Amendment right is that of "confrontation," which protects individuals from having secret charges levied against them by anonymous accusers. They have the right to confront their accusers and to be given help in securing witnesses on their own behalf. Finally, they have the right to counsel. This last provision, however, did not apply to state court cases for many years, until the Supreme Court made it applicable in cases involving the death penalty. This decision was expanded in the 1963 case of *Gideon* v. *Wainwright*, when the Court said that failure to provide legal assis-

Brooks from Monkmeyer

A trial in process. In the center, an attorney is addressing the jury (far right). Because the courts have generally banned the taking of photographs in the interests of a fair trial and due process of law, this picture is somewhat unusual.

tance to a person accused of a crime was a violation of the Sixth Amendment. Mr. Gideon was given a new trial, with legal help, and gained his freedom. Almost immediately, thousands of prisoners in states where courts were not required to provide lawyers by state law began to demand retrials. In some cases, their retrial sentences were longer than those they had first received.

THE EIGHTH AMENDMENT

Even if due process has been observed carefully in every instance, a convicted person still is protected from high fines or cruel and unusual punishment by these words of the Eighth Amendment:

> Excessive bail shall not be required, nor excessive fines imposed, nor cruel and unusual punishments inflicted.

Under this amendment, some of the horrible punishments prescribed for criminals in previous eras have been outlawed. Punishments must be both cruel *and* unusual to violate this amendment. Thus, assigning a traffic violator to work in the accident ward of a hospital might be unusual but not cruel. In a case decided in 1947, the Supreme Court ruled that a man could be electrocuted twice (the electric chair had not worked the first time) without violating the Eighth Amendment. More recently, in 1962, the Court held that making it a crime just to be a narcotics addict was against the Eighth Amendment, although the possession or sale of narcotics is a criminal offense. The Eighth Amendment was modified by court action in 1972 when the Supreme Court outlawed the death penalty in the case of *Furman* v. *Georgia* by a vote of five to four. The reasons given by the majority were that the death penalty was given so rarely that it could be considered arbitrary and, therefore, unusual, and that it was most often meted out to poor and minority group persons when it was used. This decision caused great controversy, and it led state legislatures to draft death penalty laws that would be more evenly applied.

In 1976, the death penalty was brought to the highest court once again. This time, in *Gregg* v. *Georgia*, a state law permitting the death penalty but providing all safeguards was upheld. The seven justices who approved this decision were undoubtedly aware of the widespread public support for restoration of the death penalty, and they knew also that thirty-five states had adopted new death penalty statutes since the *Furman* decision. The *Gregg* decision is an example of the way in which a popular democracy makes its will known even to judges who need not answer to the people. However, also in 1976 and again in 1977, the Court limited the application of the death penalty under laws where the penalty was made mandatory, where it was automatic for killing a police officer, and where it was imposed for rape. Despite these restrictions, the death penalty is now constitutionally approved. In 1977, the first execution in some years took place in Utah, where the supreme penalty was paid by a person convicted of murder.

The Eighth Amendment also covers excessive fines. A fine should not be so high that a person must work for years, perhaps all his or her life, to pay it off. However, a glance at some of the fines which can be levied for offenses against the federal government shows that they can be set quite high.

Finally, bail must be reasonable, since the whole bail system is designed not to keep people in jail but to make certain that they appear in court for trial. Setting a high bail can penalize poor people by keeping them in jail until their trials, while wealthier people will be able to stay free until their trials. Quite often, innocent people have been arrested in good faith by the police and legally charged with crimes, and then have had to wait months until their trials were due on the court calendar. They have then been found not guilty. In the meantime, however, they have sometimes served months in jail and have lost their jobs, while their families have gone heavily into debt. This is one of the unfortunate sides of the bail system.

THE NINTH AMENDMENT

The Ninth Amendment is less specific than those we have been studying:

> The enumeration in the Constitution, of certain rights, shall not be construed to deny or disparage others retained by the people.

This means exactly what it says: that just because some rights are specifically mentioned in the Constitution and the Bill of Rights, it does not mean that these are the only rights which Americans possess. The Ninth Amendment is not used by the Supreme Court as a guarantee of any rights. It simply recognizes our government as a limited one.

OTHER RIGHTS AND PROTECTIONS

Not so vague are the sections of the Constitution dealing with personal liberty. In Article I, Section 9, we find the following guarantees:

1. *Habeas corpus;*
2. No bill of attainder;
3. No *ex post facto* law.

The states as well as the national government are required to honor these guarantees. *Habeas corpus* (a Latin term which does not make much sense when translated literally) protects us against imprisonment for any but serious reasons. Upon the arrest of an individual, any person (a friend, an attorney, or even a stranger) may seek a writ (order) of *habeas corpus* from a judge. The writ of *habeas corpus* then is served on the victim's jailor (usually the police) and the jailor then must appear before the judge to explain why he has the person in custody. If the judge thinks the reasons are grave enough, he will permit the jailor to continue to hold the person. If not, the person must be released. This right is connected closely to the Fourth and Sixth Amendments, as you probably already have noted.

The prohibition against bills of attainder forbids Congress or the state legislatures to pass laws which deprive a person of life, liberty, property, or reputation. In English history, Parliament occasionally passed such acts, sometimes ordering the death sentence. Tyrants used this device for getting rid of their enemies, since it required no trial, no jury, and no evidence. All it took was a majority vote of Parliament, which could sometimes be induced to pass such laws. The vote "tainted" (spoiled) the victim, who then could be forbidden to inherit money or to pass it on to his children.

An *ex post facto* law is a retroactive criminal law; that is, one which makes an act a crime although it was not a crime when the person performed it. Another type of *ex post facto* law is one in which the punishment for the offense is increased. Thus, if a person went to jail under a law which stipulated a twenty-year sentence for an illegal act, and if Congress the following year increased the penalty to forty years, the prisoner would not come under the new law. If Congress decreased the penalty from twenty to ten years, however, the person convicted under the old law would benefit by it, since the *ex post facto* provision does not work against a person. This protection does not extend beyond criminal proceedings. If a civil law was made retroactive, it would have to be obeyed. In New York City some time ago a group of transit workers went on strike for higher wages. This was contrary to a state law which forbade public servants to strike and which prohibited them from receiving pay raises for several years if they did strike. In spite of this law, the workers were given a new raise and an angry citizen secured a court order setting the new pay scale aside. The state legislature then amended the act to remove transit workers from this prohibition.

The law-abiding citizen may think that all these guarantees are very remote. Most of the time this is true. Sometimes it may seem that they are used more for the protection of criminals than for peaceful citizens. We read of racketeers and subversives "taking the Fifth Amendment" or enjoying the right of *habeas corpus*. In 1966, we read that Jack Ruby, who was seen to shoot President Kennedy's assassin on television, had his first murder conviction reversed by a higher Texas court because the original judge had not granted the change of venue requested by Ruby's lawyers. It seems as if people can be so easily freed on technicalities, but it also should be remembered that all these safeguards work for *all* citizens. As one Supreme Court justice said, our liberties have been defined and extended in cases involving some not-so-very-nice people.

When Americans are asked what problems they consider most serious in their lives, high on the list is usually crime—specifically, violent crime. The reported rates of murder, assault, rape, burglary, mugging, and kidnapping have risen to epidemic proportions in the last two decades. And these are just the *reported* crimes. In some types of crime, the victim is too ashamed to report it or feels it is useless to do so, since the chances are that nothing will be done about it. A newspaper observed that out of 1,085 arrests for rape in one year in New York, there were only 18 convictions.[1]

The sheer volume of crime is enormous, rising from 5.9 million offenses in 1967 to 11.3 million offenses ten years later. Murder and nonnegligent manslaughter rose from 12,000 instances in 1967 to 18,800 in 1976, and rape increased from 27,600 cases to 57,700 offenses in the same period. There were 851 law enforcement officers killed during the first seven years of the 1970s.

Law breakers are arrested for violent and other crimes, released on little or no bail, and strike again and again. When finally brought to court and convicted, they receive light sentences and, on the average, serve only half of them. When

1. *The New York Times*, 14 February 1972, p. 28.

released, most go back to their old ways, according to studies made of the habits of felons. An FBI report on 19,000 persons released from federal prisons revealed that by the end of six years, two-thirds were rearrested, proving that recidivism, or repeated criminal offenses, is one of the major problems in America today.

Ironically, as the number of law breakers, victims, and law officers has grown, and as the cost of law enforcement has risen, so has the crime rate. It is so bad that some states have set up programs to provide money payments to crime victims for hospital expenses and lost income. Some members of Congress are urging this on a national level.

Crime is one of the nation's most urgent problems and all are involved in its solution. Judges, parole officers, social workers, and other public servants must protect *both the criminal and the victim* from denial of their rights to life, liberty, and property. The citizenry must insist that equal justice be meted out to all, regardless of wealth or any other characteristics.

The laws are there. They apply to everyone. All are assured certain freedoms and guarantees and all have the same obligation to recognize these in others. Federal and state officials are required by law to deal fairly with all people, but the people themselves have the responsibility to invoke these legal means whenever unjustly treated. It is not the law itself but the attitude of the people which determines the growth of effective government. Progress will be proportionate to public support.

AFTER-CHAPTER REVIEW

REVIEW QUESTIONS

1. Define the following names, terms, or ideas.

petit jury	Immunity Act
grand jury	due process
double jeopardy	recidivism
self-incrimination	eminent domain
habeas corpus	change of venue
indictment	

2. Vocabulary building.

retroactive
confrontation
waive
transit

3. Cases.

Malloy v. *Hogan*
Escobedo v. *Illinois*
Hawkins v. *United States*
Estes v. *Texas*
Gregg v. *Georgia*
Norris v. *Alabama*
Miranda v. *Arizona*
Bartkus v. *Illinois*
Oregon v. *Mathiason*

4. Review of the text.

a. What is the reasoning behind the protection against self-incrimination? In what instances does this apply? Should a person be forced to testify before a legislative committee? What reasons exist for and against this?
b. List and explain the safeguards provided by the Fifth Amendment.
c. Against what evils does the Sixth Amendment protect us? Describe these.
d. What is the Eighth Amendment? How does this protect us?

DISCUSSION AND PROJECTS

1. Questions for discussion.

a. Some legal experts have suggested abolishing jury trials altogether and allowing one or several judges to decide a case. Discuss the wisdom of this proposal.
b. Discuss the bail system in our country. Does this punish the poor and not the wealthy?

2. Debate topic.

Resolved: Our society is too soft on criminals. Let's bring back the whipping post!

3. Opinion poll.

Do you think that the American legal system gives too much of an advantage to the accused person and not enough to the victim?

BIBLIOGRAPHY

See Chapters 8 and 9 for related bibliography.

Asinof, Eliot. "The Trials of a Juror," *New York Times Magazine*, 12 November 1972.

Boyarsky, Nancy. *Juvenile Justice: The Legal Rights of Young People*. Encino, Calif.: Glencoe, 1977.

Clark, Todd, and Novelli, Rebecca J. *Fair Trial/Free Press: Rights in Conflict*. Encino, Calif.: Glencoe, 1977.

Corwin, Edward S. *The Constitution and What It Means Today*. Princeton, N.J.: Princeton University Press, 1974. See especially pp. 313–366.

"If Every Criminal *Knew* He Would Be Punished if Caught . . . ," *New York Times Magazine*, 28 January 1973.

"Reforming the Criminal Justice System," *Current History*, July/August 1976.

Van Den Haag, Ernest. "The Collapse of the Case against Capital Punishment," *National Review*, 31 March 1978.

Way, H. Frank, Jr. *Liberty in the Balance: Current Issues in Civil Liberties*. New York: McGraw-Hill, 1976.

Wilson, James Q. "Changing Criminal Sentences," *Harper's*, November 1977.

UPI

Dr. Martin Luther King, Jr., guided Americans closer to equality through his courageous leadership of the black civil rights movement during the 1950s and 1960s.

11

The National Supremacy Amendments and Racial Discrimination

In the years before the Civil War, a great debate raged over the relationship between the federal government and the states. Many who favored a system of federalism in which the states would be dominant believed that state governments could nullify federal law and could even secede from the Union if they wanted to. Supporters of the Union denied these claims and in 1860 elected Abraham Lincoln as their President. Lincoln believed in the preservation of the Union at all costs, even war, and led his side to victory over the seceded states.

This victory did more than preserve the old Union. It also had important constitititutional effects, since it led to the adoption of the Thirteenth, Fourteenth, and Fifteenth Amendments, which are known as the "National Supremacy Amendments." These amendments changed forever the relationship between the states and the federal government. Although at first not interpreted by the Supreme Court in a revolutionary way, as time passed these amendments, particularly the Fourteenth, had a revolutionary effect upon American life.

In this chapter, we will examine these new documents of federal power and their effects upon racial discrimination in every part of our lives. They were intended to guarantee to the black American in particular a place of equality in American life. In accomplishing this, they altered many of our notions about federal-state relations. We will study the legislation passed under the authority of these amendments, particularly the Civil Rights Acts of 1957, 1960, 1964, 1965, 1968, and 1975.

THE THIRTEENTH AMENDMENT

The Thirteenth Amendment protects us from slavery and involuntary servitude:

> Neither slavery nor involuntary servitude, except as a punishment for crime whereof the party shall have been duly convicted, shall exist within the United States, or any place subject to their jurisdiction.

This amendment was adopted in 1865, after the war, and was aimed at eliminating one of the worst evils ever to exist in society, the ownership of one person by another. Because of the amendment, four million black Americans gained their freedom from legalized bondage.

During the early history of our republic, a major problem was whether or not slavery should exist in the territories acquired by war or purchase. The free northern states wanted to keep these territories for free white labor, while the southern slave states thought that slavery should exist everywhere. Since free and slave states were almost evenly balanced in the national government, the only solution to this disagreement, short of war, was compromise. One such agreement, known as the Missouri Compromise, forbade slavery in the Louisiana Territory in return for certain concessions to the slave states.

On the basis of this document, a slave named Dred Scott later sued his master for legal recognition of his freedom, claiming that a trip he had taken with a former master into free territory made him free. Since, at the time of this lawsuit, Dred Scott lived in one state and his master in another, the case came under federal jurisdiction.

When the case of *Dred Scott* v. *Sanford* was tried, there were five southerners on the Supreme Court, including the chief justice. They overruled the other members by declaring that Dred Scott had no right to sue in federal court since he was a Negro and no Negro could be a citizen. The Court went on to say that the Missouri Compromise was unconstitutional, since Congress could not legislate against the property (slaves) of its citizens.

This dramatic decision of 1857 stirred terrible passions among the people of the North and South. It broke down all the carefully built compromises of previous years and led America one more step toward war. The *Dred Scott* case, by the way, was only the second time in which an act of Congress had been called unconstitutional, the first time being *Marbury* v. *Madison*, in 1803.

In addition to its obvious purpose, the Thirteenth Amendment also excludes things such as binding contracts which can be classified as involuntary servitude. An example of this is a contract in which a person states he will work for a certain amount of time and will allow his employer to force him to work under guard if he does not. This does not mean that people can break contracts. If they do, they can be sued for damages.

After the Thirteenth Amendment was adopted, some states tried to defeat its purpose by passing severe vagrancy laws which permitted local authorities to arrest persons (usually Negroes) who had no money. The vagrants would be fined and, since they could not pay, they would be hired out to farmers to work off their fines. When released, they would have no money and could be rearrested. The cycle could go on endlessly. In recent times, persons convicted of crimes have been required to work off their fines by forced labor for the community.

THE FOURTEENTH AMENDMENT

The Thirteenth Amendment was aimed at ending *legal* slavery, but for northern members of Congress this did not go far enough. What they thought was needed was a powerful weapon to protect the Negro from discrimination. This sentiment produced the Fourteenth Amendment. We will not quote it entirely here, since not all of it is necessary to illustrate its importance. Instead, we will break down the first section into four main parts:

1. All persons born or naturalized in the United States and subject to the jurisdiction thereof, are citizens of the United States and of the state wherein they reside;
2. No state shall make or enforce any law which shall abridge the privileges or immunities of citizens of the United States;
3. Nor shall any state deprive any person of life, liberty, or property, without due process of law;
4. Nor deny to any person within its jurisdiction the equal protection of the laws.

Some of the words in this amendment, such as privileges, immunities, equal protection, and due process, may seem vague. Nevertheless, in the last half-century, they have produced a revolution in equality.

The first part of the amendment overruled the Dred Scott decision by declaring that a person was a citizen if he was born or naturalized in this country. Americans were to have dual citizenship, on the state and federal levels. The other parts of this section were designed to insure that states would not discriminate against the Negro or any other citizen. The due process clause, which in the Fifth Amendment limited the federal government, now was used to limit state action. Although intended as a guarantee for Negroes, during its first seventy years of existence the Fourteenth Amendment was used for almost everything but Negro protection. Corporation lawyers convinced the Supreme Court that the word "person" could be applied to corporations, thus gaining for them a great deal of protection from state regulation.

The citizenship guarantee means that even children of aliens are citizens of the United States. This guarantee does not apply to children born in this country of foreign diplomats. They take the nationality of their parents.

The due process clause of the Fourteenth Amendment is intended to protect the citizen from state oppression, through the federal Bill of Rights. We know that unreasonable searches and seizures are prohibited to the states as well as to the federal government, and that in both cases the accused person has the right to know the charges against him, to be able to confront his accusers, and to have access to legal counsel. We also know that states are not bound by the double jeopardy clause, nor are their juries required to reach unanimous votes. Little by little, the Supreme Court has defined those instances when the federal Bill of Rights, under the due process clause of the Fourteenth Amendment, applies between a citizen and the state.

PROTECTION AGAINST SEGREGATION AND DISCRIMINATION

But, you must be asking, when do we get to the Fourteenth Amendment's protection of the Negro against discrimination? One of the most important cases, decided in 1896, was known as *Plessy* v. *Ferguson.* It concerned a Negro named Plessy who challenged a Louisiana law ordering railroads to have separate facilities for Negroes. Laws which kept the two races separate were known as "Jim Crow" laws or as segregation. In ruling on the question of separate accommodations, the Supreme Court stated that as long as facilities for the races were equal, they could be separate. This was called the "separate but equal" doctrine. A justice who disapproved of the Court's decision said he did not think the Constitution allowed the states to determine on the basis of color whether or not a person could enjoy his constitutional rights. The Constitution, he said, was "color-blind," and did not recognize this difference among citizens. But his voice was drowned out by the majority of the Court, which upheld Louisiana's right to legislate on the "separate but equal" basis.

Segregation became part of the supreme law of the land. Blacks were forced to ride in special seats on public transportation, were required to go to special segregated schools, and even were segregated in hospitals and in public washrooms. The "separate but equal" doctrine was in most cases only "separate." Facilities usually were not equal, particularly in education. On the lower levels of education, although there were schools, equipment was not up to white standards and teachers were not as well trained. On the higher levels, the difference was even more obvious. The Supreme Court recognized these differences in the 1930s and in 1950, but no general rule was laid down until 1954, in the revolutionary case of *Brown* v. *Board of Education of Topeka.* The Court's decision in this case reversed the *Plessy* doctrine of "separate but equal" by concluding with the thundering words, "Separate educational facilities are inherently unequal." The Court held that separate schools tend to produce a feeling of inferiority in the minority group, particularly when the schools are segregated on a legal basis.

How could this decision be carried out? About one-third of the states had fully developed segregated school systems. What could be done to integrate them? In 1955, the Court ruled that integration should take place "with all deliberate speed," but massive resistance developed in many places in the South. Some school districts integrated quickly, but most simply did not comply with the order. A crisis was reached in Arkansas in 1957 when the governor used the Arkansas National Guard to prevent integration in Little Rock Central High School. Overruling the governor, President Eisenhower ordered the Arkansas National Guard into federal service and added troops of the regular army to enforce integration. The President was successful, but much discord and hostility resulted, such as had not been seen since the days after the Civil War. Force also was used in other places. In 1962, President Kennedy used hundreds of federal marshals, as well as federal troops and the Mississippi National Guard, to secure entrance to the University of Mississippi for one student.

In 1954, seventeen states had segregated schools. Then the *Brown* decision was made. Ten years later, in 1964, less than eleven percent of black school children were attending racially mixed schools. Out of a total of 3,500,000 Negro students in these seventeen southern and "border" states, less than 400,000 were integrated with white pupils. The farther south one went, the less integration existed. In Alabama and Mississippi, less than one percent of black pupils were integrated.

This condition slowly began to reverse after 1964. One reason for the change was the passage of a number of far-reaching Civil Rights Acts, the third of which, the Civil Rights Act of 1964, hastened desegregation. The main parts of this act:

1. Forbade discrimination in public accommodations such as restaurants, cafeterias, movie theaters, motels, etc.

UPI

On August 28, 1963, more than 200,000 people gathered in front of the Lincoln Memorial in Washington, D.C. to hear Dr. Martin Luther King, Jr., give his now-famous speech, "I Have a Dream." At that time, important legislation proposed by President John F. Kennedy—the far-reaching Civil Rights Act of 1964—was pending before Congress.

There was some limitation in this, however, since the only places covered were those which had some connection with interstate commerce. Congress, in passing the law, was acting under its powers to regulate interstate commerce as well as its power under the Fourteenth Amendment. Some of the businesses exempted from coverage by this act were small boarding houses, small motels, barber shops and bowling alleys. Private clubs also were not included, although later judicial decisions generally integrated these.

2. Gave the Attorney-General the power to start court actions in cases of such discrimination when the persons injured could not afford to do so.
3. Permitted federal officials to cut off federal aid to areas which did not observe court decisions and laws prohibiting discrimination of any kind.
4. Forbade the hiring or firing of persons on grounds of

race, religion, sex, or color. Also forbade segregation at work or discrimination in union membership.

5. Created the EEOC, Equal Employment Opportunity Commission, to assist in getting compliance to the employment provisions of the act.
6. Provided for a maximum penalty of six months in jail and $1,000 fine for convicted violators.

There are scores of other sections in the act which could be mentioned, but these should give you a good idea of the scope of the statute. It stirred a great deal of interest in the country because of its broad provisions. Not only did it guarantee equality to black Americans who had been deprived of it for so long but it also provided an umbrella of protection for women, a group long discriminated against.

Until recently, women generally have been overlooked as objects of discrimination in American society. Nevertheless, they have been discriminated against in hundreds of ways, some obvious and others subtle. Among the obvious examples of discrimination have been unequal pay for identical work, slow or no promotion, and assignment of women to jobs that are less challenging than those given to men. A male college graduate could expect to start his business career as a management trainee; a female college graduate was advised to take typing and shorthand courses to equip her for a secretarial job.

This attitude has its roots in an older America, one in which the husband was traditionally the breadwinner while the wife was traditionally the homemaker. When a woman worked it was assumed that she was supplementing her husband's income and that she did not need to earn as much as a man in the same job. Of course this assumption was never really correct because it overlooked women who were single, widowed, or divorced, or who had husbands unable to support them and their children. And in recent years, with the cost of living rising so rapidly, many families could barely survive without the second income provided by a working wife. Women now make up forty percent of employed Americans, and the number of women seeking jobs outside the home is constantly increasing.

To overcome sex discrimination, in 1972 Congress passed a constitutional amendment guaranteeing that there should be no discrimination on the basis of sex. The main text of the amendment reads: "Equality of rights under the law shall not be denied or abridged by the United States or by any state on account of sex." Symptomatic of the discrimination that women still face, however, is that fact that only thirty-five states had approved this proposed amendment by 1978. Approval by thirty-eight states was necessary for ratification.

Still another form of discrimination in American life has been that directed toward the aged. Employment opportunities decline as one grows older, and forced retirement at age sixty-five (or earlier) has given the older citizen the feeling that he or she has been rejected simply because of the calendar. Recent court decisions and acts of Congress have reversed this trend. Age discrimination is now illegal, although within certain limitations, and the retirement age of sixty-five was "retired" for most workers in 1978.

Although the purpose of laws and amendments such as the above was to secure fair treatment for *all* citizens on a nationwide basis, by far the most discriminated-against group in American history has been the black Americans. Before 1964, some of the states had already acted in this area. About one-quarter of them had fair housing laws and nearly half had tried to secure equal employment rights. In addition, the Interstate Commerce Commission had ruled out segregation in interstate transportation. But no measure had such sweeping effects as the Civil Rights Act of 1964.

The act was attacked as unconstitutional, but the Supreme Court upheld the right of Congress to legislate in this manner in a 1964 case known as *Heart of Atlanta Motel* v. *United States*. The Court said that the motel catered to many people from other states and therefore would come under the power of Congress over interstate commerce. In another case, the Court ruled that a restaurant was covered even though it bought less than half its meat supply through interstate commerce.

A powerful weapon against discrimination can be found in the power of federal officials to withhold funds from states not complying with the act. Many states, particularly in the South, relied heavily on federal aid to carry out their educational and social welfare programs. About twenty percent of the money available for these purposes came from federal sources. Thus, failure to cease discriminating would endanger these programs. In many areas, school districts began to comply with the requirement, and desegregation in the South after 1964 increased greatly by comparison with previous years. This did not solve the problem of segregation in education elsewhere. Dozens of school districts lost federal funds and the desegregation plans of the United States Office of Education came under increasing attack by members of Congress.

It was not until 1970 that a real breakthrough in desegregating southern school systems came about. Then, relying upon persuasion instead of force, President Nixon urged southern leaders to end the segregated conditions once and for all. Good results were achieved in the early 1970s, to the point where over ninety percent of the black children of the eleven southern states were in desegregated schools. There were, of course, many problems not solved by this statistical fact. Sometimes all-white schools took only a few students (this is called "tokenism"), or students were segregated *within* the school. When black and white schools were consolidated, black educators often were the ones who lost their jobs. However, these problems also were being examined and partially solved by government action.

DE FACTO SEGREGATION

Another problem arising out of the civil rights movement was that of segregation in schools outside of the southern or border states. Although no laws or governmental policies separated whites and Negroes in schools, there was what is called *de facto* segregation (segregation in actual fact, if not legally) because school districts were based on the "neighborhood school" concept. In an area where white people lived, the school might be ninety percent white and ten percent black, while the school a few blocks away in a black neighborhood might be just the reverse.

"Racial imbalance" was attacked by civil rights leaders and education officials, who saw the solution to the problem in busing children from one school to another. Busing was widely attacked by parents, civic groups, and legislators. Resistance to it sometimes took the form of picketing or even

UPI

In Muscogee County, Georgia, thousands of students ride buses as a result of a court order requiring that every school in the district be 70 percent white and 30 percent black. Although busing is not popular, it is almost the only way to achieve immediate school integration in areas where housing is not integrated.

the establishment of hastily set up private schools which, the groups said, were created not to discriminate against blacks but to keep white children near their homes.

Civil rights leaders said schools in poorer, nonwhite areas were inferior to those in white neighborhoods. Buildings were older, teaching staffs were not as experienced, and equipment such as books and other educational aids was often of poor quality. Many white citizens had no objection to busing nonwhite children out of these neighborhoods to attend white-dominated schools, but they objected strenuously to having their children bused into slum area schools. They simply did not want their children in the same inferior schools from which the nonwhites were trying to escape.

During the 1950s, 1960s, and 1970s, many white persons (and a fair number of blacks) left city areas in what has been called the "flight to the suburbs." There were many reasons for this mass exodus, among which were a desire for home ownership and the hope of escaping air pollution and high crime rates. No doubt a desire to secure a better education than that offered in urban areas was also a factor. Whatever the motives, the result has been that in some areas the city schools are dominated by nonwhites while the schools in the surrounding suburban areas are almost all white. In the city of Detroit, for example, for every five white public school children there were twelve black, while in the three surrounding counties whites outnumbered blacks in the schools twenty to one. Conditions of this sort exist throughout the nation and have led federal court judges to order cross-county busing, bringing students into urban areas and busing others out to suburban areas to balance out classrooms on a racial basis. The Supreme Court has overturned most of these efforts, most notably in a 1974 case *(Milliken* v. *Bradley)* affecting Detroit and the three surrounding counties.

The Court generally has upheld the use of busing plans within political units and between districts where it can be shown that discrimination exists. The Court has also stressed the need for additional educational help for deprived and previously deprived minorities. A nine-to-zero decision in 1977 required school districts to comply with federal court orders in providing remedial education to minorities who needed it.

Blacks and whites remain segregated primarily through housing patterns. Where this is caused by racial discrimination, much can be done. After the murder of Dr. Martin Luther King, Congress passed the Civil Rights Act of 1968, an act which outlawed most discrimination in housing. This law helped stimulate black and other minority groups to seek housing in the suburbs for better educational, environmental, and employment opportunities. Where segregation is the product of economic factors, the federal government has tried to promote some integration through rent subsidies.

All over the country, questions have been raised: Can racial equality be achieved by federal law? Can discrimination be ended by judicial decree or by order of the Health, Education and Welfare Department? There are about 60 million school children, about 50 million white and about 10 million black or other minorities. Does racial equality mean that one-sixth of the seats in each classroom must be filled by minorities? Black and Hispanic persons make up twelve and eleven percent of the population, respectively. How can the rights of these minorities be protected—in education, housing, and employment—without creating a police state based on thousands of petty regulations which invade every aspect of our lives? The answers to these questions lie in the future course of American history.

The assault on segregation in education had the good effect of making education one of the highest goals Americans could aspire to, whether white or black. Over the years, blacks began to approach whites in educational attainment. In 1960, the average number of years of education completed by all white persons was 10.9, and by black persons was 8.0. By 1976, whites were completing 12.4 years and blacks 11.1. Of course, statistics about educational differences can be misleading. A statistical table prepared by the Census Bureau showed that more blacks were enrolled in schools in proportion to their population than whites. Fifty-seven out of every hundred blacks between the ages of three and thirty-four were enrolled, while only fifty-two out of every hundred whites of the same age were enrolled. These figures, however, must be balanced against other tables which showed that for every two whites who dropped out of school, there were three blacks. What can definitely be said is that black Americans are striving, and are making gains.

Far behind both blacks and whites in educational attainment are two other groups, Indians and Hispanics. Mexican Hispanics, or Chicanos, are especially deprived in education, as are Puerto Ricans. Approximately one of every four Mexican-Americans has received less than five years of schooling. Puerto Ricans are not far ahead of this figure, about one of every five having been in school less than five years.

One method used to balance inequality of opportunity is known as "affirmative action." Essentially this means that businesses, schools, and other institutions are expected to compensate for past unfairness by giving some extra help to minority candidates for jobs or higher education berths. In some cases minority candidates have received special training or tutoring to help them qualify. In other cases they have been hired or admitted to schools on a quota system. For example, a medical or law school might set aside a certain number of places especially for black, Asian, or Hispanic persons. Standards of admission for this group would not be as high as for white applicants, and thus a white college graduate with a law school admission test score of 600 might be refused entry while a minority person could qualify with a score of 525. White students have challenged this practice in the courts, calling it "reverse discrimination." And in the *Bakke* decision of 1978, the Supreme Court agreed with them. The Court ruled that strict quota systems are unfair, even when established for honorable reasons, and required that candidates be evaluated on an individual basis. At the same time, however, the Court upheld the general concept of affirmative action and urged American institutions to continue and expand their efforts in this direction.

THE FIFTEENTH AMENDMENT

The most sacred weapon anyone can possess in a democratic republic such as ours is the right to vote. It can win respect for an idea when all other methods fail. Therefore, it is vital to our country's future that this right be protected for all, because denial of it to any person can lead to denial of it to all. The third member of the national supremacy triumvirate of amendments is the Fifteenth, which guarantees the right to vote regardless of ethnic or racial background:

> The right of citizens of the United States to vote shall not be denied or abridged by the United States or by any state on account of race, color, or previous condition of servitude.

After the Civil War, Congress required the former states of the Confederacy to adopt constitutions which provided for universal manhood suffrage before they could come back into full partnership with the other states of the Union. Many states did this, but still there was fear that once they had returned to the Union they might then repeal the right to vote from their constitutions. Moreover, even after the Civil War, many northern states denied Negroes the right to vote. To solve these twin problems, Congress adopted the Fifteenth Amendment.

For the next few decades, very large numbers of Negroes enjoyed the vote throughout the country, including the South.

Religious leaders of many faiths were among the 25,000 people who marched 54 miles from Selma to Montgomery, Alabama, in 1965. The marchers, who were protected by National Guard units called out by President Lyndon Johnson, wanted to encourage black Southerners to register to vote.

Indeed, you may be surprised to learn that at one point during the 1870s there were eight blacks in Congress, while in the Eighty-ninth Congress of 1965–1967 there were only six. With the election of the Ninety-third Congress of 1973–1975, the number increased to sixteen. It has remained at about that level through the Ninety-sixth Congress (1979–1981).

A movement to deny the vote to the Negro began in the 1890s. It took many different forms, but the goal was still the same. The state constitutions of South Carolina and Louisiana were changed to make it difficult for Negroes to vote. Other states, including North Carolina, Alabama, and Oklahoma, followed suit. In some cases, exclusion took the form of difficult literacy tests and of tests requiring a person to read and explain some part of the Constitution. Tests like this were permissible, said the Supreme Court. However, the tests were not satisfactory to poorly educated white persons, since their chances of failure were as great as those of the blacks. To get around this, the "grandfather clause" was invented. This clause exempted from the tests all those whose grandfathers had been voters. Thus, whites were permitted to vote, while blacks, most of whose grandfathers had been slaves, had to take the tests. The low percentage of Negro voters afterward attests to the success of this program.

If exclusion did not work, another weapon was ready in the form of a poll tax. Although not high by our standards, even a tax of a dollar or two could impose a hardship on low-income families. Curiously enough, some students of voting have concluded that the poll tax may have kept more whites than blacks away from the polls.

Efforts made by members of Congress to protect Negro voting rights were defeated in Congress. One bill, sponsored by Henry Cabot Lodge in the late nineteenth century, would have permitted federal officials to exercise some supervision over elections in southern states. The bill passed the House, but was defeated in the Senate. In 1915, however, the Supreme Court ruled the grandfather clause unconstitutional. But this still left the black in the hands of a white examiner who could ask easy questions of whites and stump blacks with difficult questions.

Another powerful factor in reducing Negro voting influence was the device known as the "white primary." A primary is an official election held within a political party to determine which member will be chosen to represent that party in the regular election. Since the Democratic party was so dominant in various parts of the South, whoever was nominated within the party was assured almost automatically of election. Laws were passed to forbid Negro voters from taking part in Democratic party primaries. These laws were declared unconstitutional by the Supreme Court because they violated the Fourteenth Amendment's guarantee of equal protection. But only state governments were forbidden to discriminate against citizens in this way. A private group could do so, without being subject to the amendment's restrictions. Thus, southern leaders went through the motions of setting up the Democratic primary as a private organization, which then could discriminate in its voting practices. The Supreme Court permitted this for a few years, but finally disapproved it in the 1940s.

The percentage of black voters in the southern states was woefully low compared with the number of potential voters in them. Between eighty and ninety percent of black adults were not registered to vote. An effort was made to solve this problem through the Civil Rights Act of 1957, which:

1. Created a civil rights commission to investigate discrimination in voting and to report on this to the President and Congress;
2. Prohibited all persons from interfering with anyone's right to vote;
3. Gave the Attorney-General power to protect voting rights by securing injunctions against those who interefered with voting;
4. Provided imprisonment or fines or both for violating this law.

This act helped, but civil rights advocates were sure it was not enough. Another civil rights act was passed in 1960 to provide further guarantees against discrimination. This act:

1. Required voting records to be preserved for a stated period of time after the elections were held;
2. Permitted federal judges in certain cases to certify Negroes as eligible to vote if a pattern of voting discrimination had been found;
3. Make it a federal crime to bomb or burn any building or even to threaten to do so. (This provision was placed in the act because of bombing and arson incidents in which members of minority groups had been terrorized. It is not designed to protect minority groups only.)

The Civil Rights Act of 1964 included many provisions designed to protect minority group voting rights, in addition to the other broad sections we have already studied. It provided the Attorney-General with the power to review literacy examination papers and it exempted from literacy tests any potential voter who could prove that he had a sixth-grade education. In addition, it required registration boards to administer their requirements fairly to all who came to register.

One year later, the Civil Rights Act of 1965 became law, giving broader powers to the federal government in the area of voting. Under the terms of this act, voting examiners would be appointed by the federal government if:

1. The Attorney-General stated that he had received complaints of discrimination from twenty or more residents of a given voting area;
2. A federal judge ordered it on the basis of information about discrimination;
3. A literacy test was used;
4. Less than fifty percent of the potential voters of a given voting area were registered.

Thus, if any complaints were filed, or if literacy tests were being administered, or if less than half the eligible voters were unregistered in any county or other type of voting district, the federal government could appoint election examiners. These examiners would talk to potential voters to find out if they were qualified to vote and if it appeared that they were, the state government would be required to let them vote. In 1970, the life of the Civil Rights Act of 1965 was extended for five more years, during which the use of all literacy tests was suspended.

The 1975 Voting Rights Act extended the earlier bill by seven years, and had the following effects:

1. The literacy test was banned permanently;
2. Voting protections were extended to Alaskans, Asians, Indians, and Hispanics requiring that voting information should be in both English and their native language in areas where they number more than five percent of the total voters on record.

Voter registration since 1960 has greatly increased among minorities. Black registration in the South, for example, was then limited to twenty-nine out of every hundred persons. By 1976, this figure had grown to sixty-three out of every hundred persons. The figures for white registration were sixty-one out of every hundred persons in 1960 and sixty-eight in 1976.

To encourage voting and extend the suffrage, Congress enacted the Twenty-fourth Amendment, which outlawed the poll tax in federal elections. This amendment was ratified in 1964 and was followed two years later by a Supreme Court decision outlawing the use of a poll tax (amounting to $1.50) in Virginia's state elections. One after another, the poll taxes of other states fell and one more obstacle to voting was removed.

The federal government, through its judicial, legislative, and executive branches, has accomplished a near-revolution in the status of minorities during the last two decades. This, of course, would not have been possible without the support of millions of white Americans sympathetic to the cause of minorities. Even more important, minorities themselves have led the fight for equal rights. The number of black elected officials has grown from fewer than one hundred in the early 1960s to 1,200 in 1969, and to 4,300 in 1979.

In this way, black people have followed the example of dozens of other minority groups, such as Jews and Italians, in seeking an end to unequal treatment. And they have shown other minorities, by example, the way to full participation in American life. Granted that much remains to be done. The increase in black elected officials over the last twenty years is a good thing, but there are 520,000 elected officials in the country, so that the 4,300 blacks in office make up less than one percent. Nevertheless, black Americans continue to "keep on keeping on," as Rosa Parks, a dauntless heroine of early civil rights struggles, remarked recently. Blacks have suffered more and for a longer time than any of the other minorities. Their time has been long in coming, but it is now at hand. All Americans can welcome it not only in the spirit of justice but also as a reaffirmation of the rights of all.

AFTER-CHAPTER REVIEW

REVIEW QUESTIONS

1. Define the following names, terms, or ideas.

"legal person"	"grandfather" clause
"separate but equal" doctrine	poll tax
	white primary
EEOC	literacy tests
de facto segregation	affirmative action
"tokenism"	

2. Vocabulary building.

involuntary servitude	integration

segregation
desegregation
ethnic

3. Cases.

Dred Scott v. *Sanford*
Plessy v. *Ferguson*
Milliken v. *Bradley*
Heart of Atlanta Motel v. *United States*
Brown v. *Board of Education*

4. Review of the text.

   a. What were the consequences of the *Dred Scott* decision?
   b. In your own words, make a list of all the guarantees provided by the amendments studied in this chapter.
   c. What purposes did the Fourteenth Amendment serve at first?
   d. Write an outline of the relationship between education and the races from the Civil War to the present day.
   e. Discuss the Civil Rights Act of 1964. What were its provisions and what were the main weapons it gave the federal government against discrimination?
   f. Describe the methods used to deny the right to vote to blacks.
   g. List the major provisions of the Civil Rights Acts of 1957, 1960, 1964, 1965, 1968, and 1975 with respect to voting rights. What were the overall effects of these measures?

DISCUSSION AND PROJECTS

1. Questions for discussion.

   a. What is meant by "National Supremacy" when we describe the Thirteenth, Fourteenth, and Fifteenth Amendments? What is their significance for the future of federalism?
   b. If you had been a school official in 1955, how would you have interpreted the words "with all deliberate speed"?
   c. What is the difference between integration and desegregation? Can a person believe in desegregation and yet refuse to accept integration? Explain, using specific examples.

2. Debate topics.

   a. Resolved: Voting is a state matter; the states should be allowed to control it.
   b. Resolved: Integration should be fostered by federal laws which establish quotas on how many members of each race should work, live, or go to school in a certain area.

3. Opinion poll.

   Should busing be adopted to achieve racial balance in the schools?

BIBLIOGRAPHY

See Chapters 9 and 10 for related bibliography.

Berger, Raoul. "The Imperial Court," *New York Times Magazine*, 9 October 1977.

Corwin, Edward S. *The Constitution and What It Means Today.* Princeton, N.J.: Princeton University Press, 1974. See especially pp. 382–435.

"Changing Black America," *Current History*, November 1974.

Fribourg, Marjorie. *The Supreme Court in American History.* New York: Avon Books, 1969. Chapter 8.

Jenkins, Herbert. *Keeping the Peace.* New York: Harper & Row, 1970.

Martz, Carlton S. *The Promise of Equality: Equal Rights and Opportunities.* Encino, Calif.: Glencoe, 1977.

Miller, Loren. *The Petitioners: The Story of the Supreme Court of the United States and the Negro.* Cleveland: Meridian Books, 1967.

Okun, Arthur M. "Equal Rights but Unequal Income," *New York Times Magazine*, 4 July 1976.

Vocational Foundation, Inc., and Gilder, George. "To Be Young, Black, and Out of Work," *New York Times Magazine*, 23 October 1977.

Vista from Monkmeyer

A VISTA volunteer discusses working and living conditions with Navajo migrant farm workers in a field of broomcorn ready for harvesting in New Mexico. VISTA is a federally funded antipoverty program that was started during the administration of President Lyndon Johnson. In 1971, under President Richard Nixon, it was combined with the Peace Corps and several other federal volunteer programs in an agency known as ACTION.

12

Government and the Citizen

Hardly a day goes by in which we do not have some form of contact with the federal government. The food we eat, the mail we receive, the highways we travel on, and even the television channels we watch are connected in some way with the federal government. All of them are subsidized, directly or indirectly, by the taxes Americans pay. Is the product worth the price? Just what are we and our families getting for our money? What benefits does it secure for us in national defense, education, veterans' benefits, protection of health, and social welfare? In this chapter, we will examine these and other questions. We will begin with the money question. Where does federal revenue come from and how is it spent?

SOURCES OF REVENUE

The power to tax rests with Congress, as you know from Article I, Section 8 of the Constitution. Moreover, Congress may impose tariffs and may authorize the sale of federal property to obtain revenue. It also may permit the executive branch to borrow money and in certain cases to collect fines or confiscate goods. In this paragraph, then, are summed up all the money-raising methods Congress can and does use to support the national government: taxation, tariffs, sale of land or other properties, borrowing, fines, and confiscation.

At one time in our history the tariff and the sale of public land made up the greatest portion of our national revenue. Now they are only a small part of government income. The main sources of federal revenue today are taxes: personal income taxes, employment or payroll taxes, corporate income taxes, excise taxes, estate and gift taxes, and other miscellaneous taxes.

THE TAX SYSTEM

The history of the graduated income tax, which takes a smaller percentage of low incomes and a larger percentage of higher incomes, is an interesting one. Although many considered it inequitable that a larger percentage should be taken from one person's income than from another's, a graduated income tax was levied on the people of the Union during the Civil War. The Supreme Court upheld this act as a valid war measure. The tax was eventually dropped, however, because the federal government found itself with a problem that sounds unbelievable today—the government's income was exceeding its expenses, and so it was ending up with a surplus of revenue every year.

Toward the end of the nineteenth century, however, the government once again was looking for new funds. In the 1890s, Congress added various provisions to a tariff bill to reinstate the income tax, but the Supreme Court declared this part of the bill unconstitutional in an 1895 decision known as *Pollack* v. *Farmers' Loan.* The Sixteenth Amendment was adopted in 1913 to overcome this obstacle. It reads:

> The Congress shall have power to lay and collect taxes on incomes, from whatever source derived....

These few words started a national revolution in government financing, although they were not expected to do so. The first income tax law was very modest, providing for a tax of one percent on incomes above $3,000. Since an overwhelming majority of the American people earned nowhere near this sum, the tax left them untouched. A few years later, though, the tax went up to four percent on incomes over $1,000.

From these small beginnings came the present tax system under which we live. Today, taxes are one of the average American's biggest expenses and greatest worries. Each year, taxes take an increasingly large share of a person's income. Even when tax cuts occur in the personal income tax rate,

Mimi Forsyth from Monkmeyer

A taxpayer makes a note of the hours during which Internal Revenue Service employees will be available to help him prepare his income tax return.

federal Social Security taxes might be raised or state sales taxes or municipal property taxes or any one of a dozen nuisance taxes. The average American spends a good third of every eight-hour working day earning money to pay taxes of one kind or another.

The late Senator Hubert H. Humphrey led Americans in complaining not only about the high rate of taxation but also about the confused tax structure. The entire tax system, he said, is "complex, overlapping, and fragmented." In addition to expense and confusion, the American tax system tends to add fear to the citizen's burden. An IRS tax audit is one of the most frightening potential experiences Americans can contemplate, even though most will never face it. Out of 82,500,000 tax returns filed by individuals in 1977, only a little more than two percent were audited, that is, reviewed

Form **1040** Department of the Treasury—Internal Revenue Service
U.S. Individual Income Tax Return **1978**

For Privacy Act Notice, see page 3 of Instructions | For the year January 1–December 31, 1978, or other tax year beginning , 1978, ending , 19

Use IRS label. Otherwise, please print or type.
Your first name and initial (if joint return, also give spouse's name and initial) | Last name | Your social security number
Present home address (Number and street, including apartment number, or rural route) | Spouse's social security no.
City, town or post office, State and ZIP code | Your occupation

Do you want $1 to go to the Presidential Election Campaign Fund? Yes No
If joint return, does your spouse want $1 to go to this fund? . . Yes No
Note: Checking Yes will not increase your tax or reduce your refund.
Spouse's occupation

Filing Status
Check only one box.
1 Single
2 Married filing joint return (even if only one had income)
3 Married filing separate return. If spouse is also filing, give spouse's social security number in the space above and enter full name here ▶
4 Unmarried head of household. Enter qualifying name ▶ See page 6 of Instructions.
5 Qualifying widow(er) with dependent child (Year spouse died ▶ 19). See page 6 of Instructions.

Exemptions
Always check the box labeled Yourself. Check other boxes if they apply.
6a Yourself | 65 or over | Blind
b Spouse | 65 or over | Blind
Enter number of boxes checked on 6a and b ▶
c First names of your dependent children who lived with you ▶
Enter number of children listed ▶

d Other dependents: (1) Name	(2) Relationship	(3) Number of months lived in your home	(4) Did dependent have income of $750 or more?	(5) Did you provide more than one-half of dependent's support?

Enter number of other dependents ▶
Add numbers entered in boxes above ▶
7 Total number of exemptions claimed

Income
Please attach Copy B of your Forms W-2 here.
If you do not have a W-2, see page 5 of Instructions.
Please attach check or money order here.

8 Wages, salaries, tips, and other employee compensation . . . 8
9 Interest income (*If over $400, attach Schedule B*) . . . 9
10a Dividends (*If over $400, attach Schedule B*) , 10b Exclusion
10c Subtract line 10b from line 10a . . . 10c
11 State and local income tax refunds (*does not apply unless refund is for year you itemized deductions*) . . . 11
12 Alimony received . . . 12
13 Business income or (loss) (*attach Schedule C*) . . . 13
14 Capital gain or (loss) (*attach Schedule D*) . . . 14
15 Taxable part of capital gain distributions not reported on Schedule D (see page 9 of Instructions) . . 15
16 Net gain or (loss) from Supplemental Schedule of Gains and Losses (*attach Form 4797*) . . . 16
17 Fully taxable pensions and annuities not reported on Schedule E . . . 17
18 Pensions, annuities, rents, royalties, partnerships, estates or trusts, etc. (*attach Schedule E*) . . . 18
19 Farm income or (loss) (*attach Schedule F*) . . . 19
20 Other income (state nature and source—see page 10 of Instructions) ▶ 20
21 **Total income.** Add lines 8, 9, and 10c through 20 . . . ▶ 21

Adjustments to Income
22 Moving expense (*attach Form 3903*) . . . 22
23 Employee business expenses (*attach Form 2106*) . . 23
24 Payments to an IRA (see page 10 of Instructions) . . . 24
25 Payments to a Keogh (*H.R. 10*) retirement plan . . . 25
26 Interest penalty due to early withdrawal of savings 26
27 Alimony paid (see page 10 of Instructions) . . . 27
28 **Total adjustments.** Add lines 22 through 27 . . . ▶ 28

Adjusted Gross Income
29 Subtract line 28 from line 21 . . . 29
30 Disability income exclusion (*attach Form 2440*) . . . 30
31 **Adjusted gross income.** Subtract line 30 from line 29. *If this line is less than $8,000, see page 2 of Instructions.* If you want IRS to figure your tax, see page 4 of Instructions . . . ▶ 31

☆ U.S. GOVERNMENT PRINTING OFFICE : 690-738 Form 1040 (1978)

(a)

Form 1040 (1978) Page 2

Tax Computation

32 Amount from line 31 32

33 If you do not itemize deductions, enter zero . . . . .
If you itemize, complete Schedule A (Form 1040) and enter the amount from Schedule A, line 41 33

Caution: If you have unearned income and can be claimed as a dependent on your parent's return, check here ▶ ☐ and see page 11 of the Instructions. Also see page 11 of the Instructions if:

- *You are married filing a separate return and your spouse itemizes deductions, OR*
- *You file Form 4563, OR*
- *You are a dual-status alien.*

34 Subtract line 33 from line 32. Use the amount on line 34 to find your tax from the Tax Tables, or to figure your tax on Schedule TC, Part I 34

Use Schedule TC, Part I, and the Tax Rate Schedules ONLY if:

- *The amount on line 34 is more than $20,000 ($40,000 if you checked Filing Status Box 2 or 5), OR*
- *You have more exemptions than those covered in the Tax Table for your filing status, OR*
- *You use any of these forms to figure your tax: Schedule D, Schedule G, or Form 4726.*

Otherwise, you MUST use the Tax Tables to find your tax.

35 Tax. Enter tax here and check if from ☐ Tax Tables or ☐ Schedule TC 35

36 Additional taxes. (See page 11 of Instructions.) Enter total and check if from ☐ Form 4970, ☐ Form 4972, ☐ Form 5544, ☐ Form 5405, or ☐ Section 72(m)(5) penalty tax . . . 36

37 **Total.** Add lines 35 and 36 . . . . . ▶ 37

Credits

38 Credit for contributions to candidates for public office . . 38

39 Credit for the elderly *(attach Schedules R&RP)* 39

40 Credit for child and dependent care expenses (attach Form 2441) . 40

41 Investment credit *(attach Form 3468)* 41

42 Foreign tax credit *(attach Form 1116)* 42

43 Work Incentive (WIN) Credit *(attach Form 4874)* 43

44 New jobs credit *(attach Form 5884)* 44

45 Residential energy credits (see page 12 of Instructions, attach Form 5695) . . . 45

46 **Total credits.** Add lines 38 through 45 46

47 **Balance.** Subtract line 46 from line 37 and enter difference (but not less than zero) . ▶ 47

Other Taxes

48 Self-employment tax *(attach Schedule SE)* 48

49 Minimum tax. Check here ▶ ☐ and attach Form 4625 49

50 Tax from recomputing prior-year investment credit *(attach Form 4255)* 50

51 Social security (FICA) tax on tip income not reported to employer *(attach Form 4137)* . . 51

52 Uncollected employee FICA and RRTA tax on tips *(from Form W-2)* 52

53 Tax on an IRA *(attach Form 5329)* 53

54 **Total tax.** Add lines 47 through 53 . . . . . ▶ 54

Payments

Attach Forms W-2, W-2G, and W-2P to front.

55 Total Federal income tax withheld 55

56 1978 estimated tax payments and credit from 1977 return . 56

57 Earned income credit. If line 31 is under $8,000, see page 2 of Instructions. If eligible, enter child's name ▶ 57

58 Amount paid with Form 4868 58

59 Excess FICA and RRTA tax withheld (two or more employers) 59

60 Credit for Federal tax on special fuels and oils (attach Form 4136) . 60

61 Regulated Investment Company credit *(attach Form 2439)* 61

62 **Total.** Add lines 55 through 61 . . . . . ▶ 62

Refund or Due

63 If line 62 is larger than line 54, enter amount **OVERPAID** . . . . . ▶ 63

64 Amount of line 63 to be **REFUNDED TO YOU** . . . . . ▶ 64

65 Amount of line 63 to be credited on 1979 estimated tax . ▶ 65

66 If line 54 is larger than line 62, enter **BALANCE DUE.** Attach check or money order for full amount payable to "Internal Revenue Service." Write your social security number on check or money order . . ▶ 66
(Check ▶ ☐ if Form 2210 (2210F) is attached. See page 14 of instructions.) ▶ $

Please Sign Here

Under penalties of perjury, I declare that I have examined this return, including accompanying schedules and statements, and to the best of my knowledge and belief, it is true, correct, and complete. Declaration of preparer (other than taxpayer) is based on all information of which preparer has any knowledge.

▶ Your signature Date ▶ Spouse's signature (If filing jointly, BOTH must sign even if only one had income)

Paid Preparer's Information

Preparer's signature ▶ | Preparer's social security no. | Check if self-employed ▶ ☐

Firm's name (or yours, if self-employed), address and ZIP code ▶ | E.I. No. ▶ | Date ▶

(b)

Form **W-4** (Rev. December 1978) Department of the Treasury Internal Revenue Service

Employee's Withholding Allowance Certificate
(Use for Wages Paid After December 31, 1978)
This certificate is for income tax withholding purposes only. It will remain in effect until you change it. If you claim exemption from withholding, you will have to file a new certificate on or before April 30 of next year.

Type or print your full name | **Your social security number**

Home address (number and street or rural route)

City or town, State, and ZIP code

Marital Status ☐ Single ☐ Married ☐ Married, but withhold at higher Single rate
Note: *If married, but legally separated, or spouse is a nonresident alien, check the single block.*

1 Total number of allowances you are claiming . . . .
2 Additional amount, if any, you want deducted from each pay (if your employer agrees) . . . . $
3 I claim exemption from withholding (see instructions). Enter "Exempt" . . . .

Under the penalties of perjury, I certify that the number of withholding allowances claimed on this certificate does not exceed the number to which I am entitled. If claiming exemption from withholding, I certify that I incurred no liability for Federal income tax for last year and I anticipate that I will incur no liability for Federal income tax for this year.

Signature ►.. **Date ►**.., 19.........

by IRS officials for data other than arithmetical or other basic errors. But most people who are audited usually wind up paying extra taxes to the government. Chances of an audit grow with increased income, and people who itemize their deductions rather than taking the standard deduction are also more apt to be audited.

There are several ways citizens may prepare their tax returns. These are explained thoroughly in the instruction booklets which accompany the tax forms sent yearly to each family. Since it would be difficult for most people to raise a lump sum for taxes in April of each year, money is withheld from each worker's paycheck all year long. The withholding rate varies according to a person's basic salary or wage and the number of his dependents. The great shuffling of papers each year just before the April fifteenth deadline is the American taxpayer trying to determine whether the government has taken too little or too much of his money during the past year. Rarely is just the right amount taken. Therefore, at this point, either a refund is made to the taxpayer, or the taxpayer pays more to the government.

Critics contend that the withholding tax system disguises the real size of the tax because it is less painful than lump sums and that it permits tax increases to be imposed more easily on the people. A $78 annual tax increase, for example, can be described as only $1.50 a week. And, if the withholding system collects more taxes than are needed, the refund often is looked upon as a government windfall.

Supporters of the system say that high taxes are going to be with us for a long time, at least for as long as we earmark one dollar for the federal budget out of every four dollars of national income. The most efficient and convenient way to discharge our tax obligation is on a "pay as you go" basis.

Economists measure government spending by comparing it with the overall income of the nation. The overall income is called the Gross National Product (GNP) and is the sum of all the goods and services produced in the entire country in one year. The GNP in 1977 was more than two trillion dollars.

Some 82,500,000 Americans file individual tax returns every year, but not all of them yield income for the government. Some people have such low incomes and such high expenses that they owe no taxes. All of the amount withheld therefore is returned to them and those whose income is below subsistence level actually receive assistance in a kind of reverse income tax. Congress has also made provisions to ease tax burdens for persons with disabilities and for the aged.

The graduated income tax on individuals accounts for more than forty percent of the revenue of the national government (forty-five percent in 1963 and forty-three percent from 1970 to 1976).

The second most important source of revenue is in the form of social insurance taxes and payments made by workers, businesses, railroad employees, and civil servants for such social services as retirement, disability programs, and medical care. The biggest example of these social insurance payments is the payroll or employment tax, with one part paid by the employee in the form of Social Security withholding and the other paid by the employer. This tax accounted for more than one-quarter of the national governmental income during the 1970s.

Third in importance is the income tax on corporations which, in the 1970s, amounted to some fifteen percent of government income. Excise taxes on automobiles, tobacco, gasoline, alcoholic beverages, and many other items accounted for about seven percent. Lesser sources of revenue include estate taxes and gift taxes. The estate and gift taxes do not

Receipts and expenditures of the federal government

	Fiscal Year				
	Actual			Estimated	
	1975	1976	1977	1978	1979
Receipts by source (in billions):					
Individual income taxes	122.4	130.8	156.7	178.8	190.1
Corporate income taxes	40.6	41.4	54.9	58.9	62.5
Social insurance taxes and contributions	86.4	92.7	108.7	124.1	141.9
Excise taxes	16.6	17.0	17.5	20.2	25.5
Estate and gift taxes	4.6	5.2	7.3	5.6	6.1
Customs duties (tariffs)	3.7	4.1	5.2	5.8	6.4
Miscellaneous	6.7	8.0	6.5	6.9	7.2
Total	281.0	299.2	356.9	400.4	439.6
Expenditures by purpose (in billions):					
National defense	85.6	89.4	97.5	107.6	117.8
International affairs and finance	6.9	5.6	4.8	6.7	7.7
General science, space, and technology	4.0	4.4	4.7	4.8	5.1
Energy	2.2	3.1	4.2	7.8	9.6
Natural resources and environment	7.3	8.1	10.0	12.1	12.2
Agriculture	1.7	2.5	5.5	9.1	5.4
Commerce and housing credit	5.6	3.8	—	3.5	3.0
Transportation	10.4	13.4	14.6	16.3	17.4
Community and regional development	3.7	4.7	6.3	9.7	8.7
Education, manpower, and social services	15.9	18.7	21.0	27.5	30.4
Health	27.6	33.4	38.8	44.3	50.0
Income security	108.6	126.6	137.0	147.6	160.0
Veterans benefits and services	16.6	18.4	18.0	18.9	19.3
Law enforcement and justice	2.9	3.3	3.6	4.0	4.2
General government	3.1	2.9	3.4	4.1	4.3

Receipts and expenditures of the federal government (Cont'd)

	Fiscal Year				
	Actual			Estimated	
	1975	1976	1977	1978	1979
Revenue sharing and general purpose fiscal assistance	7.2	7.2	9.5	9.9	9.6
Interest	31.0	34.6	38.1	43.8	49.0
Allowances (for government employee pay raises and for contingencies)	—	—	—	—	2.8
Undistributed offsetting receipts	-14.1	-14.7	-15.1	-15.6	-16.0
Total	326.1	365.6	401.9	462.2	500.2
Budget surplus (+) or deficit (-)	-45.1	-66.4	-45.0	-61.8	-60.6

Source: Office of Management and Budget.

touch most people, since exemptions under them are high. An estate is not taxable under federal law (state laws are a different matter) unless it is more than $60,000.

TARIFFS

The tariff once accounted for the bulk of our government's income, but now customs receipts (as tariff charges are called) are rather insignificant, contributing only about one percent. Today, the question of a tariff is not one of America's biggest problems, although it once was and could be again.

Tariffs are placed on imports for two reasons—to raise revenue and to protect the industries at home which manufacture the same products. An American tool manufacturer who makes a hammer might charge two dollars for it. A foreign firm, because of lower labor costs, might be able to make it, ship it, and sell it in the United States for one dollar. The American manufacturer, therefore, might demand a tariff of one hundred percent on imported hammers, to bring their price up to his. The workingman is caught in the middle. If he wants to buy a hammer, he finds that "high tariffs mean high prices," so he might favor reduction in the tariff rate. But if the rate is reduced too far, he might find that American manufacturing firms are going out of business, or are being forced to pay lower wages. Then he would find that "high tariffs mean high wages." The mottoes placed in quotation marks were used during the nineteenth century to win support for or against a high tariff.

Another dilemma connected with the tariff was the problem of America's foreign trade. If we imposed a high tariff on the goods of a nation, it would do the same to ours. A way out of the situation was suggested in the 1890s through the principle of reciprocity; that is, if one nation would lower its tariff on some of our goods, we would lower our tariff on some of its goods. This principle did not take hold completely until 1934, with the passage of the Reciprocal Trade Agreements Act. Under this law, dozens of treaties have been made to encourage tariff reduction and thereby to promote greater international trade.

In its commercial dealings with other nations, every nation tries to maintain a favorable balance of trade. That is, it tries to export more than it imports. During the last few years the United States has not been able to do this. As a result, the country has suffered from what is called a "balance of payments" deficit. We are spending more overseas—for petroleum, certain minerals, and on military and economic assistance to other nations—than we are getting back. Efforts to correct the balance of payments deficit are being made by the federal government, but it is too early to know whether or not the trend will be reversed.

BUDGET DEFICITS

The only other revenue producer large enough to discuss is borrowing. When the federal government cannot balance its budget, that is, when its expenses exceed its income, the condition is called a deficit and must be made up either by cutting expenses or by borrowing. From the 1930s to the 1970s, our government has had a deficit most of the time. In fact,

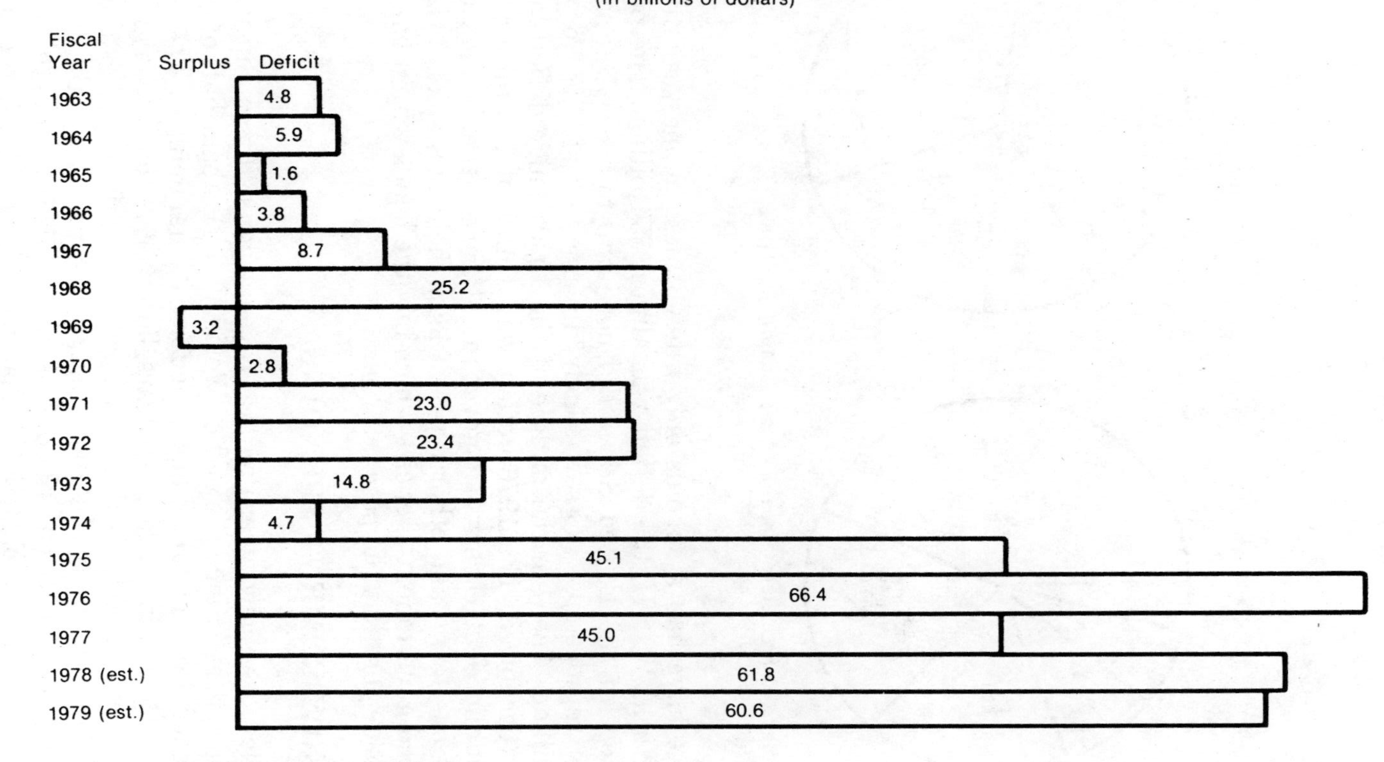
THE BUDGET GAP
One year of surplus—sixteen years of borrowing
(in billions of dollars)
Fiscal Year
Surplus
Deficit
1963
4.8
1964
5.9
1965
1.6
1966
3.8
1967
8.7
1968
25.2
1969
3.2
1970
2.8
1971
23.0
1972
23.4
1973
14.8
1974
4.7
1975
45.1
1976
66.4
1977
45.0
1978 (est.)
61.8
1979 (est.)
60.6
Source: Office of Management and Budget.

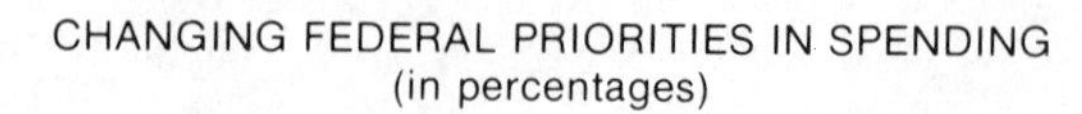

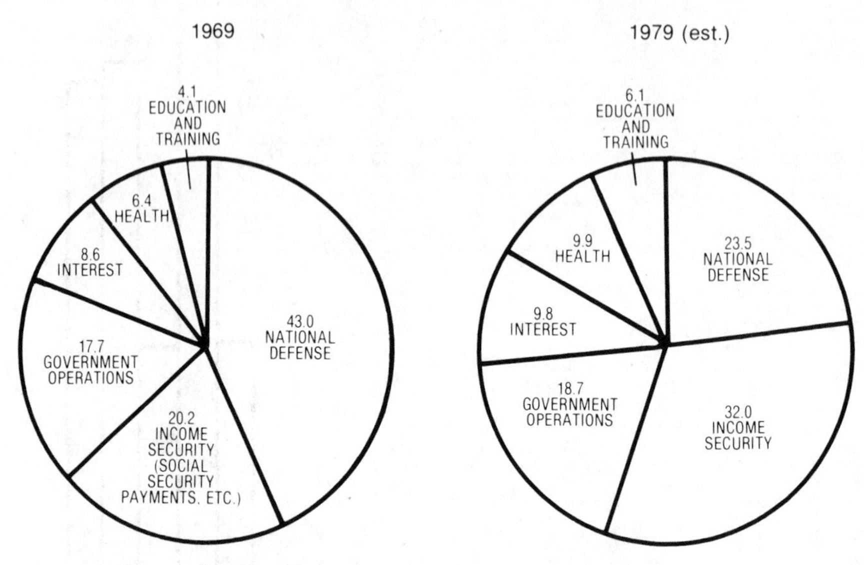

Source: Congressional Record, 4 October 1978, p. S17092.

we have had a surplus only a few times. In one year during World War II, the deficit was almost $54 billion. The public debt of the United States did not jump to over $700 billion in rapid steps. It grew slowly, in amounts of three or four billion. Then, in the middle of the 1970s, huge deficits were experienced. The 1976 deficit was a high of $66 billion. The public debt consists of government bonds (the savings bond is one form) and other types of loans held by banks, citizens, and government agencies which buy the bonds with money set aside for that purpose.

GOVERNMENT SPENDING

Now we know where federal revenue comes from. But where does it go? Since the end of World War II, about half of every federal dollar raised has gone for national defense. The trend has slowed in the last few years, however, so that now a greater proportion of federal money goes to human resources than to national security. In 1963, forty-seven percent of the federal budget went to national defense, while in 1973 only thirty-one percent was allocated for that purpose. By 1977, the figure was down to twenty-four percent. (The actual dollar amount was increased during the period, however.) More than forty-nine percent of the national budget of 1977 went for human needs such as education, health, and Social Security. Another sizable expense in the national budget is the interest on the national debt, which accounted for about seven percent of the budget of 1977. Other governmental outlays include expenditures for agriculture, housing, conservation, and transportation needs. The remainder of government spending is divided among space research expenses, foreign aid, general costs of running the government, and revenue sharing, which will be examined in a later chapter.

National defense and its related costs are the prices of our continued existence as a free nation. Our commitments all over the world are so great that we must provide hundreds of thousands of soldiers and other armed forces personnel to scores of countries. These military personnel must be supplied with the best possible weapons, food, housing, and other essentials. In addition, we have undertaken the exploration of outer space, a task which becomes more expensive as we grow in knowledge. Twenty years ago no one could have predicted that space research and other space-related activity would be a big item in our budget, yet by 1977 $4.4 billion was set aside for it. Because it is related to national security, the space program has had important effects upon improving the nation's ability to defend itself and its allies. We will consider these subjects more fully in a later chapter.

There is little we can do about the interest on the national debt except to pay it and to hope that taxes and other revenues increase in the near future to the point where income will at least balance expenses. After expenses such as national defense, space research, and the national debt interest payments are taken care of, what is left over goes for the direct or indirect benefit of Americans. In the remainder of this chapter, we will see how the federal dollar goes for education, veterans' benefits, and health, welfare and housing programs.

AID TO EDUCATION

For many years, the question of "federal aid to education" was debated sharply throughout the United States. Nothing in the Constitution gave the federal government any specific author-

The rising cost of government
(in millions of dollars)

	1969	1979	Percentage increase
National defense	79,418	117,779	49%
Education and training	7,538	30,421	304%
Health	11,758	49,677	322%
Income security	37,281	160,024	329%
Interest	15,793	48,991	210%
Government operations	32,760	93,282	185%

Source: *Congressional Record*, 4 October 1978, p. S17092.

ity in education, yet aid from the central government is actually older than the United States itself. In 1785, under the Articles of Confederation, the Land Ordinance which divided the territory of the Ohio Valley into townships set aside part of the land for the maintenance of public schools. In 1862, the Morrill Act provided for land grants of many thousands of acres to the states to help them establish colleges for agricultural instruction.

More recently, these basic acts have been followed by several far-reaching federal acts aimed at fostering growth at all levels of education. Every phase of education, from school lunches, to scholarship assistance, to funds for school construction has been covered. We will consider federal aid to education in three main categories: aid to veterans, aid under the National Defense Education Act of 1958, and through the Elementary-Secondary Education Act of 1965.

During World War II, Congress passed legislation known as the "GI Bill of Rights," providing for educational assistance to all veterans, depending upon their length of service. This legislation caused a tremendous revolution in education. Millions of ambitious Americans were given the opportunity to improve themselves by obtaining an education. Veterans of World War II, and of the Korean and Vietnam conflicts, have received more than $36 billion in education and training aid in the thirty years following the victory of 1945. They have repaid

AVERAGE NUMBER OF YEARS OF SCHOOL
COMPLETED BY AMERICANS

Year	Years
1940	8.6
1950	9.3
1960	10.6
1970	12.1
1975	12.3

Source: U.S. Bureau of the Census.

their government handsomely. Surveys indicate that high school graduates earn far more in their lifetimes than do those who did not complete their secondary education. Surveys also show that college graduates average twice as much annual salary as do those with only high school education. Since the higher the income, the greater the taxes paid, educational aid to veterans has become more an investment than a gift from federal sources.

Education was aided a second way through the National Defense Education Act of 1958. It enabled scholars and students to improve their skills in mathematics, science, and other subjects. Loans and grants were made available to schools and to individuals who wished to pursue their education in fields related to national defense.

The first two programs we have studied are not related solely to education. They deal also with veterans' benefits and national defense. Because education had always been regarded as a state responsibility, there was much resistance to direct federal aid to education. It was welcomed only as long as it was not aimed at education alone. But resistance had weakened by 1965, enabling Congress to pass the broad Elementary-Secondary Education Act. This act provides for federal grants, primarily to schools in low-income areas, but actually it covers almost all school districts throughout the country. It provides aid for private and parochial schools as well as for public schools. Congress voted about $1.3 billion to start it off, and by

1977 the Health, Education, and Welfare Department was spending more than $6.4 billion for this phase of its work out of a total educational expenditure of $13.8 billion.

AID TO VETERANS

We find one of the most acceptable and consistent forms of assistance to citizens in the field of federal aid to war veterans. Members of the armed forces contribute their time and sometimes far more to defend their country. Throughout its history, a grateful country has rewarded them for it. This reward has taken several forms, including land grants after the Revolutionary and Civil Wars, cash bonuses, and the education aid we already have studied. In addition, pensions have been voted to older veterans, usually for service-connected injuries. Hospital care is offered to all veterans regardless of the nature of their illnesses, although limited space makes it necessary to base admittance on the relation of the illness to their military service and to their financial needs. Veterans are offered the opportunity to purchase inexpensive life insurance and at death are provided with a grave at government expense. In these ways, the nation shows its gratitude to the more than 29.6 million veterans living today.

SERVICES FOR ALL CITIZENS

Federal interest in the American citizen extends beyond grants of money to individuals or groups. It covers a wide range of activities, from protection against impure food and drugs to security against kidnapping. Let us examine some of the agencies involved in these activities—the Food and Drug Administration, the U.S. Customs Service, and the Public Health Service.

In 1962, the American public was shocked to learn of a drug called thalidomide which, when taken as a supposedly harmless sleeping pill by expectant mothers, deformed many of their babies. The worst and most numerous cases occured in West Germany. Only a few were found in the United States, since the drug was being used only experimentally here. Because of strict federal regulation of drugs and the vigilance of a doctor in the Food and Drug Administration, "watchdog of the consumer," further tragedy was averted.

The thalidomide incident illustrates the far-ranging duties of the FDA. It operates under authority given it by many laws, but the main acts governing it are the Pure Food and Drug Act of 1906 and the Food, Drug, and Cosmetic Act of 1938. Under these laws the manufacture, sale, or advertisement of impure foods, drugs, or cosmetics is forbidden. The FDA constantly is testing and investigating to make sure that labels are not misleading and that products are not injurious. It has forbidden the use of certain lipsticks, prevented the sale of contaminated cranberries, and stopped the operation of some patent medicine companies which made excessive claims for their products. It also keeps a close watch on "quack" doctors and on other persons who claim unusual abilities to heal.

The U.S. Customs Service protects us from illegal or dangerous imports such as radioactive materials or illicit drugs. It works with many American and international agencies to keep these items under control. A related agency, the Public Health Service, has helped to conduct research projects showing a relationship between smoking and lung cancer. The agency also sends teams of investigators to determine the cause of epidemic illnesses, such as "Legionnaires' disease" (a type of pneumonia) which broke out in parts of the country in the late 1970s. A few other areas of federal concern are mental health, auto safety, blindness, and air pollution. For each of these, federal programs have been undertaken to help state and local governments, and to establish federally operated clinics or research centers.

The federal government's interest in public health has been stimulated greatly during the past forty years of this century. This concern is matched by federal interest in social welfare. Social welfare, for our purposes, may be defined as government assistance:

- To the aged and the jobless;
- To widows, children, and the disabled;
- To those in need of medical care;
- To those who lack proper housing.

Jim Cron from Monkmeyer

People in a New York City unemployment office, filling out forms to apply for unemployment compensation or waiting for interviews with the job counselors.

An examination of these areas will show the amount of progress made in them.

SOCIAL SECURITY

During the Great Depression of the 1930s, many Americans suffered from illness and undernourishment. Local governments were unable to help. Older citizens sometimes were seen outside restaurants, rummaging through garbage cans. To help the unemployed and the elderly, the Social Security Act of 1935 was passed. It accomplished a number of purposes:

- It provided for a federal-state system of unemployment compensation, under which each state would set up unemployment agencies with the help of federal funds. This was to be paid for by a payroll tax on businesses;
- It provided federal help to the states for widows, dependent children, disabled workers, and those over sixty-five;

- It set up a compulsory retirement insurance system, which we call "Social Security," for persons in certain industries throughout the country.

The act of 1935 has been amended frequently over the years to increase the number of persons covered under the insurance, to raise the benefit payments, and to make other changes, such as lowering the eligibility age under certain conditions from sixty-five to sixty-two. The system requires employees to contribute a certain percentage of their salary every year, the amount being matched by the employer. In 1967, the percentage was 4.4 percent of the worker's salary, taken from the first $6,600 of his income. Thus, the maximum tax was $290.40. Anything earned over $6,600 was not subject to the tax. By 1978, these figures had been raised to 6.05 percent of one's pay taken from the first $17,700. The maximum tax, therefore, was over $1,100. Again, anything earned over $17,700 was not taxed. But, since most Americans did not make nearly $17,700 a year, this meant a drain of more than six percent of their salaries all year long. By 1981, the rate is scheduled to go to 6.65 percent of $29,700.

The program has been expanded to include widows, dependent children, and disabled persons. If a worker covered by this insurance dies, his widow and children can receive Social Security benefits. These benefits vary according to the amount paid into the system, but eventually could total more than $787.50 a month as the maximum family payment for the worker with the widest coverage. If a worker becomes disabled, he or she can receive benefits on a level with those due at age sixty-five. Because of increased services, the program is now called OASDHI — old age, survivors, disability, and health insurance. The Social Security Administration insures over 120 million workers in one form or another, and paid out over $75 billion in 1976. This money was sent to more than 33 million persons every month.

MEDICAL CARE

One important reason for increasing Social Security taxes is the establishment of "Medicare," federal assistance for medical services. The Medicare program was set up in 1965, after years

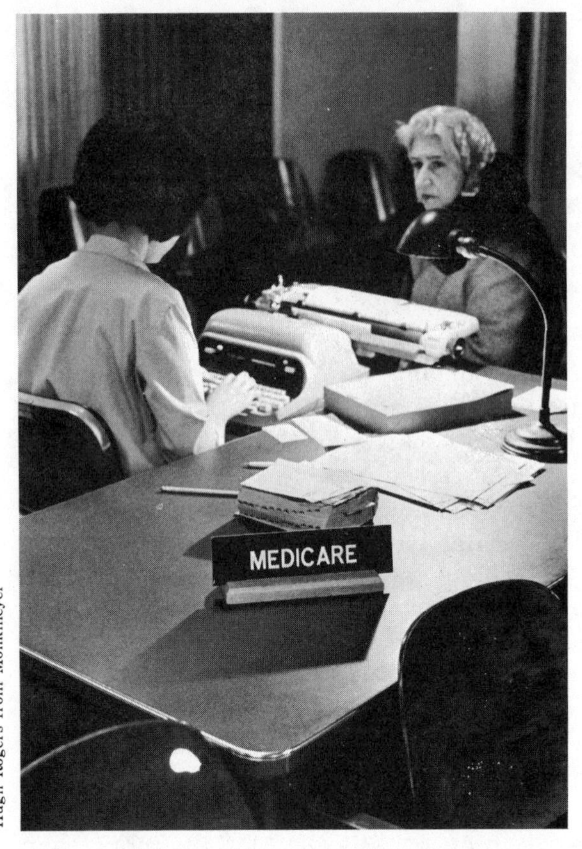

Hugh Rogers from Monkmeyer

A woman filing a claim for assistance under the Medicare program.

of dispute in and out of Congress. It provides medical care funds for the elderly, and is divided into two parts, one voluntary and the other provided automatically. The automatic part of the Medicare program provides coverage for hospital treatment, nursing home care in some cases, and other services which the elderly would find difficult, if not impossible, to purchase themselves. The voluntary part ($7.20 per month) pays the greater part of doctors' fees and covers other expenses, such as nursing visits and medical equipment. In addition to care for the aged, federal health programs exist to aid the states in caring for crippled or retarded children and in helping the "medically indigent" (that is, those too poor to pay for medical help out of their own pockets). Federal health insurance plans for government employees and their families bring the number of Americans being aided in their pursuit of health up to the tens of millions.

HOUSING

Another area of recent federal interest is housing. During the 1930s, the Federal Housing Administration was set up to guarantee private lenders (such as banks) against the loss of money lent to home buyers or builders. Lenders would be insured by the FHA against losses and therefore would be more willing to lend their funds to approved persons. Similarly, after the war, veterans were permitted to apply for mortgage loans guaranteed by the Veterans' Administration. These and other laws have helped millions of Americans to buy or improve their homes.

To aid in public housing (government-owned apartments provided to persons of low income), the federal government has set up a system of loans and grants to local communities. The Public Housing Authority (PHA) supervises the work, but the local government actually owns and operates the property.

The federal government's entrance into the fields of housing, education, and unemployment is fairly recent. Prior to it, the work was handled almost entirely by the states, which still finance or administer most programs. Through this cooperative effort we have a perfect example of federalism in action, the federal government using money extracted from all parts of the nation and distributing it among the states on the basis of need. The states, in turn, know best how to handle their problems on a more localized level. Although there are many flaws in this system, it has the advantage of recognizing the peculiar needs of each of the fifty states.

AFTER-CHAPTER REVIEW

REVIEW QUESTIONS

1. Define the following names, terms, or ideas.

   withholding taxes   Reciprocal Trade Agreements Act

GNP	Land Ordinance of 1785
net income	FDA
Morrill Act	FHA
OASDI	PHA

2. Vocabulary building.

windfall	reciprocity
tariff	deficit

3. Cases.

   Pollack v. *Farmers' Loan*

4. Review of the text.
   a. List and explain the major ways by which the federal government raises revenue.
   b. What are the major forms of taxation? Explain each.
   c. List the reasons for and against the withholding tax system.
   d. Discuss the tariff and the effects it can have depending upon whether it is low or high.
   e. List and explain the major expenses of the federal government.
   f. What steps were taken by the federal government to aid education from the year 1785 to the present? Explain these.
   g. Give five examples of veterans' benefits.

DISCUSSION AND PROJECTS

1. Questions for discussion.
   a. Can taxation limit the liberties of the individual?
   b. If you were in a position to do something about it, how would you alter our tax structure? Are there any untaxed items you would tax? Are there any taxed items you would tax more heavily? Would you lower or eliminate taxes on any other items? Explain.
   c. What are the functions of agencies such as the FDA and the U.S. Customs Service? What are their effects upon American life?
   d. Discuss the federal Social Security program. What are its aims? How well does it seem to be achieving these?

2. Debate topics.
   a. Resolved: The graduated income tax is unfair and should be replaced by some other form of taxation.
   b. Resolved: We need more federal aid for housing, education, and social welfare.
3. Opinion poll.

   Is the United States becoming a welfare state?

BIBLIOGRAPHY

"About Tax Cheating — What the IRS Chief Says," *U.S. News & World Report,* 3 April 1978.

"Budget Deficits Year after Year and No End in Sight," *U.S. News & World Report,* 2 February 1977.

Dale, Edwin L., Jr. "The Security of Social Security: The Young Pay for the Old," *New York Times Magazine,* 14 January 1973.

Dudar, Helen. "The Price of Blowing the Whistle," *New York Times Magazine,* 3 April 1977.

"If the IRS Calls You in for a Tax Audit," *U.S. News & World Report,* 11 April 1977.

Proxmire, William. "The Devastating Truth about Government Giveaways," *Reader's Digest,* March 1978.

"Taming a 148-Billion Dollar Federal Giant: Will Anything Work?" *U.S. News & World Report,* 15 May 1977. Deals with HEW.

Wolff, Anthony. "Of Rats and Men," *New York Times Magazine,* 15 May 1977. Discusses the FDA's testing of saccharin.

In addition to the above sources, every federal agency within the government seeks to publicize its activities and provides brochures without charge to those who ask about their operations. The U.S. Government Printing Office is the largest publisher in the country and will place the name of any persons who request it on a mailing list for its publications called *Selected U.S. Government Publications.* Send a postcard to the Superintendent of Documents, U.S. Government Printing Office, Washington, D.C. 20402.

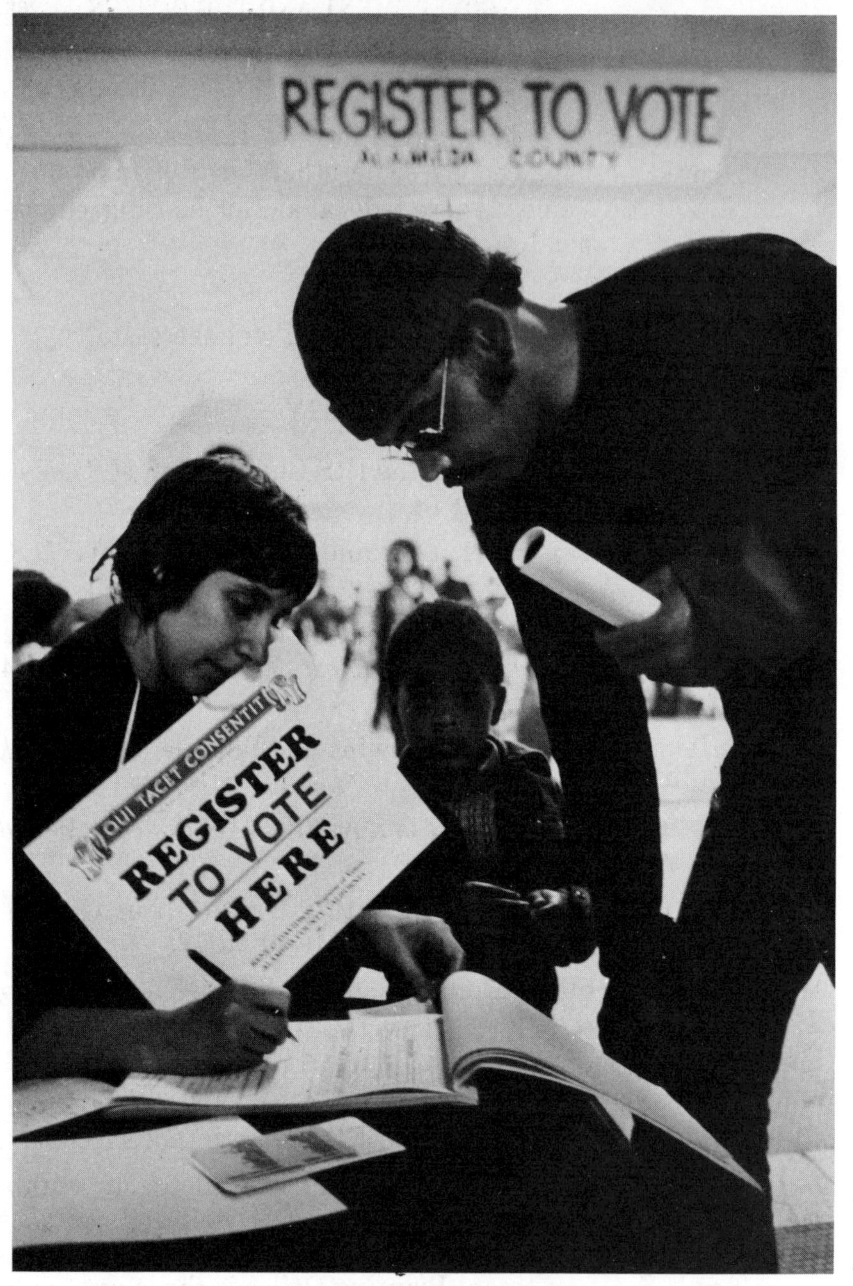

Stephen Shames from Black Star

In our democratic republic a vote represents a small but very real share of power, a fact that too many Americans seem to forget. No presidential election in this century has attracted more than 73.2 percent of eligible voters, and usually the turnout has been much smaller than that. Only about 54 percent bothered to vote in 1976.

13

State and Local Governments and the Political Process

There are many people in American who lament the "death" of the states. They complain that the federal government is gradually "taking over" functions and responsibilities once the exclusive domain of the states. It is true that the federal government has taken a very active part in many new areas, as we saw in Chapter 12, but any obituary written about the states is a little premature.

As the federal government has increased its revenues and expenses in the last two decades, so have the state and local governments. They cannot be viewed as subordinate or inferior in any sense. In terms of revenue and expenditure they are partners. During the 1975–1976 fiscal year, for example, the federal government's revenue was $325 billion while that of all state and local governments was $304 billion. This was matched by federal expenditures of $391 billion and state expenditures of $305 billion. In employment, as we have seen, state and local workers outnumber their federal counterparts more than four to one. The federal government is large and growing, but the workhorse of domestic government in America is not the federal government but the states and their subdivisions.

In this chapter, we will study state government, local government, and the political process as it concerns them and the national government. Let us begin with the states, bearing in mind that, since there are fifty of them and each is a sovereign unit under federalism, they will differ in many ways.

Each state has a constitution with many of the same features as the federal Constitution, such as the separation of powers and the inclusion of a bill of rights. Every state has a governor chosen by the people, a legislature (although the names for it vary from state to state), and a judiciary (with names different from those of the federal judiciary).

GOVERNORS

The state governor is chosen for two or four years by popular vote and is paid from $10,000 to $85,000 a year. He or she may or may not be re-elected indefinitely, since some state constitutions put a limit on the number of terms, just as the Twenty-second Amendment does on the Presidency. To run for office, a candidate must satisfy varying age and residence requirements and must be a citizen. The governor usually is provided with an official residence.

Governors may be impeached, although few have been during the past century, and in thirteen states may be recalled. The recall is a process by which, if a certain percentage of the voters petition for it, an official must stand for re-election immediately. Although a great power, it was used successfully only once in the United States against a governor, almost half a century ago.

The governor of a state has the power to enforce the laws, call out the state's National Guard when it is not in federal service, compile a budget, call special sessions of the legislature, veto bills, pardon criminals, supervise state administrative agencies, and make appointments to various offices. In some cases, his or her powers (within the state borders) are greater than the President's. In most states, for example, governors have an "item" veto; that is, they may veto part of a bill without rejecting it altogether, as the President must do if he disapproves of part of a bill. On the other hand, the governors sometimes find their hands tied in administering the government since the heads of many state agencies are elected rather than appointed. Attorneys-general and secretaries of

Ella T. Grasso (left) became governor of Connecticut in 1975. Although several women have served as state governors following their husbands' terms in office, she was the first to be elected to a governorship on the basis of her own efforts and accomplishments. Dixy Lee Ray was the first woman to be appointed to a full five-year term on the Atomic Energy Commission (now the Nuclear Regulatory Commission). She became Chairman of the AEC in 1973, and in 1976 she was elected governor of the state of Washington.

state often are elected and therefore independent of the governor; sometimes they are members of the opposition party. In New York, the comptroller (a position similar to that of Secretary of the Treasury) was for many years a Democrat, while the governor was a Republican.

STATE LEGISLATURES

The legislatures of our states sometimes seem bewilderingly different. The pay is different, the terms of office are different, and even the names applied to these lawmaking bodies vary. In one state, legislators are paid $32,000 a year, while in another they receive $1,200. Still others are paid on a daily basis, sometimes as little as five dollars a day. In some states, when one becomes a state legislator, it obviously is not for the financial rewards! These low salaries prohibit worthy persons without other sources of income from serving.

Some state legislatures meet for a specified length of time, such as sixty days, after which they must disband. Not all legislatures assemble annually; in fact, many states meet every two years, or biennially. To overcome these restrictions, legislators use legitimate parliamentary devices to extend the life of the session beyond its time limit or governors call special sessions. All state legislatures are bicameral except one, Nebraska, which has a unicameral (one-house) legislature. The upper house is called the Senate, while the lower house may be referred to as the Assembly, General Assembly, House of Delegates, or, most generally, House of Representatives.

State legislatures have great powers. The following is but a partial list of the many things they can do:

- Provide care for the elderly, the sick, the mentally ill, orphans, retired persons, etc.;
- Approve all legislation applying to the state;
- Set up educational institutions of all kinds;
- Regulate firearms;
- Issue charters to corporations, enabling them to engage in business;
- Provide for conservation of natural resources;
- Set up recreational areas in the form of campsites, hunting preserves, etc.;
- Regulate business, pass mininum wage laws, and establish safety regulations;
- Issue licenses for driving machinery, selling an item, or hunting;
- Determine conditions for divorce;
- Provide for housing and highway building and maintenance;
- Regulate labor, including the power to permit workers to be employed in an industry without joining a union;
- Establish voting regulations in elections, including federal elections, except that when federal laws clash with state statutes the federal law is obeyed;
- Establish standards for licensing teachers, doctors, lawyers, and other professional groups;
- Finally, the legislatures can and often do delegate many

Local courthouses are often picturesque examples of Americana; they are also the source of most of the justice dispensed in the United States.

of these responsibilities to counties, cities, and other divisions within the state.

STATE COURTS

It is important that we realize the extent of work done by the states. The majority of court cases in the United States, whether civil or criminal, start and finish in the courts of the states. But in our country there is no such thing as a "typical" state court system, since there is as much variety in the judicial branch as there is in the legislative branch. The duties are the same in each state court system, however, even though the names of the courts and their jurisdictions differ. Among the lowest courts of the states are those run by a justice of the peace, usually in rural areas, and those run by a municipal court judge, usually in urban areas. These judges, even though they often have no training in the law, try persons accused of lesser offenses, such as vagrancy or traffic violations. Many of them are farmers or business people elected to their posts for a specified term. The legal profession does not hold these offices in high esteem, so efforts are being made to upgrade requirements for "J.P.'s" or to eliminate them entirely.

Between these and the higher courts of a state are the specialized courts, such as juvenile court, small claims court,

Heron from Monkmeyer

A juvenile court hearing in California. In most states, legal proceedings involving juveniles (generally defined as persons under eighteen) differ considerably from proceedings involving adults. Usually there is no jury, and the judge has very broad discretionary powers.

and others which take care of one particular set of problems. There are also the "trial" courts, which handle civil problems or more serious crimes and are like the District, Appellate, and Supreme Court system of the federal government. The names vary, but the work remains the same. In some states, the major trial court is called "Superior Court," "District Court," or a like name, while the highest court usually is referred to as the "Supreme Court." In New York, however, the lowest court is called the Supreme Court and the highest is known as the Court of Appeals. In West Virginia the highest court is called the Supreme Court of Appeals, while in Massachusetts it is called the Supreme Judicial Court.

State judges usually are elected officials. They serve for varying amounts of time, from two years to life. Although criticized, the system of electing judges still is practiced in more than three-quarters of the states. The rest of the states permit other methods, such as appointment by the governor or by the state legislature. Judges are subject to impeachment and some can be recalled, if the state constitution allows for it.

State responsibility in law enforcement and in other judicial functions is so vast that courts are kept busy. Most courts are overloaded and behind schedule. Trials involving civil matters, such as one party suing another over a broken contract, may be delayed by two or three years. Witnesses may have died or records may have disappeared by the time the case comes up on the court's calendar, so that sometimes the outcome is very different from what it might have been had the case been tried right away. The remedy for this is to have more judges and more courts. But even when this is done, there still are long delays.

Even though given top priority, criminal trials also proceed slowly through the state courts. This is because of the frightening rise in crime over the past few years and also because of the increasing efficiency of law enforcement agencies in tracking down and arresting offenders. Still, the crime rate is outstripping our population increase and our ability to apprehend criminals. Law enforcement officials report that the total number of crimes committed has risen from 3.3 million in 1960 to 11.3 million in 1976. Since our population increase has not matched this increase in crime, the only conclusion to be drawn is that there is far more lawlessness in society today.

Because transportation has improved rapidly in the past century, the states have had to cooperate more closely with one another to prevent criminals from skipping from one state to another. The federal Constitution recognized this problem by providing for interstate extradition (sometimes called rendition), the right of one state to demand the return of a fugitive who has fled to another state to avoid prosecution. Most states are very cooperative in the rendition process, since they know that some day they may want to use it themselves.

FEDERAL-STATE AND INTERSTATE RELATIONS

The states' need for cooperation brings us to other examples of the way in which they fit into the federal system. We know that the states are, in a sense, second to the federal government: state courts may be overruled by the federal courts, state laws are void if they conflict with national law, and the federal government has first call on the people of the states for military purposes. But the federal government has obligations to the states, too. In the Constitution, the federal government is required to guarantee a republican form of government to each state, to protect the states in general from invasion, and to guard them against domestic rebellion (Article IV, Section 4). In addition, Congress alone may not decide to split any state into two or more parts to increase the number of states. If new states are to be created out of existing ones, the state legislatures concerned must approve the change also.

Just as there are federal-state obligations, so there are state-state duties. One of these, interstate extradition, we have already seen. In addition, Article IV, Section 1, of the federal Constitution provides that "Full Faith and Credit shall be given in each State" to the acts of another. Suppose you are hurt in an accident in your home state and you sue the person who injured you. Assume that the courts of your state rule in your favor, granting you an award of $1,000. Could the guilty party move to another state to escape paying? Not too easily. The authorities of the other state would be required to help you collect your money. Unfortunately, this might be expensive and time-consuming, but the "full faith and credit provision" would be on your side.

The provision is not an unlimited one, however. Even if your state does not require a pistol permit you cannot bring a weapon into another state without observing its laws on firearms. Or, if you are a lawyer and have a license to practice law in California, you still must satisfy New York requirements in order to practice law in that state. The same principle applies to doctors, teachers, motorists (except transients), and so on.

Thus, when you go to another state, you are subject to its laws, not those of the state you left. This rule works both ways, since the new state may not discriminate against you simply because you are not a native. In Article IV, Section 2, the Constitution states, "The Citizens of each State shall be entitled to all Privileges and Immunities of Citizens in the several States." If you move to a job on a farm in Minnesota from your home in Wisconsin, you cannot be paid less for your work than the laws of Minnesota guarantee for its citizens.

New York Port Authority

Loading docks at Newark, New Jersey, part of the Port of New York Authority.

Or if you come from Washington and open a business in Oregon, the Oregon authorities cannot make you pay higher license fees than other Oregon businessmen pay. The United States Supreme Court many times has overruled such discriminatory laws on the basis of the "privileges and immunities" clause.

Interstate cooperation, a practice necessary for the fulfillment of American life, takes many other forms. States may cooperate with each other in matters such as transportation and health through agreements called "interstate compacts." These are federally approved pacts among states which join together to solve problems by pooling their resources. On the Atlantic coast, for example, New York and New Jersey formed the Port of New York Authority to improve their airport facilities and bus transportation, and to satisfy other important needs. Scores of other compacts exist to deal with problems such as water pollution, conservation, and highway development.

The main reason for these compacts is economy: the states must cooperate to get the most out of each dollar they spend.

Revenue sources of the states include some of those available to the federal government (such as personal income taxes and borrowing), but states are barred from levying tariffs.

STATE REVENUES

States raise revenue in a variety of ways, including state personal income taxes; state corporate taxes; sales taxes; liquor, cigarette, and gasoline taxes; license fees; fines; and gambling taxes. All of these taxes vary greatly in the amount of revenue they take in and in the method used. Hawaii has a sales tax of four percent, Kentucky charges five percent, and Indiana two percent. Some states also have turned for additional revenue to lotteries and to the establishment of legalized off-track betting parlors.

Aid from the federal government makes up an important part of state income (about $20 out of every $100 raised by states and local government in the early 1970s). This type of aid is available to states and localities for everything from housing to highways. It may seem unusual to you that the federal government should tax the citizens of a state and then later return the money to the state in the form of aid. Why not let the state tax more and avoid the roundabout way of going from citizen to federal treasury and back to the state? This is a good point and everyone admits that this process adds to bureaucratic costs, but it does have advantages. It helps to distribute the wealth from prosperous states to those which are poorer. About two-thirds of the states receive more money from the federal government than their citizens pay to it. Thus, one-third of the states help the rest improve their highways, educational systems, and other facilities.

Until recently, there were many problems connected with federal aid to the states. Most of the money was in the form of "grants-in-aid," grants for specific purposes (such as highways or conservation projects) which might not have been the most important needs of the state. Still, the state went after the money because it was available, in this way diverting its own funds to match those of the federal government when this was required and using up vast amounts of time and manpower to prove that it was eligible for the program. In

Tom Bradley, mayor of Los Angeles, administers a city of almost three million people, larger than many independent countries. Bradley has been an active mayor, as well as an influential voice in the Democratic party.

addition, the money went to the states for the most part, and not to the local governments which often needed it more.

In 1971, President Nixon proposed general revenue-sharing as part of his "New American Revolution," designed to give the state and local governments greater control over their wealth. "The fact is," the President said, "that we made the federal government so strong it grows muscle-bound and the states and localities so weak they approach impotence."[1] A year later, Congress approved a $30 billion revenue-sharing bill, to be spread over five years. Two-thirds of this money was earmarked for the local governments and the rest was for the states to use almost as they saw fit. Budgets could be balanced, taxes cut, transportation improved, and police and fire protection increased. The great advantage of this system was the flexibility it provided to local governments to

1. *New York Times*, 23 January 1971, p. 12.

meet their own needs in their own ways. Recognizing the popularity of revenue-sharing, Congress and the President have maintained the program at between six and seven billion dollars a year during the later 1970s.

State income is spent directly and indirectly. Direct state spending can be in the form of highway construction, college building, or general governmental expenses. Indirect expenses are those which go to local communities in the form of state aid for local educational, medical, or welfare projects. In affairs directly touching the citizen, the local government carries the ball, with federal and state help or supervision, of course. Thus, we cannot be concerned only with the fifty-one governments of the federal system. We also must view the tens of thousands of local governments which exist in America. They provide police and fire protection, sanitation and educational services. They build and supervise our parks and playgrounds, run many of our medical facilities, and provide local transportation. And these vital concerns are a daily need for us all.

LOCAL GOVERNMENTS

By what right, you may ask, do these thousands of local governments exist? They exist because the states created them. All the counties, municipalities, townships, and school districts exercise their powers by reason of charters or acts of the state legislatures. Almost all of our states are divided into counties. There are more than three thousand counties in America, and their functions include maintaining jails, courts, public records, and hospitals. Each has some kind of political system, sometimes consisting of a chief executive and a county board elected by the people.

Municipalities are villages and cities, population centers which have charters granted by the state setting forth their duties and limitations. In some states, a few hundred people can ask for a charter; in others, thousands are needed. The important thing is that these units have geographical boundaries and special charters. Some cities, such as New York and Los Angeles, are larger than most countries represented in the United Nations. And they are almost as difficult to govern! Others consist of a handful of people. But they all are linked together by common characteristics: they have charters and specially designated boundaries, and they exist only because the state permits them to.

Local governments have been created to perform those duties closest to the people—keeping birth records; providing for a citizen's health, protection, and welfare; issuing marriage licenses; and recording the cause and time of death. Thus, their services run from the cradle to the grave.

Local units have one other common characteristic—they are growing constantly. When this country was first formed in the 1780s only a small percentage of Americans (about one out of twenty) lived in urban areas. By 1920, more than ten out of every twenty Americans lived in urban areas (areas with more than 2,500 population), and in 1970 about fifteen out of twenty were classified as urban dwellers.[2]

The growth of cities has taken place because of a number of vital factors: an agricultural revolution which permitted American farmers to produce more food with fewer and fewer workers, an industrial revolution which brought people to the cities from rural areas and from overseas as immigrants, and the "population explosion" of the last two centuries. Cities and work areas now sprawl across state boundaries without respect for the old ideas of federalism. People who live, pay taxes, vote, and have their children educated in one area often work and are taxed again in another area. Children cross town and district lines to secure educations, parents cross state lines to go to work, and as a result the hard boundaries have weakened. The automobile and mass transit have contributed greatly to this mobility.

Overflowing from the urban areas or from what may be called the central cities are suburban areas, also called "bedroom communities" because so many people live there but work in the central city. These suburban areas still fall within the definition of "urban" because they have populations much larger than 2,500 persons in their political units. In some metropolitan areas, these political units number in the hundreds, when you take into consideration school districts,

2. U.S. Bureau of the Census, *Statistical Abstract of the United States: 1971*, 92nd ed. (Washington, D.C., 1971), p. 17.

water districts, fire districts, county governments, incorporated towns, and so on. A Bureau of the Census count indicates that there are more than 78,000 local governments in the United States. These are broken down as follows: school districts, 15,700; special districts, 23,800; townships, 17,000; municipalities, 18,500; and counties, 3,000.[3] Special districts are those set up for a specific purpose, such as providing fire, water, or recreation services to a community. Municipalities are cities, that is, urban places of widely varying size.

To keep up with the times, the federal government's Office of Management and Budget (OMB) has redefined the terms "urban" and "rural" for census purposes. These are now known as "metropolitan" and "non-metropolitan" areas. A more elaborate term for a metropolitan area is Standard Metropolitan Statistical Area, or SMSA. Everyone in the nation lives either within a SMSA or outside of one. The OMB has defined a SMSA as a geographical region which includes at least one city of 50,000 or more persons, or a series of adjoining places which have a total population of more than 50,000 and are located in a surrounding county containing 75,000 persons. Integration of county and city for economic purposes is necessary for a SMSA, but location within the same state is not. One of the largest SMSAs is "Philadelphia, PA—NJ," including almost five million people in five Pennsylvania counties and three New Jersey counties. The largest urban place in the SMSA is called the "central city" and usually gives its name to the SMSA. As of mid-1977, the OMB had designated 281 SMSAs in the United States.

Going even beyond the SMSA in size and in area is the SCSA, or Standard Consolidated Statistical Area, made up of two or more contiguous (adjoining) SMSAs. There are thirteen SCSAs in the United States, the largest being "New York—Newark—Jersey City, NY—NJ—Conn" with 16.6 million persons.

SMSA and SCSA are terms developed by the OMB for governmental purposes. Other sources use different terms, and

3. U.S. Bureau of the Census, *Statistical Abstract of the United States: 1977*, 98th ed. (Washington, 1977). Figures are rounded to add exactly to 78,000.

see our clustering cities in even broader perspective. The term "Megalopolis" was applied some years ago to the eastern seaboard running from Massachusetts to Virginia. Colloquially, the area is sometimes called "BosWash" because it extends over a distance of six hundred miles, from north of Boston to south of Washington, D.C. Within this area, one out of every five Americans lives and works—a total of approximately 40 million persons. The Megalopolis has been created by the spread of urban and suburban areas, resulting in overlapping. State boundaries are ignored as people work, live, and seek recreation across state lines every day, paying little heed to the old divisions.

LOCAL FINANCES

Local governments are financed by sales taxes, license fees, state aid, federal aid, and most of all by property taxes. The property tax is one source of revenue which state and federal governments leave almost entirely alone, since it makes up such a large part of local government income. Each dwelling in the local area is assessed (or valued) at a certain amount of money. The tax rate is based on an annual rate, perhaps $4 for every $100 of assessed valuation. On a property assessed at $10,000, therefore, the real estate tax would be $400 a year.

Property taxes vary widely from city to city, and sometimes there are differences even within the cities. Property taxes are taxes on property, not on people, and therefore do not take into account the individual's ability to pay. A retired person pays the same rate as a fully employed and high-salaried worker. Some critics have called this practice unfair and various communities have responded by giving tax reductions to poor, retired, or handicapped home owners.

THE ORGANIZATION OF MUNICIPAL GOVERNMENTS

Cities in our country are governed in a variety of ways. One method is the mayor-council system. Under this form of government, the voters elect a mayor and a city council, which is the local legislature. The council may tax, spend, and borrow within limits set by the charter. It also may make local laws, which are called ordinances.

In many areas of city government, problems are not *political* but *administrative.* In other words, there are no great political principles involved in the collection of refuse or in the need for efficient firefighting forces or in the many other day-to-day chores of city government. Therefore, a good administrator or manager might be better equipped to govern a municipality than a popular political leader might be. The mayor-council system is the most popular, but other methods have been suggested and put into use, among them the commission and council-manager plans.

Under the commission system, several commissioners (often five) are elected by the voters. Each commissioner is the head of a city department, and when the entire commission meets it forms the governing council of the city. The people also elect someone to be their official mayor, but he or she does not have the powers of a mayor under the mayor-council system. Unlike a strong mayor, for instance, he or she has no veto power.

The council-manager plan begins with a city council. The council hires a professional administrator, known as a manager, to run the city from then on. The manager is therefore an employee of the council and can perform his or her duties without political considerations. The council sets down the general policies, approves taxation and spending, and, of course, removes the manager if he or she proves unsatisfactory.

Regardless of their form of government, the problems of most municipalities are universally the same: housing, unemployment, pollution, health, nutrition, crime, and traffic. To solve some of the major urban problems, the Eighty-ninth Congress created the Department of Housing and Urban Development (HUD) and the Department of Transportation. These agencies, coupled with the Department of Health, Education, and Welfare, created in 1953, have led a three-pronged assault on the above-mentioned problems.

Federally sponsored programs authorizing large sums of money for particular neighborhoods to help them improve themselves so that they might inspire other areas have been introduced in some ghetto areas of large cities. Other programs aim at helping underprivileged people to become self-supporting. Federal and state training agencies have been created, offering vocational and other forms of education. Food stamps have been distributed to millions of Americans in all parts of the nation to improve their health through proper nutrition. By 1976, some eighteen million Americans were receiving food stamps to allow them to stretch their food dollars farther.

THE POLITICAL PROCESS

The cornerstone of all American governments is the political process. Even in those local governments which have tried to free themselves from the mayor-council form, the selection of commissioners or council members is part of the political process. In America, politics is the art of self-government, the effort on the part of active groups to secure control of the government so that their principles may prevail.

We have two major political parties, which are organized from the smallest district up to the county, state, and national level. In each of these districts there are committees and chairmen chosen by the party members to represent them, to screen candidates for public office, and to express party ideas. It is difficult to say just what the Republican or Democratic parties stand for, since their ideas have changed over the years and the words now mean different things to different people. We now say that the Democratic party often stands for a strong central government while the Republican party often favors state initiative. Yet there are many Democrats who favor the states and many Republicans who support a powerful central government.

Let us take a recent specific example, the approval by a recent Congress of federal funds for elementary and secondary education. The House of Representatives approved this federal aid to education by a vote of 185 to 76. Of the 185 lawmakers who approved it, 144 were Democrats and 41 were Republicans. Twenty-nine Democrats and 47 Republicans were lined up against the bill. Every Democrat who voted against it came from a southern or border state, so we might be inclined to say that southern Democrats think the states should be left alone to work out their own educational futures.

Andrew Sacks from EPA

Senator Hubert H. Humphrey campaigning in the Democratic presidential primary in Wisconsin in 1972.

Yet this would not be true, since 42 of the Democratic members of Congress voting *for* federal aid came from southern and border states. Since 41 Republicans favored the bill and 47 disapproved it, no clear-cut conclusions can be drawn.

Although overall party tendencies are hard to define, we find some interesting answers when looking at the vote by states. Not one New York member of Congress, Democrat or Republican, voted against federal aid. In New York State, both parties agreed on this issue. But in Ohio, five Democrats and no Republicans voted for the bill, while no Democrats and seven Republicans voted against it. So federal aid to education is a political issue in Ohio, and there is a struggle between the two parties. Finally, in the Texas delegation, twelve Democrats voted for it, five Democrats voted against

Jean-Claude LeJeune

High school girls campaigning for local candidates in Chicago.

it, and four Democrats said they opposed it although they did not vote. So in Texas, federal aid to education is an issue which shows disagreement *within* a party.

The above illustration is given to show that the Democratic and Republican parties are not strongly controlled organizations with rigid, unchanging nationwide ideas. They vary from place to place, from time to time, and from person to person. Of the 435 members of the House, only 261 were there to vote on the issue. Since the vote was taken at the end of October, most of the remaining members were campaigning busily for re-election and were not present. Many of them publicly indicated their approval or disapproval; others "ducked" the issue for one reason or another.

It has been said that the first job of politicians is to get elected. As soon as they win public office, they begin running again for the next election. But they must spend some time in their home districts, "mending fences," as the saying goes. To win election or to secure re-election, a person seeking office usually must follow these steps: win nomination from his or her party, campaign actively for the office, and secure more votes than his or her opponents. Let us examine these steps.

CAMPAIGNING FOR OFFICE

Parties nominate their candidates in a number of ways. Sometimes, party leaders "caucus," or meet to select their nominee. At other times, the primary may be used. Or there may be a mixed system of caucus and primary. A primary is an election held within a party to select candidates for public office. If only party members are allowed to vote, it is a "closed primary." If it is open to all registered voters, it is an "open primary."

Campaigning for office in the United States is a long and costly operation, involving the expenditure of huge sums of money and months of strenuous work. More than $74 million was spent by congressional candidates running in the 1974 general elections. Some $45 million was spent by House candidates and nearly $30 million by candidates for the Senate. As an example of a state race, the 1974 gubernatorial election in New York cost $4.1 million in the primary, and $5.2 million in the general election.[4]

In 1976, the presidential election campaign was unique in American history in that it was to a great extent financed by the public. Of the $114 million raised, $46 million came from private sources and about $68 million was contributed by the federal government from a fund created by an act of Congress. The money in this fund results from a decision made by taxpayers at the time they file their income tax returns each year. If they check a certain box on the tax form, the government automatically sets aside one dollar (two if it is a joint return) to be used for presidential election expenses. About one of every four taxpayers uses the check-off system.

This method of public financing of presidential elections gives all candidates a chance, not just wealthy persons or persons with wealthy backers. Some observers believe that public financing made possible Jimmy Carter's "miraculous"

4. Herbert Alexander, *Financing Politics* (Washington: Congressional Quarterly Press, 1976), p. 239.

transformation from a little-known governor of Georgia in 1975 to a recognized candidate and an upset winner in 1976.

Beginning in 1971, Congress passed a great deal of legislation designed to reform campaigning for public office. The 1971 Federal Election Campaign Act, as amended in 1974 and 1976 and altered by Supreme Court decisions, is the basic law of the land. Among the provisions of this act were those which:

- Created a Federal Election Commission of six persons to be appointed by the President and confirmed by the Senate;
- Required that contributors and contributions be made public;
- Authorized the check-off system to provide for public financing of presidential campaigns;
- Provided taxpayers with a tax reduction for any donation made to a bona fide candidate, up to a limit of $12.50;
- Set dollar limits on the amount of money persons could contribute to campaigns either for themselves or others.

The act got off to a shaky start when the Supreme Court, in the case of *Buckley* v. *Valeo* in 1976, ruled certain provisions unconstitutional. Among these was a section limiting contributions by individuals. The Court argued that spending money on political campaigns was a form of speech and was therefore protected by the First Amendment. However, the Court did permit limitations on overall spending for a campaign if the candidate accepted public financing, so the ultimate effect of the decision was to place some limits on contributions by donors and candidates. Some public financing is available as "matching" funds—that is, amounts which match those contributed to candidates by private sources.

Private funds come from a variety of sources, individual contributions being the basis. In addition, political action committees representing labor, business, professional, and other groups make voluntary contributions. Direct-mail advertising is an effective method of fund-raising, as are television, radio, and newspaper appeals.

What campaign reformers are trying to avoid is the situation in which large donors "buy" a candidate with their contributions. A large donor might be an industry, a union, or a pressure group. Or it might be an individual seeking a reward in the form of an ambassadorial post or other high office. This situation can be avoided by broadening the number of contributors who support a candidate's bid. Millions of Americans give $5, $10, or $25 to their candidate to help get his or her message across. They expect nothing in return except good government. But the vast majority do not contribute, and in this way leave the door open for those unscrupulous donors who try to "buy" candidates.

THE VOTER CHOOSES

When the campaigning is over, the task of selecting the man or woman best suited for elective office rests with the voter. Voters turn out at the polls every year, on the first Tuesday after the first Monday of November. In leap years, they elect a President, an entirely New House of Representatives, and one third of the U.S. Senate. They also may elect a state legislature and numerous other officials. In other years, if elections are staggered in their state, the voters will elect city and state officials.

In a recent election, voters in one state were required to vote for:

Governor and lieutenant-governor (of the state);
Comptroller (of the state);
Attorney-general (of the state);
Chief judge of the (state) Court of Appeals;
District attorney (of the county);
Representative (in the federal House of Representatives);
Councilman (of the city);
Senator (of the state);
Assemblyman (of the state);
Three delegates to the state constitutional convention.

Voters therefore were required to select thirteen elected officials. In addition, they had to vote on one "proposition," one "question," and eleven amendments to the state constitution. They had to make a total of twenty-six important decisions within the three-minute time limit set by the state election law. This allowed them less than seven seconds for each choice. Thus, no conscientious voter can go into the polling booth without first examining the candidates and the issues closely and making choices beforehand.

The list given above is not an unusual one, except for the delegates to the constitutional convention. It illustrates the difficult job of self-government Americans have before them. It is hard to know what each candidate for each office stands for. Sometimes, election officials and the candidates themselves do their best to make it hard for the citizen. Election officials, for example, thoughtlessly permit proposals on which the voters must decide to be printed in very small letters and in very obscure language. They do this under the authority of the state legislature, of course, and the busy citizen most often simply ignores the issues. Candidates often avoid public contact which will force them to state squarely what their views are on public issues. They send out blaring sound trucks, and they plaster walls with their pictures; but all we learn from this noise and this outrage to the eyes is that they are candidates "of the people," or that we can "believe in Senator Lackluster," or that "Representative Foofram gets the job done."

Thoughtful citizens ignore this silliness and concentrate on the issues. They can keep up with men and women in public life by getting a package of index cards and writing down the name of a public figure on each. When they read or hear something about the particular official, they can jot down a few words about it. Over the course of a few years, believe it or not, these citizens are the local experts on that particular candidate. And instead of being swayed by appearances, they can, as Governor Alfred E. Smith often said, "look at the record."

But with so many difficulties confronting the voter, it is somewhat understandable (if not excusable) that American elections are very poor examples of interest in the democratic process. We are happy if sixty percent of those eligible to vote in the United States actually go to the polls. The election of 1964 was a record turnout, with some 70 million Americans going to the polls. But over 40 million eligible voters did *not* go to the polls. In the elections of 1966, less than fifty percent of the voters turned out to elect the Ninetieth Congress. The 1968 presidential election brought out sixty percent of the voters eligible, while the 1972 turnout was fifty-five percent and the 1976 was fifty-four. In 1976,

Voter turnout in U.S. presidential elections

(in percentages of eligible voters)

Election	Turnout	Election	Turnout	Election	Turnout
1824	26.9	1876	81.8	1928	56.9
1828	57.6	1880	79.4	1932	56.9
1832	55.4	1884	77.5	1936	61.0
1836	57.8	1888	79.3	1940	62.5
1840	80.2	1892	74.7	1944	55.9
1844	78.9	1896	79.3	1948	53.0
1848	72.7	1900	73.2	1952	63.3
1852	69.6	1904	65.2	1956	60.6
1856	78.9	1908	65.4	1960	64.0
1860	81.2	1912	58.8	1964	61.8
1864	73.8	1916	61.6	1968	60.6
1868	78.1	1920	49.2	1972	55.6
1872	71.3	1924	48.9	1976	54.4

Sources: *Congressional Record*, 10 April 1973, p. S7030; U.S. Bureau of the Census.

81 million Americans went to the polls, but this was out of a voting-age population of 150 million, so 69 million failed to use their right.

VOTER APATHY

Political scientists have made careful studies of voting apathy and have set forth many reasons for it. Some people are away on business, others cannot satisfy residence requirements, many are ill, some (such as blacks, as we have seen in Chapter 11) actually have been prevented from voting, and others are indifferent. In many cases, it is a combination of these factors. There are ways of overcoming voter apathy, however, and some states have adopted them. Relaxation of the residence requirements for voting is one method. Another is extension of absentee balloting, whereby citizens who know they will be out of town may mail a paper ballot to the board of elections. To overcome illegal prohibitions against voting, strong enforcement of state and federal laws is needed. More education in civic duty is also needed to arouse the lazy or the indifferent.

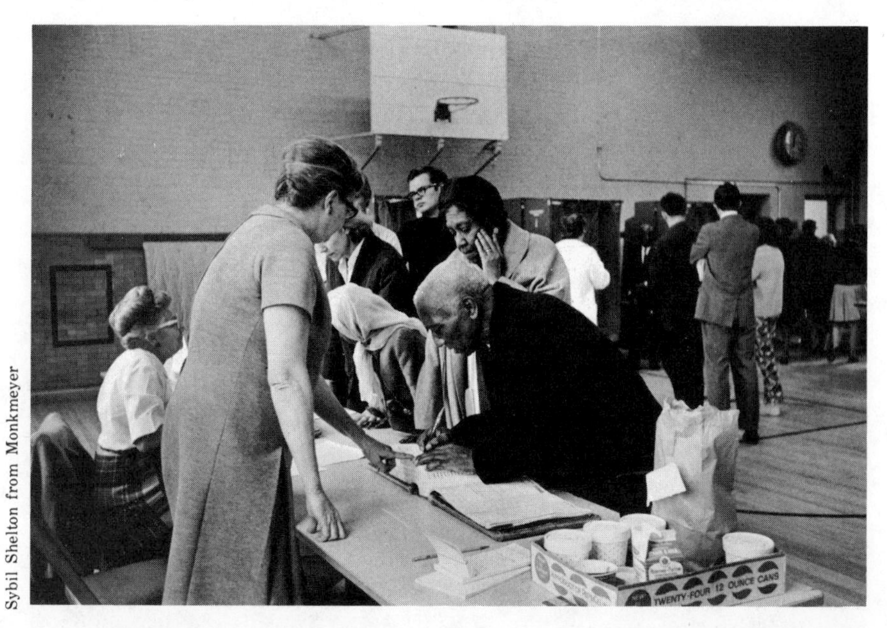

Sybil Shelton from Monkmeyer

At a polling place in New Jersey, voters sign the register before receiving their ballots. In most precincts, election officials are volunteers from the community who are paid only a nominal sum for a long day's work.

Many persons think that their vote means very little, forgetting that it takes two votes to beat their one. An amazing number of elections have been decided by one or a few votes. In a recent election held in Nassau County in New York State, two candidates ran for a judicial office and received the following votes: Candidate A—53,371; Candidate B—53,366. But there were several votes in question and the election went into the courts. The courts added a few votes to Candidate B's total and took a few away from Candidate A, and the election ended in a tie. A handful of the hundreds of people who stayed home in that election could have altered the result.

Voters sometimes excuse themselves by saying that there is no choice among the candidates. They protest by staying away from the polls. This is their right, of course, but many do not know that it is also their right to use the "write-in" procedure. Voters may write in the name of anyone they wish for any office on the paper ballot or on a section of the voting machine, depending on which form their state uses. Some years ago, a state governor was elected by write-in balloting. In one city in Brazil a few years ago, the citizens were so dis-

Voter participation in recent presidential elections
(in percentages of voting-age population)

	1968 Election	1972 Election	1976 Election
Sex:			
Male	69.8	64.1	59.6
Female	66.0	62.0	58.8
Racial or ethnic background:			
White	69.1	64.5	60.9
Black	57.6	52.1	48.7
Hispanic	unknown	37.4	31.8
Age:			
18 to 20	33.3	48.3	38.0
21 to 24	51.1	50.7	45.6
25 to 34	62.5	59.7	55.4
35 to 44	70.8	66.3	63.3
45 to 64	74.9	70.8	68.7
65 and over	65.8	63.5	62.2
Residence:			
Metropolitan area	68.0	64.3	59.2
Non-metropolitan area	67.3	59.4	59.1
Number of school years completed:			
8 or fewer	54.5	47.4	44.1
9 to 11	61.3	52.0	47.2
12 (through high school)	72.5	65.4	59.4
More than 12	81.2	78.8	73.5
Employment:			
Employed	71.1	66.0	62.0
Unemployed	52.1	49.9	43.7
Not in labor force (in school, retired, working in home, etc.)	63.2	59.3	56.5

Source: U.S. Bureau of the Census.

gusted with their politicians that they wrote in the name of a rhinoceros in their zoo and elected him to the city council. (He was disqualified, however, because he was on loan from another zoo and was not a bona fide resident of the city.)

Voting is a serious obligation, as well as a sacred right, in a democratic republic. In other countries it is taken more seriously, with the result that more people turn out in elections. Elections are held even in dictatorships, although only for their propaganda value. In the Soviet Union, the Communist rulers insist that citizens vote, although they have no choice of candidates and cannot express disagreement without betraying themselves to the Russian secret police. The use of the Australian or secret ballot in this country protects our citizens from any prying. It should be used by as many of us as possible to determine our future and that of our children.

In this chapter, we have examined the make-up of state and local governments, their functions, and their problems. We also have seen the close connection between local and national politics. After all, as we now know, government begins on the lowest level. The federal system, with its divided authority, may seem confusing. But by sharing the power, the American people actually are safeguarding their liberties. There is little likelihood that one vast tyranny can emerge from so many different parts. In addition, state governments usually know more about local conditions than the national government does. Some states have too much water, for example, and need flood control aid; others have too little water and need irrigation projects. In any case, the states are in the best position to know.

AFTER-CHAPTER REVIEW

REVIEW QUESTIONS

1. Define the following names, terms, or ideas.

"item" veto	interstate compact
rendition	HUD
grants-in-aid	revenue-sharing
Australian ballot	write-in vote
SMSA	SCSA

2. Vocabulary building.

municipality comptroller biennial contiguous

3. Review of the text.

a. Compare the office of governor with that of President. In what ways are they similar? In what ways different? Which has more power in specific instances?
b. Compare the federal Congress with the state legislatures with respect to duties, salaries, sessions, etc.
c. Describe the state court system. What kinds of cases do they hear? How are they named? How are judges of the state courts different from and similar to federal judges?
d. Make a list of those things which the federal government owes to the states and those which the states owe to each other.
e. What are the major sources of revenue and the major expenses of the states?
f. Describe the duties and powers of local governments.
g. List and explain the main forms of municipal government.
h. Describe the main features of the election campaign legislation of the 1970s.

DISCUSSION AND PROJECTS

1. Questions for discussion.

a. Discuss the many varieties of government which exist in our country. Would another system of government solve the problems of overlapping responsibilities? Explain.
b. Discuss the grants-in-aid and revenue-sharing systems. What are the advantages and disadvantages of each?
c. How can the cities solve their problems? Is federal aid the answer? Explain your answer.
d. What is a political party? Should political parties represent general ideas or should they stand for specific programs? Discuss your answer.

2. Debate topics.
   a. Resolved: All eligible voters should be forced to vote under penalty of a fine.
   b. Resolved: All elections should be publically financed, not just the presidential elections.
   c. Resolved: The federal system is anachronistic. Let's abolish the states!

3. Opinion poll.

   Would you devote the rest of our life to a career in politics?

BIBLIOGRAPHY

Alexander, Herbert E. *Financing Politics.* Washington: Congressional Quarterly Press, 1976.

"American Political Reform," *Current History,* August 1974.

Barone, Michael. "Nonlessons of the Campaign," *New York Times Magazine,* 28 November 1976.

The Future of the City. Washington: Congressional Quarterly Press, 1974.

Goodall, Leonard E., and Sprengel, Donald P. *The American Metropolis.* 2nd ed. Columbus, Ohio: Charles E. Merrill, 1975.

Helfand, Gary, ed. *Metropolitan Areas, Metropolitan Governments.* 2nd ed. Dubuque: Kendall/Hall Publishing, 1976.

Jacob, Herbert. *Urban Justice.* Englewood Cliffs, N.J.: Prentice-Hall, 1973.

Riordan, William L., ed. *Plunkitt of Tammany Hall.* New York: E. P. Dutton, 1963.

Hugh Rogers from Monkmeyer

The steelworks of this Pennsylvania town produce a commodity that is essential to the economy of the nation, yet they also pollute the streams, sky, and soil with their wastes. Our extraordinary industrial growth over the last hundred years has brought us great benefits, including the highest standard of living in the world; at the same time, it has presented us with one of our greatest challenges for the future—the restoration of a healthful environment for all Americans.

14

The Federal Government and the Nation

Just as government touches our individual lives, so it touches the entire life of our society. It regulates the immigration of persons to our shores, has great influence over business enterprises, controls farm production, regulates the labor movement, and seeks ways to preserve and utilize our natural resources in the most efficient way. Covering each field briefly, we will discuss immigration, business regulation, agriculture, conservation, and labor in this chapter.

IMMIGRATION

All Americans are immigrants. Even the Indians are said to have come from Asia across the Bering Strait when Alaska and Asia were connected by a land bridge. What concerns us here is the migration of European, African, and Asian people to the United States from the seventeenth century to the present. Significant European migration began in 1607, while African migration started in 1619, with the arrival of twenty Negroes at Jamestown, Virginia. Thereafter, the population of the country swelled from both sources until, by the time of the first census in 1790, there were nearly four million persons in the United States, one-fourth of whom were black. By this time not all Americans were migrants, though. Many had been born here, and could boast of being "native" Americans.

Immigration from Africa officially ceased when Congress forbade the slave trade after 1807, although hundreds of

Immigration to the United States by decades

Decade	Number of Immigrants	Decade	Number of Immigrants
1970s (est.)	4,000,000	1890s	3,700,000
1960s	3,300,000	1880s	5,250,000
1950s	2,500,000	1870s	2,800,000
1940s	1,000,000	1860s	2,300,000
1930s	530,000	1850s	2,600,000
1920s	4,100,000	1840s	1,700,000
1910s	5,700,000	1830s	600,000
1900s	8,800,000	1820s	150,000

Source: U.S. Immigration and Naturalization Service.

thousands of African slaves were smuggled into the country after that date. Within the next one hundred years, about forty million persons came to the United States, some from Asia but the vast majority from Europe. Until the last few decades of the century, most of the immigration came from Great Britain, Ireland, Germany, and the Scandinavian countries. By the end of the nineteenth century, however, millions of people from Italy, Poland, Russia, and other parts of eastern and southern Europe were beginning their journey westward. This wave increased right up to 1914 and the beginning of World War I.

During and after the 1920s, migration declined, mostly because of the passage of federal legislation limiting the amount of immigration. Let us review the course of federal regulation of immigration over the last century and a half.

At first Congress did very little to regulate immigration. Problems arising from uncontrolled immigration became the problems of the large eastern cities, especially New York, Boston, and Philadelphia. When regulation came, it was based on restriction by some *quality* or personal characteristic of the individual to which Congress objected. For example, paupers, the contagiously diseased, lawbreakers, immoral persons, and political radicals were forbidden to enter the country. In addition, exclusion by race was introduced with the Exclusion Act of 1882, preventing Chinese immigration. Japanese immigration was virtually stopped by the "Gentlemen's Agreement" of 1907, whereby the Japanese government agreed to forbid Japanese laborers to come to the United States in return for American agreement that segregation of Japanese in California schools would be stopped. This agreement and a new Immigration Act of 1907 resulted in the near exclusion of Asians from the United States.

It was not until the 1920s that a second type of restriction became law, namely restriction by *quantity*. The first efforts at quantitative restriction came in the form of two laws of the 1920s which established quotas for each country sending persons to the United States. These quotas were based on the percentage of persons of that national origin in the country as of 1920. An overall limit of 150,000 immigrants was set for each year. The figures were especially drawn to retain the ratio of ethnic groups then in the nation. Great Britain and Ireland, for instance, could send about 66,000 and 18,000 persons respectively, while Poland and Italy, because they had fewer immigrants already in this country, could send only about 6,500 and 5,700 persons respectively. The acts therefore favored immigrants from the Northern and Western European countries. Countries in the Western Hemisphere, however, were exempted from the quota system.

During the decade of the 1920s, 4,107,209 persons came to the United States as immigrants. Then the Immigration Act of 1924 went into full effect in 1929, and during the entire decade of the 1930s only 528,431 persons entered. The ten-year total was less than the annual total in most years before World War I. In fact, in some years as many people left the country as entered it.

In 1952, the legislation of the 1920s was somewhat modified by the McCarren-Walter Act. Racial restrictions were ended by a clause which permitted every country to send at least one hundred persons to the country annually. But the quota system was preserved, and thus immigrants from Northern and Western Europe continued to be favored. Other legislation of this era allowed for the admission of displaced persons (those whose lives had been disrupted by World War II) and for refugees fleeing political and economic misery.

Immigration to the U.S. by country, 1820-1975

	Number of persons
All countries	47,099,000
Europe	35,961,000
Austria	4,312,000
Belgium	201,000
Czechoslovakia	136,000
Denmark	363,000
France	742,000
Germany	6,954,000
Great Britain (including England, Scotland, and Wales)	4,852,000
Greece	629,000
Ireland	4,720,000
Italy	5,270,000
Netherlands	356,000
Norway	855,000
Poland	503,000
Portugal	411,000
Rumania	166,000
Russia	3,354,000
Spain	246,000
Sweden	1,270,000
Switzerland	346,000
Yugoslavia	106,000
Other European countries (including Bulgaria, Finland, etc.)	167,000

The number of persons entering the country during the 1950s and 1960s averaged more than 250,000 a year.

The Immigration Act of 1965 changed the character of American immigration drastically. Under the new law, an overall quota was fixed at 170,000 persons in any given year, plus another 120,000 persons a year from Western Hemisphere nations. Children, parents, husbands, and wives of American citizens had priority regardless of the quota, and top priority was given to skilled workers and refugees. Thus,

Immigration to the U.S. by country, 1820–1975 (Cont'd)

	Number of persons
Asia	2,275,000
China	488,000
India	107,000
Japan	391,000
Turkey	382,000
Other Asian countries (including the Middle East and Southeast Asia)	906,000
Western Hemisphere	8,348,000
Canada	4,048,000
Central America	263,000
Mexico	1,912,000
South America	607,000
West Indies	1,408,000
Africa (not including persons brought to the U.S. illegally as slaves)	104,000
South Pacific (including New Zealand and Australia)	135,000
Country not specified	386,000

Source: U.S. Immigration and Naturalization Service.

there was still a limitation on the number of persons who could enter the country in any year, but the discriminatory national origins system was ended.

Following the Immigration Act of 1965, immigration from such Northern and Western European countries as Britain, Sweden, Germany, and Ireland declined, while immigration from such Southern and Eastern European countries as Greece, Italy, Czechoslovakia, and Portugal increased.

In 1976, for example, more than 10,000 persons were admitted from Portugal, while the total number of persons from Germany, Ireland, and Sweden combined was only 9,700. Even more dramatic increases came from Asia and Latin America, particularly the Caribbean area. In 1976, the leading nations contributing immigrants to the United States were Mexico and the Philippines.

In spite of the liberalization of the laws, many people from foreign countries still find their way to the United States blocked. Some of them have taken the drastic step of entering the country illegally. Mexicans, Chinese, Arabs, Greeks, and many others make their way across the Rio Grande, sneak across the Canadian border, or fly in from the Caribbean islands. During the 1960s, the annual average of aliens expelled from the country was 140,000; during the 1970s, the annual average jumped to 700,000.

The problem of illegal aliens reached grave proportions during the last years of the 1970s. No government agency could estimate with accuracy the true number of persons residing in the nation illegally, but the figure of six million is accepted by the Immigration and Naturalization Service (INS). Since about two-thirds of these illegal aliens hold jobs, many Americans feel that they are cheating the nation's native-born and naturalized citizens who cannot find employment. It is true that a great many undocumented immigrants provide cheap labor in jobs that are unattractive to Americans, whose employment expectations are much higher. However, studies indicate that some illegal residents hold down good jobs, not just minimum-wage work, and that they are often able to avoid paying taxes on their earnings.

Mexicans make up the largest ethnic group responsible for illegal entry in recent years. In 1976, 871,000 deportable aliens were apprehended by the U.S. border authorities, and of these 848,000 were Mexican nationals. The main argument offered by Mexicans for their incursions is economic. Those who come simply have no way of supporting themselves or their families at home.

The United States has long been one of the freest countries in the world in accepting migrants, especially those in need.

In the years since the 1950s, Hungarian, Cuban, Czechoslovakian, and Vietnamese fleeing Communism, and persons from other countries fleeing other forms of tyranny, have been welcomed to this land. Among these recent arrivals were the Vietnamese who fled Communist reprisals following the end of the Vietnam War. About 150,000 refugees had come to the United States from Vietnam by the beginning of 1977. The years 1978 and 1979 also saw the arrival of many people from Iran whose lives had been disrupted by political turmoil in that country.

The goal of most immigrants to the United States is citizenship. To achieve this, each alien must indicate such desire to the Immigration and Naturalization Service. A residence of five years is required, and the person must be able to demonstrate good character, freedom from criminal activities, and a knowledge of American government. If an alien fails to live up to the regulations prescribed, he or she may be deported, that is, sent back to the country of origin. If all the requirements are fulfilled, the alien is allowed to become a "naturalized" (in contrast to a natural-born) citizen. These new Americans then may participate in every phase of American life except one—they may not serve as President of the United States.

The labor of immigrants, added to that of the native-born, built the United States. The millions who poured into our cities provided the muscle that built the factories, skyscrapers, and railroads which characterize our country today. Many immigrants became famous in industry; the names Bulova, Cudahy, and Carnegie are well known to Americans today because of their connections with a product or an industry. Business has been the cornerstone of American life since the earlier settlements. Indeed, even the early settlements were often business ventures begun by investors who wanted to develop the New World for profit. Before the Revolution, business was regulated by the British Parliament under very strict rules. These rules many times were ignored by the colonists or were not enforced by the British. When the British did decide to enforce them, they created one of the causes of the Revolution.

Profile of Indochinese refugees to the U.S., 1975

	Percentage		Percentage
Total number entering in 1975: 130,000		Elementary school	18%
		Unknown or none	24%
Sex:		Occupation of heads of households:	
Male	55%		
Female	45%	Medical	7%
Age:		Professional, technical, or management	24%
Under 18	46%		
18 to 44	44%	Clerical, sales or service	19%
Over 45	10%		
Education (persons over 18):		Agricultural, fishing, or forestry	5%
College or above	20%	Machine trades	9%
High school	38%	All other	36%

Source: Adapted from U.S. Department of State statistics.

Recent immigration to the U.S. from selected areas

	Number of persons		Number of persons
Total immigration:		From Europe:	
1965	297,000	1965	113,000
1970	373,000	1970	116,000
1975	386,000	1975	74,000
From Asia:		From Africa:	
1965	20,000	1965	3,000
1970	93,000	1970	8,000
1975	133,000	1975	7,000
From South America:		From the West Indies:	
1965	31,000	1965	38,000
1970	22,000	1970	61,000
1975	23,000	1975	67,000

Source: U.S. Immigration and Naturalization Service.

GOVERNMENT REGULATION OF BUSINESS

After the Constitution was adopted, new problems arose. One had to do with the right of contract and another with the interstate commerce clause. In the famous *Dartmouth College* case, the Supreme Court ruled that the state of New Hampshire could not revoke the charter of Dartmouth College, because that would violate the contract clause in the Constitution, the clause protecting agreements among individuals, governments, and groups. Years later, the contract clause was used by the Supreme Court to overrule laws made to regulate business. If a worker made an agreement with an employer not to join a labor union or to work seventy or eighty hours a week, this was a contract and the state and federal legislatures did not have the right to interfere with it. This position, of course, hurt working people and slowly was modified over the years. The Court later upheld the "sanctity of contract," but ruled that Congress and states could protect the interests of working people against unfair practices.

Another problem arising in the dealings between government and business concerned interstate commerce. In the nineteenth century, the question arose whether a state could regulate commerce, in view of the power of Congress. Could a state, for instance, tax a product which merely was being transported across it? In answer to this, the Supreme Court announced the "original package" doctrine, which stated that as long as an item was in its original form or had not been sold, it could not be taxed. Imagine the confusion there would be if the "original package" doctrine had not been stated. An automobile manufacturer sending a car from Michigan to Florida could be taxed by half a dozen states. The "package" may be taxed, however, at its final destination.

Toward the end of the nineteenth century, American industry really began to grow. Oil, steel, railroad, and other industries became larger and more powerful. In these, and in other businesses, trusts were created. Trusts were business combinations designed to gain control of all or most of the activities of a particular industry. These combinations often hurt the workingman and the consumer, since the companies participating in them could pay low salaries and charge high prices without fear that competing firms would interfere.

Congress responded to this danger by passing the Sherman Anti-Trust Act of 1890 and the Clayton Anti-Trust Act of 1914. These acts forbade monopolies which restrained trade in order to reduce competition, prohibited price discrimination, and tried to prevent large companies from buying stock (ownership) in other companies. They were designed to promote competition and were passed at a time when almost every industry in America was dominated, and sometimes completely controlled, by one trust or another.

But just because a company was big did not mean that it was unfair. The Supreme Court stated this in the judicial doctrine known as the "rule of reason," which declared that only *unreasonable* restraints of trade were illegal. There are some jobs which must be done and which best can be done by a large company, even if it is a monopoly. In this respect, the Court looks favorably on such "good" monopolies as gas, electric, and telephone companies and other public utilities.

The Justice Department is very zealous in supervising American business to insure against the reduction of competition. A few years ago, it secured Supreme Court approval to force the Du Pont Company to sell the securities it owned in General Motors, the auto manufacturer. It also took action against the Aluminum Company of America, the American Telephone and Telegraph Company (AT & T), and the Eastman Kodak Corporation to challenge what the government called monopolistic practices. Bear in mind, though, that these companies were not guilty of crimes. They were doing what businesses naturally do—expanding. And the government was doing what it was supposed to do—regulating. If government and business representatives disagree, the courts decide at what point expansion should be regulated.

There have been criminal practices among businesses, however. One of these is known as "pooling." A pool is an agreement among competing companies to fix prices or to divide a territory so that each company has its exclusive section. Even when companies are not acting illegally, the federal government has quickly opposed activities that appear to be unfair to the consumer.

In 1962, President Kennedy made a speech expressing

his anger over an increase in steel prices. Among the weapons he used to bring pressure to bear against the steel industry were the possibility of antitrust suits, a possible Congressional investigation, and a threat to remove all government business. The steel companies lowered prices, indicating how powerful the federal government had become. They claimed, however, that their increase was modest and necessary. They also accused the President of undermining confidence in business and pointed out that, as a result of the affair, prices on the stock market dropped. We see here the interaction between business and finance. A year later, the steel industry increased its prices and the federal government did nothing. Notice in this case how even the *threat* of governmental intervention was enough to bring about a desired action. Many Americans were frightened to see this display of federal power, but others saw that it meant protection against possible business abuses.

The financier or investor is the person who puts up the money to start, operate, or expand a business. He or she may be a worker who buys a share of stock now and again, or the president of a bank or insurance company which lends large sums of money to corporations. Investing in business is very widespread. More than thirty million Americans own stock in businesses. The stockholders are part owners of the business and share in its profits through dividend increases and higher market value for their shares. Similarly, they are tied to company misfortunes and will be a part of the corresponding decline unless they have the foresight to sell out beforehand. The more cautious invest in bonds, which are loans to corporations. A bondholder is merely a creditor and has no voice in running the company. A fixed rate of interest is paid and this payment has priority over all other company obligations, stockholders included. The bondholder also has first chance at any assets remaining, in the event of company dissolution. In short, a stockholder takes more risk but the rewards could be greater, while the bondholder chooses security above possible financial gain.

During the early part of this century, unfair tactics were practiced by unscrupulous dealers in the stock market. For example, a small group of men would agree to buy large amounts of stock in a company to force the price up. They would start rumors that the company was going to become very prosperous. This would set off a buying wave as other investors climbed aboard the bandwagon. When the price was high enough, the original investors would sell their stock at a great profit. These substantially large sales would trigger a price decline. Unsuspecting citizens who had bought in at unrealistically high prices now would find themselves holding securities worth much less than the original purchase price. To eliminate such unscrupulous practices, Congress set up the Securities and Exchange Commission in 1934. The SEC regulates stock exchanges by licensing and supervising them. It also investigates price manipulation of the type just described.

Another financial need satisfied by the national government in this century was in banking. There was a time in this country when some banks were merely "fly-by-night" businesses. They accepted money from their depositors, and invested it in loans to companies and persons without making sure that these borrowers were good credit risks. When depositors lost confidence in the bank and tried to draw their money out, a "run on the bank" resulted. This often meant disaster for the bank and for those depositors who were not among the first to withdraw their funds.

To remedy this and other ills, banking laws were passed. In 1913, the Federal Reserve Board was set up to give some central control to banking. The country now is divided into twelve districts, and banks may affiliate with the Federal Reserve branch in their district. The Federal Reserve system also has the power to expand the amount of money in circulation to enable banks throughout the country to meet their changing business needs. Another beneficial measure was the creation of the Federal Deposit Insurance Corporation (FDIC) in 1933. It insures the savings accounts of individual depositors against failure or fraud. Examiners of the FDIC appear at irregular intervals at a member bank and immediately begin to check its money supply and its loans and mortgages, to make sure that it is being run according to good banking standards.

The American people are among the hardest working people in the world and need this kind of protection. In 1978, over ninety-two million of them were employed in the civilian labor force, which does not include members of the armed forces. They are not just a numerous work force; they are very productive and ingenious workers. The security of these workers and their families in their persons and their homes is the major function of government on all levels.

GOVERNMENT AND AGRICULTURE

Farmers, because they feed us all, occupy a place of special importance among the workers of the nation. Their position, however, has changed greatly during the course of our history. At one time, about ninety-four out of every one hundred persons were employed in farming. Today the number has fallen to four out of one hundred. Yet in spite of the decreasing numbers of farmers, the food production of the United States continues to increase to meet the needs of the population. In fact, the major problem facing the American farmer in this century has been overproduction.

We often speak of the "Industrial Revolution" as having caused great changes in the world. This was true, but we cannot overlook the fact that an "Agricultural Revolution" which came before and continued during the Industrial Revolution was just as important. Indeed, it was only when machines and new agricultural techniques were applied to farming that farm labor could be released to work in the new factories of the industrial age. So great were the effects of scientific achievements on farming that during many years of the twentieth century an agricultural surplus was produced. Because so much food was available, food prices and farmers' incomes were low. Government programs were set up to help the farmer borrow money or learn better farming methods. But increased efficiency only made the problem worse.

Farmers began to look to the federal government for other forms of aid. They were in a position to do this because, although they were not numerous, farmers were spread out among states of relatively low population. This gave them great strength in the U.S. Senate, since that body is not based on population. During the 1920s and 1930s, when farm prices dropped very low, several federal programs were undertaken to aid the farmer. One of these was the Agricultural Marketing Act of 1929, which set aside half a billion dollars to lend to farmers, enabling them to keep their goods off the market until prices rose. The act worked poorly, so in 1933 the Agricultural Adjustment Act was passed, setting up a program of paying farmers to keep their goods off the market. Farmers were told to plow under their crops and to kill their livestock rather than to sell them at low prices. Millions of pigs, sheep, and other domestic animals were slaughtered and farmers sometimes destroyed as much as a third of their crops. The farmers were to be paid through a tax on the food processers, such as canners and packers. This tax was declared unconstitutional by the Supreme Court, however, in the case of *United States* v. *Butler*, since it was not a valid use by Congress of its taxing power.

A second agricultural act was passed in 1938 without the tax system of the first law. Under this act, the farmer was paid by the Department of Agriculture for not growing crops. Thus, farm production would be reduced and soil would be conserved. The crops which were produced would be sold at prices guaranteed by the government and farmers would have an income on a par with the incomes they had been getting before World War I.

The system of paying farmers to keep land out of production was fairly successful in reducing America's agricultural surplus. Lower production and the gift or sale of wheat and other crops overseas had brought the surplus under control. In fact, some agricultural experts were worried that it had gone too far. The cost of keeping farm prices up and land out of cultivation was high, and going higher. Total costs of the Agricultural Department rose from $8.3 billion in 1970 to $13.7 billion in 1977.

The system had other disadvantages. Money was not distributed among those farmers who most needed it, but rather went to aid those who often were fairly prosperous already. One farmer demonstrated this by purchasing an expensive auto and touring cities with signs on the car pointing out that the general taxpayer had paid for it. Another farmer in New Mexico rented several hundred acres of land from the state for less than $200, and then applied to the federal government for funds to keep the land out of cultivation. For his uncultivated rented land he received almost $5,000. There were cases of some farms receiving as much as $4 million in subsidies, and of others, far more numerous, receiving as little as $200. To overcome this difficulty partially, Congress in 1970 limited the amount of money any farmer could receive for not growing certain crops.

American farmers, however, are quite different from almost all other Americans in that, while they could probably do without the rest of us, the rest of us could not do without them. We tend to take for granted the ability of so few to feed so many. Fewer than four out of every one hundred Americans live on the farm, but they keep 2.7 million farms operating to feed their fellow citizens.

The federal government has been most successful in agriculture in such areas as conservation, electrification, guaranteeing mortgage loans for farmers, and supplying information on the latest scientific progress in farming. Conservation, in particular, has been a subject of keen interest for the national government as well as for the states and private groups.

CONSERVATION

When this country was first settled, its soil, forest, and wildlife reserves were untouched, as were its rivers and mineral resources. But during the last three and a half centuries, these resources have been depleted seriously. In some areas, our soil is exhausted, our forest lands are scarred, the great herds of animals have disappeared, our rivers are polluted, and our mineral resources are running out. In many cases, not much can be done. We cannot restore mineral resources which took millions of years to form, and we have little hope of bringing back the countless buffalo, elk, deer, and horses which once roamed the continent. We have upset the ecological balance of nature (*ecology* meaning "the study of living things in their total environment"). In other cases, if we act quickly, we can do something to restore the ecological balance.

Soil exhaustion and deforestation go hand in hand, since trees act as brakes to keep topsoil from blowing away or from being washed away by rain. Because wood plays such an im-

Paul Kirouac from Monkmeyer

Unfortunately, this stream in upstate New York is all too typical of America's waterways —even those in remote, rural places.

portant part in our lives, our timber lands are among our most valuable resources.

Theodore Roosevelt was the first President to recognize the importance of conserving our forest resources. More than one-third of the country is now set aside for that purpose. This forest land can satisfy our needs only if we use it carefully and replace cut timber with new trees. Both private and governmental groups are now doing this. The United States Forest Service administers almost one-fourth of our forests. Operating under the Department of the Interior, it fights fires, controls disease in trees, and studies the usefulness of trees in preventing floods. Closely allied with it is a Department of Agriculture agency, the Soil Conservation Service. Although the earth is vast and soil is plentiful, mankind actually lives off the top six inches, or topsoil. The remainder will not grow enough to sustain life. Topsoil has been wasted recklessly over the past three and two-thirds centuries.

Since the 1940s, Congress has passed numerous laws and has appropriated a great deal of money for soil conservation programs. These programs have been very effective in preserving the land we have left and in reclaiming some of that exhausted by wasteful farming. Great strides also have been made in solving water problems. Millions of acres, once thought too dry to grow crops, now are recording great gains in fertility through irrigation.

Water is a major problem the world over. Although particularly blessed by the existence of many vast water systems, the United States still is battling problems of flood and pollution control. Flood control became an important national interest about fifty years ago. The most important project in this area was the creation of the Tennessee Valley Authority (TVA) in 1933. A series of dams was built along the Tennessee River, keeping floods under control and harnessing the flow of water to provide hydroelectric power for the people of nearby states. Dams have been built in other states, but no program as comprehensive as the TVA has been introduced yet for our other river systems.

In the last decade, water pollution has become a major problem. A river should be a source of health for those it serves, but our rivers are becoming health hazards through the indiscriminate use of them to carry off industrial and sewage wastes. As a result of this dumping, the waters stagnate and cannot support fish or be used for irrigation or drinking purposes. To solve this problem, federal and state programs have been set up to examine ways of treating waste to prevent it from causing pollution. Stiff laws are being enforced against violators who fail to conform to standards of waste treatment. In this way, hopefully the rivers can be cleansed and returned to their former useful purposes.

But even if all our existing water resources can be restored, will they be enough to satisfy the needs of our growing population? Experts say "no"; something more must be done to provide for our water needs. A way must be found to extract salt from the ocean cheaply enough so that the fresh water produced can be made available to meet man's increasing needs. Since the 1950s, the federal government also has been in this business. Desalinization plants have been built throughout the country and now are producing desalted water for limited use.

The main problem in the desalinization program is the cost of producing the pure water. It is more expensive to secure fresh water from the ocean than to obtain it from ordinary sources. In the 1950s, desalted water cost more than ten times the price of fresh drinking water. It is much less costly now, but still is more so than fresh water. The Office of Water Research and Technology administers this program under the Interior Department.

To protect the environment by unifying the federal forces marshalled against pollution, the Nixon administration, in cooperation with Congress, created the Council on Environmental Quality in 1969. This EOP agency sees the entire picture of the environment in relation to the needs of Americans and reports to the President on progress and problems. Early in 1970, the President established the Environmental Protection Agency (EPA) to take care of the day-to-day needs of Americans as far as pollution is concerned. Cities which dumped poorly treated sewage into rivers, lakes, or the oceans were ordered to clean up or face federal penalties. Industries which polluted the water or air were forced to stop fouling the environment.

In a bipartisan and urgent manner, Republicans and Democrats have banded together to place curbs on pollution. Laws requiring autos to be relatively more pollution free have been passed, cleaner fuels are being developed as quickly as possible, and international cooperation to save the earth from the specter of stagnation has been urged.

Pollution is not the problem of the United States alone, of course, nor is it a problem confronting only countries with advanced standards of living. In the 1970s it has become popular to refer to Earth as a spaceship which must depend upon itself for its own support. Nothing can be wasted any more without causing damage to some other part of the system or danger to the entire spaceship and its riders.

Along with the fact that people are spoiling their environment by waste is the fact that even if they do use their resources in the most efficient and pollution-free manner possible, their numbers are so great that they may well run out of fuel, food, and even space in the next few generations or centuries. World population has grown amazingly in the last few decades and, although it is difficult to arrive at

Jean-Claude LeJeune

The skyline of Chicago, photographed from the littered shore of Lake Michigan.

accurate figures, the estimate is more than four billion persons. Food and fuel production must be improved to keep pace with this growth or the East will face famines of huge proportions and the West will face energy crises of equally serious dimensions. Governments throughout the world have begun working on these problems as well as on projects to foster family limitation.

In the long run, whatever positive contributions or mistakes the government makes will affect the country's working people to the greatest extent.

THE TECHNOLOGICAL REVOLUTION

The twentieth century has been the greatest century of change in world history. In fact, if a person lost contact with the world for ten years or so, he might find it difficult to see how the world he left was related to the world he returned to. This was not always so in the past, since conditions of travel, living, eating, and working were very similar from ancient times to the eighteenth century. Since that time, new sources of energy, new inventions, and new materials have revolutionized the world. The steam engine, electricity, motor vehicles, computers, aircraft flight, radio and television, space travel, synthetic materials, new drugs, new foods, and thousands of other developments have brought about undreamed-of changes.

Perhaps the entire revolution can be symbolized by the automobile. This invention—or development, since it consisted of so many different inventions—has changed most people the most. The motor vehicle employs more people, directly or indirectly, and uses more raw materials than any other industry in the country. It has been responsible for the creation of the sprawling suburbs, by allowing Americans to travel greater distances between home and work with less inconvenience and expense than any other form of transportation. Together with the bus and the truck, the automobile has placed the railroad in a crisis situation. For every five people who traveled by railroad in 1920, there was only one fifty years later. The automobile also has contributed to pollution and traffic problems. Suggestions have been made to ban the auto in some cities or parts of cities or to ration gasoline in order to conserve fuel and reduce pollution. The automobile has been responsible for far more deaths than all the wars of the country, with an average of 51,000 persons a year dying in motor vehicle accidents during the first seven years of the 1970s. However, the recent figures are better than previously, thanks to the national speed limit of fifty-five miles an hour imposed in 1973. In 1972, 56,000 persons died in auto accidents; by 1976, the figure was 46,000.

In spite of its drawbacks, the automobile is the preferred method of transportation for most Americans. It is possible, as the federal government is now encouraging, to develop standards for more efficient and less polluting engines and fuels. The automobile affords its owner far more independence than any other mode of transportation. It enables the citizen whose hours don't coincide with those of public transportation to move about freely, and it transports the aged and the infirm to hospitals rapidly and inexpensively. It is, therefore, a mixed blessing, a tool which can be used or abused, depending upon the good or poor sense of the person employing it.

The great technological changes of modern times revolutionized working conditions throughout the United States and the world. Machines made it possible for fewer and fewer workers to produce greater quantities of goods than ever before. The computer, which only began life in the 1950s, already has influenced man by its benefits, its expansion of human knowledge, and the problems it has caused. The American standard of living is the direct result of the economic system we live under, a system based upon the partnership of management and labor for the production of goods and services to satisfy needs.

THE LABOR MOVEMENT

The standard of living of American workers has not been always as satisfactory as it is for most today. There were times when conditions of work, salaries, and other factors made life very hard for the wage earner. Men worked incredibly long hours for low pay, while conditions for women and children were even worse. These conditions were due partly to the selfishness of early businessmen, but also to the inevitable economic difficulties associated with the changeover from an agricultural to an industrial society.

To overcome these difficulties, a twofold movement was begun. First, laborers in many industries began to organize into labor unions; and second, all levels of government were petitioned to request passage of laws correcting conditions of labor. At first, both these efforts were failures. But during the last third of the nineteenth century, at least some labor unionization was achieved.

In 1886, the American Federation of Labor was founded, consisting of about two dozen unions. The AFL was not a union, but rather a kind of union of unions. Its membership grew greatly during the next thirty years, so that by World War I it had over two million members. It declared that it would not become a political party and nominate its own candidates. Instead, it would follow the voting policy of rewarding its friends and punishing its enemies. Historically, the AFL and other unions have usually supported Democratic party candidates, but they have broken tradition and crossed over to Republican candidates if they felt that this was in their best interests.

The AFL was composed of unions made up of skilled

workers such as bookbinders, bricklayers, and electrical workers. But large numbers of unskilled workers remained outside, a situation which continued until the Congress of Industrial Organizations was founded. The CIO began as a committee of the AFL, but it became independent in 1938. In 1955, the two unions merged to become the AFL-CIO with a membership of about seventeen million.

These and smaller unions fought the battles of labor with every weapon at hand. To achieve their goals they went on strike, picketed, organized boycotts and, on occasion, resorted to violence. Businessmen fought back with lockouts (closing the doors of the company until the workers' needs forced them back to work), blacklists (sending the names of union workers to other businessmen so that they would not be hired), and their own brand of violence. In addition, businessmen had another weapon in the injunction, which is a court order forbidding a certain action. If a strike occurred, lawyers for businessmen would claim that this action restricted trade and therefore was illegal under the Sherman Anti-Trust Act, which forbade conspiracies in restraint of trade.

The Supreme Court accepted this argument and its acceptance, together with its decisions on the "sanctity of contract" and other principles, hurt the cause of labor. Here are two examples. In New York State, bakery workers labored for long hours in the early 1900s. To help them, the state legislature voted to limit their work to sixty hours a week. The Supreme Court said that the act interfered with the right of bakery owners and their employees to make free agreements, and was therefore unconstitutional. Similarly, when Congress legislated to forbid interstate shipment of products made by child labor, the Court ruled against it. In fact, two child labor laws were declared unconstitutional in 1918 and 1922.

In spite of these setbacks, however, changes were taking place. The Clayton Anti-Trust Act contained provisions which exempted labor unions from injunctions unless there was danger or damage to property, permitted striking and picketing, and declared that labor unions could not be considered as subject to the antitrust laws. Twenty years later, the Norris-LaGuardia Act of 1932 went even further in exempting labor unions from injunctions.

Jean-Claude LeJeune

United Farm Workers Association members and their supporters march through the streets of Chicago. They are asking people not to shop at a local supermarket chain because the markets buy lettuce from growers who refuse to hire union members.

The basic labor law in our country was yet to come, however. This was the National Labor Relations Act (sometimes called the Wagner Act) of 1935, which set up the NLRB (National Labor Relations Board) to supervise labor relations, review union qualification to represent workers, and prohibit unfair practices by businessmen. In addition, the famous Section 7a of the National Industrial Recovery Act guaranteed the worker's right to join a union and to bargain collectively with his or her employer.

The new system worked so well that labor unions grew remarkably strong. After World War II, it was estimated that more than twenty out of every one hundred people employed was a union member. Meanwhile, abuses had crept into the labor union movement and to correct these the Taft-Hartley Act was passed in 1947. This act prohibited labor unions from making contributions to political parties, eliminated collection of union dues by employers, forced labor leaders to take oaths

UPI

Ford Motor Company officials, left, and representatives of the United Auto Workers, right, face each other across the bargaining table. They are negotiating the workers' demands for wage increases and improved fringe benefits, such as health, insurance, and retirement plans.

swearing that they were not Communists, and provided for two other vital items—the "union shop" and the "cooling-off period." Let us examine these last two provisions more closely.

After passage of the Wagner Act, many labor unions operated in what were called "closed shops"; that is, shops (businesses) where only union members could be employed. To get a job, then, a person had to be a member of a union even before he was hired. The Taft-Hartley Act replaced the closed shop with the "union shop," in which the company could hire nonunion employees but these new employees would have to join the union within thirty days. Another important part of the 1947 act was Section 14b, which said that state legislatures had the right to permit the "open shop"; that is, one where a person may or may not join a union, depending on his or her views. Under Section 14b, half the states passed what were called "right to work" laws providing for the "open shop," in which union and nonunion members worked side by side.

Labor leaders disapproved of these laws, since they felt the labor union movement could grow only if workers were forced to join unions through the "union shop" plan. As a result, some state legislatures repealed their "right to work" laws, but efforts by national leaders—such as President Lyndon Johnson—to repeal that entire section of the Taft-Hartley Act have failed.

A second important aspect of the law was the "cooling-off period." When a union went on strike, the President could ask for a legal injunction which would suspend the strike for eighty days during which labor and management would, with the help of federal mediators, negotiate to end the strike. The union members would vote on the matter during the eighty-day period and, if nothing was settled, the strike would continue. The President was to use this power only in strikes which he thought would endanger the safety of the nation, and his power was limited to those eighty days. But he also could ask Congress for other legislation if it seemed necessary. President Carter invoked the cooling-off feature to bring a record-breaking coal strike of 1978 to a halt, successfully placing pressure on labor and management for a quick settlement.

During the late 1940s and the 1950s, public attention remained sharply focused on the labor union movement. Some union leaders seemed to be acting more for their own interests than for the interests of their members. Union funds occasionally were unaccounted for. Union leaders sometimes enjoyed huge salaries and, ironically, treated the laborer much the same as some of the businessmen of the nineteenth century had, denying the laborer the right to speak and to vote freely in labor matters.

To overcome this threat, which Robert F. Kennedy called "the enemy within," Congress passed the Landrum-Griffin Act of 1959. This act provided for secret elections in unions, permitted free speech and freedom of assembly to union members, granted equal rights to debate and, in general, tried to bring the governing processes of labor unions more in line with the procedures Americans use in electing their political leaders. It also gave union members more control over their dues and other payments to their unions.

Most American workers do not belong to unions, fewer than one out of every five persons employed being a member. Unions usually have appealed to "blue-collar" workers engaged in crafts, construction work, manufacturing, and so on.

"White-collar" workers, such as secretaries and salespersons, generally have been less attracted to unions.

During the 1960s, minority groups complained that they were not represented fairly in unions. By the 1970s, government, union, and industry plans to provide for more black membership in unions were introduced, resulting in improved positions for them and other minorities. They have benefited by enjoying a greater share in the fruits of union membership, although minorities still lag behind whites in wage-earning. This is partly due to seniority, an important factor in job retention and job placement. Job seniority protects more established workers but jeopardizes those who have just come on to a job. "Last hired, first fired" is the motto expressing it. In recent years, the Supreme Court has upheld seniority as a principle, even when it has had the effect of forcing companies to let minority workers go in cutbacks.

The labor movement in America almost always has aimed only at improvement of salaries and working conditions. It has not, as in so many countries, tried to make radical changes in government and society. Thus, the labor union movement believes in America and in its free enterprise system. It seeks mainly to secure for its followers a larger share of the profits of this free enterprise system.

This attitude is reflected generally among businessmen, farmers, and other workers not associated with unions. There is a combination of respect for everyone else mixed with a desire to make fair gains for one's own group. Not every person feels or acts this way at all times, of course. There are many who think only of their own selfish ends. But there are more fair-minded people than not, people who believe that fruitful cooperation is better than cut-throat competition.

One of the greatest enemies of all Americans, whether wage earners, businessmen, retired persons, or the unemployed, may be summed up in the word "inflation." Inflation in the form of rapidly rising prices and interest rates causes workers in some industries to demand higher wages. If these raises are secured, then workers in other industries demand similar increases. To pay for these, manufacturers and others raise their prices, which then wipes out some of the wage gain. Workers then begin anew to demand higher wages, and a

Jean-Claude LeJeune

Although inflation hurts everybody, those who suffer most are retired persons living on pensions or savings. Prices go up and up, but their incomes remain the same.

wage-price spiral is started. For several decades, such a wage-price spiral has existed in the United States.

To combat this inflationary cycle, which bites deeply into the earnings and pensions of everyone, the federal government has tried many solutions. Among the methods used have been efforts to cut federal spending, a wage and price freeze, and presidential requests to unions and businesses to hold the line on wage demands and price increases. This last method, known as "jawboning," has been the one preferred by most Presidents. And it may have had some success, particularly when the American inflation rate is compared with that of other nations. The inflation rate is measured by the Consumer Price Index, or CPI, which sets one year as a base of 100 and compares prices in later years against that base. Thus, using 1967 as the base of 100, let's say that a certain item cost $1.00 in that year. Ten years later, the CPI in the United States was 170, meaning that in 1976 it would cost $1.70 to buy the item that sold for $1.00 in 1967. Actually, a ten-year Consumer Price Index of 170 is not bad, since most major nations had higher rates of inflation as

Consumer Price Index for selected items, 1967–1977
(using 1967 as base of 100)

Year	Food	Rent	Wearing apparel (cost + upkeep)	Transportation	Medical care	Entertainment	All items	Purchasing power of consumer dollar
1967	100.0	100.0	100.0	100.0	100.0	100.0	100.0	1.000
1968	103.6	102.4	105.4	103.2	106.1	104.7	104.2	0.960
1969	108.9	105.7	111.5	107.2	113.4	108.7	109.8	0.911
1970	114.9	110.1	116.1	112.7	120.6	113.4	116.3	0.860
1971	118.4	115.2	119.8	118.6	128.4	119.3	121.3	0.824
1972	123.5	119.2	122.3	119.9	132.5	122.8	125.3	0.798
1973	141.4	124.3	126.8	123.8	137.7	125.9	133.1	0.752
1974	161.7	130.6	136.2	137.7	150.5	133.8	147.7	0.678
1975	175.4	137.3	142.3	150.6	168.6	144.4	161.2	0.621
1976	180.8	144.7	147.6	165.5	184.7	151.2	170.5	0.587
1977	192.2	153.5	154.2	177.2	202.4	157.9	181.5	0.551

Source: Bureau of Labor Statistics, U.S. Department of Labor.

measured by the Index. In Great Britain, for example, it took $2.52 to buy in 1976 what sold for $1.00 in 1967.

The federal government of the 1980s has a role which the nation's founders probably did not intend it to have, that of acting as umpire between the many different economic groups which make up our country. Capital and labor, the farmer and the railroad, corporations and state governments, banks and their depositors, stock exchanges and stockholders—all have experienced federal intervention in the past one hundred years. In other words, the federal government has tried to act as an honest arbitrator between all the conflicting interest groups in the nation. Trying to balance these different interests is a difficult task. If, for example, the right to strike were limited severely, laborers might suffer from business tyranny; but if striking were permitted to become lawless and unlimited, business would be ruined. Thus, the needs of all concerned must be considered. No one boasts that the federal government, in its role as umpire, is doing the best job that could be done. But in view of the difficulty of the task, it is doing an amazingly efficient job.

AFTER-CHAPTER REVIEW

REVIEW QUESTIONS

1. Define the following names, terms, or ideas.

qualitative immigration restriction
national origins quota system
Federal Reserve System
Landrum-Griffin Act "original package" doctrine
FDIC
EPA
Council on Environmental Quality
"union shop"
"open shop"
"jawboning"
"rule of reason"
SEC
Taft-Hartley Act
contract clause
Clayton Anti-Trust Act
TVA
AFL-CIO
NLRB
"closed shop"
INS
CPI

2. Vocabulary building.

trust
stock
desalinization
blacklist
monopoly
bond
disparity
boycott
pooling
pollution
lockout
ecology
dissolution

3. Cases.

Dartmouth College case
United States v. *Butler*

4. Review of the text.

a. Describe federal regulation of immigration.
b. What was the early position of the federal courts toward government regulation of business? How did this change?
c. Outline government regulation of stock exchanges and banks.
d. Review the farm problem and federal attempts to solve it.
e. Outline the development of organized labor in the United States. What were its problems and how did it solve them?
f. Review the major pieces of labor legislation approved by the federal government.

DISCUSSION AND PROJECTS

1. Questions for discussion.

a. Discuss the role of the federal government in the economic life of the nation today.
b. Discuss the conservation problem in America and the ways to solve it. Why is it so vital that our timber, water, and soil resources be carefully used?
c. Discuss trade unionism. Should every wage earner in America be a member of a union? Explain your answer.
d. Which of the following do you approve of: open, closed, or union shop? Explain your reasons for the choice.

2. Debate topics.
   a. Resolved: Let us open the door to millions of immigrants again.
   b. Resolved: The labor movement has grown too powerful in America.
3. Opinion poll.

   Should the federal government continue to subsidize the farmer?

BIBLIOGRAPHY

Boggess, Louise. *Journey to Citizenship.* New York: Funk & Wagnalls, 1967.

Canby, Thomas Y., and Raymer, Steve. "Can the World Feed Its People?" *National Geographic,* July 1975.

"A Clean America: Will People Pay the Price?" *U.S. News & World Report,* 7 February 1977.

"Controversy over the Proposed 'Labor Reform Act,'" *The Congressional Digest,* January 1978.

"A Growing Rush to Solar Energy," *U.S. News & World Report,* 4 April 1977.

Laird, Melvin P. "The Energy Crisis: Made in USA," *Reader's Digest,* September 1977.

Lavine, Sigmund A., and Casey, Mart. *Water Since the World Began.* New York: Dodd, Mead, 1965.

Midgley, Elizabeth. "Immigrants: Whose Huddled Masses?" *Atlantic Monthly,* April 1978.

"Telephone Monopoly: Good or Bad?" *U.S. News & World Report,* 22 November 1976.

"What to Do about Energy Crisis—Advice from Five Experts," *U.S. News & World Report,* 18 April 1977.

White, Peter T. "This Land of Ours—How Are We Using It?" *National Geographic,* July 1976.

"The World Energy Crisis," *Current History,* March 1978.

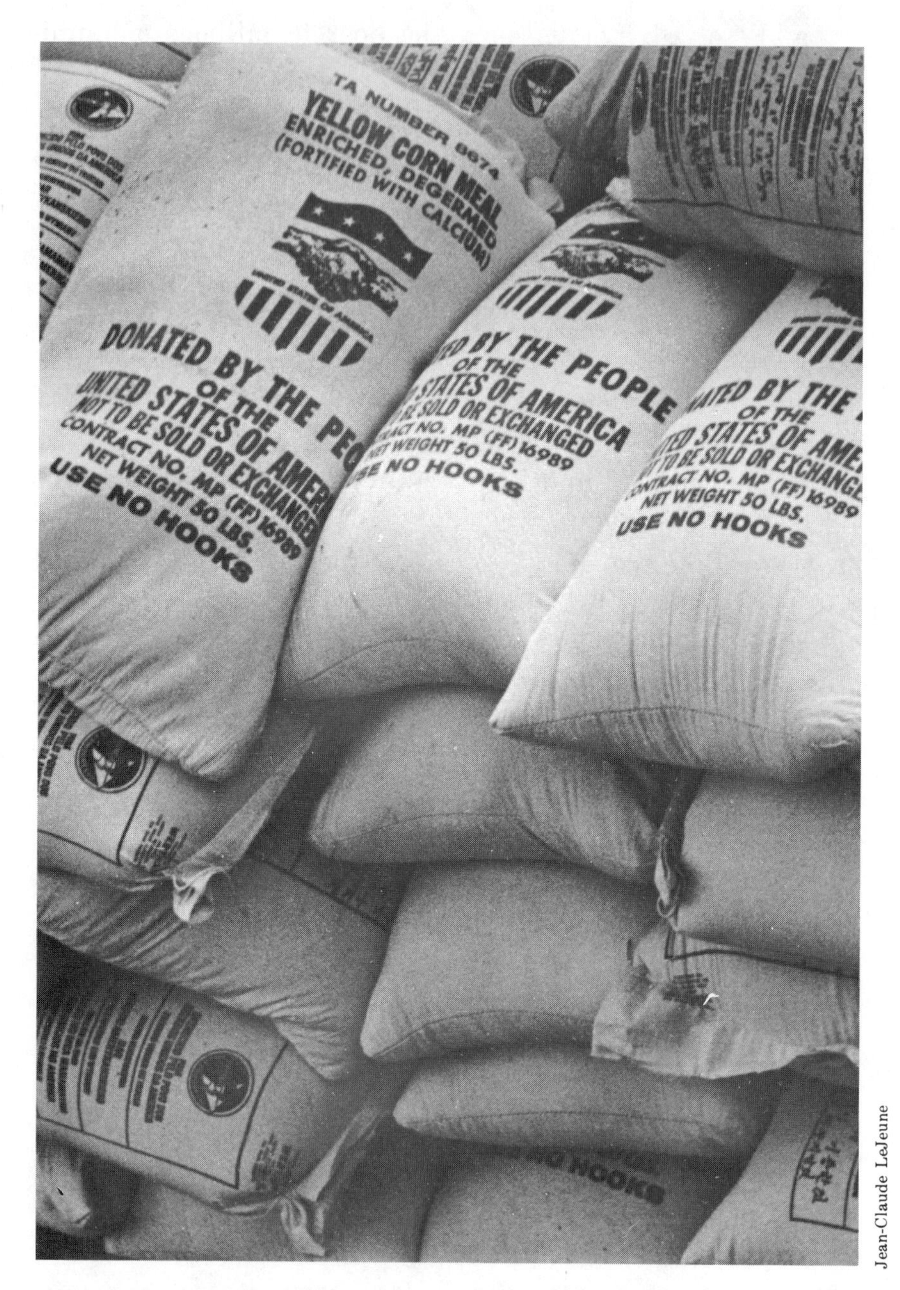

Jean-Claude LeJeune

Fifty-pound sacks of American corn meal, piled up at the docks and waiting for shipment to hungry people somewhere in the world.

15

The United States and the World

During the first hundred years of our nation's existence, its sons and daughters blazed their way across the wide continent to the Pacific, organizing the wilderness into the Federal Union. No frontier was too remote, no region too dangerous to halt the inevitable expansion of the first century. The expansion continued during the second century, but in a different way. The Pacific was crossed and outposts were manned from Hawaii to Micronesia and from the Philippines to South Korea. Across the Atlantic, Americans guarded a partitioned Berlin, patrolled the Mediterranean, and poured their lives and knowledge into Europe, Africa, and the Near East.

Pick up any newspaper and scan the columns. America is involved in nearly every corner of the earth, sometimes for traditional political and economic reasons, other times for purely humanitarian reasons. Is there famine in Bangladesh? American food is on the way. An earthquake in Nicaragua? Medical facilities are airlifted to Managua. Floods in Holland? American troops are rushed to the dikes. Everywhere we turn we see signs that America has become what Jefferson said it should be—an Empire for Liberty. Americans now feel responsible for the health and safety of their fellow men all over the globe. This is a wonderful feeling—and a grave responsibility. For the first time in the history of the world, a nation powerful enough to control it by force is anxious to free it from poverty, disease, and fear.

None of the other great empires of the world—Rome, Persia, France, Britain, Russia—have had this spirit. It is unique to us. What other empire in all the world has ever been armed as we have been and has not used these arms? None. What other empire in the world has ever possessed the means to seize the wealth of the world and has not? None. Far from enriching ourselves, we have offered to the rest of the world some $230 billion worth of our labor and goods since the end of World War II. This is a record of service to mankind which no other nation can match.

In this chapter, the United States in its relation to the world will be considered. We will study who makes our foreign policy, how it is carried out, and what it is.

FOREIGN POLICY MAKERS

The President has the final responsibility for American foreign relations. In carrying out his task, however, he has considerable help. The Department of State is one of the prime agencies for this, since it is responsible for the day-by-day conduct of relations with other nations. The Secretary of State, therefore, is a key man in the President's Cabinet. Under the direction of such Secretaries as Dean Acheson and George Marshall (under President Truman), John Foster Dulles (under President Eisenhower), Henry Kissinger (under Presidents Nixon and Ford), and Cyrus Vance (under President Carter), the foreign policies of the United States have evolved in the past thirty years.

At the State Department, these men have been assisted by undersecretaries and deputy undersecretaries concerned with political or economic matters, and with assistant secretaries for African, Latin American, European and other areas. They are kept informed by our representatives abroad, and they in turn pass the information on to their chiefs. Eventually, if the President's attention to a matter is needed, the information goes to him.

Other parts of the executive branch also are vitally concerned with foreign affairs. The Commerce, Treasury, and Agriculture Departments must be aware of international conditions which will affect their areas of interest. Many independent agencies (the Tariff Commission, for example) are also concerned.

Let us use as an example two actual transactions which

took place during the administrations of Presidents Kennedy and Nixon concerning the sale of American wheat to Russia. The decisions to allow these sales had enormous effects upon many agencies of government:

1. They showed the Russians that we recognized their need for food and that we would not let our disagreements stand in the way of supplying them—this part concerned the President and the State Department;
2. Such sales, which amounted to hundreds of millions of dollars, helped our own economy—here the Treasury and Commerce Departments entered the picture;
3. They reduced our own surplus of wheat and aided our farm program—which affected the Department of Agriculture.

These are only a few of the agencies which were concerned with the matter. Many others were kept very busy too, including those dealing with public relations, because trading with Russia was not very popular with a large part of the American people.

We now come right to "the boss," the American people, who play a vital though indirect role in the conduct of foreign affairs. Every two years they elect an entirely new House of Representatives and one-third of the Senate, and the persons they select for these positions usually reflect their views on foreign policy. They also express themselves by letters and telegrams to members of Congress, Cabinet officials, and the President; by letters to the editors of newspapers; by picketing when it seems necessary; and by demonstrating in large numbers when moved to more direct action. Our elected leaders are very sensitive to public opinion, and prove it by the faith they place in public opinion polls, which they sometimes pay for out of their own pockets.

Congress's role in foreign affairs is as important as that of the President, as we saw earlier. Congress controls the purse-strings, and the Senate's power over treaties and appointments is final. Thus, a look at our machinery for dealing with the rest of the world reveals that no one person or agency or branch is responsible solely for it. Like the other aspects of our national life, this is a shared function and is subject to checks and balances.

Two examples, one from the administration of President Wilson and the other from that of President Roosevelt, will illustrate this sharing process. Most treaties in our history have been approved, although usually in the form that the Senate wants and not exactly as the President desires. After World War I, President Wilson went to Paris to help draft the treaties ending the state of war with Germany and its allies. The Treaty of Versailles of 1919, which ended the war with Germany, was the subject of bitter debate in the Senate and throughout the country.

The question of Senate ratification was made difficult by the fact that President Wilson was a Democrat and the Senate was under Republican control. A minority of both parties in the Senate opposed the treaty because it required us to join the League of Nations. A majority of both parties favored this, but wanted to make certain that congressional powers were not weakened by our membership in the league. They attached several amendments to the treaty which guarded the right of Congress to declare war. These amendments proved unacceptable to the President, who urged Democratic Senators to vote against ratification, thus defeating the treaty. The chairman of the Senate Foreign Relations Committee, Senator Henry Cabot Lodge, did not get along personally with the President and this certainly did not improve matters.

Twenty-five years later, when the question of American membership in the United Nations arose, President Roosevelt used Wilson's methods as an example of what to avoid. He recognized the need for bipartisan support for his policies and took Republican leaders into his confidence. By the time the question came to Congress, Roosevelt had died and President Truman continued his policy. American entrance into the world organization was approved, but American troops could not be called upon by the UN without the approval of Congress and the President.

America's entrance into the UN marked a turning point in its history. The United States entered into full permanent partnership with other nations in hopes of securing a free and peaceful world. Using the year 1945 as a turning point, let us review America's foreign relations from two aspects, from independence to 1945, and since 1945.

AMERICAN FOREIGN POLICY TO 1945

During the Revolutionary War, the United States entered into an alliance with France which was very useful, since it guaranteed French help in the war against Great Britain. But it was to be a perpetual alliance, joining us to France in a mutual defense pact. During President Washington's eight years in office, it became obvious that this kind of alliance was damaging to American interests. When Washington left office, he pleaded with his fellow citizens to avoid all permanent alliances but to be ready to enter into temporary agreements when they were necessary. Washington's advice was followed for a century and a half.

The French alliance was dissolved in 1800 and thereafter the country played a lone role in world affairs. Sometimes this long period in our history has been called "isolationist," but that term is misleading. We did not divorce ourselves from world affairs; we just did not enter into perpetual alliances which would hamper our freedom of choice.

In the 1820s, fearing that a European alliance was planning to recover Spain's Latin American colonies, President Monroe issued the Monroe Doctrine, warning Europe that the United States would not tolerate European efforts to reestablish colonial governments in the New World. Britain was sympathetic to this view and a treaty had even been suggested in which both countries would join in protecting the new nations of Latin America. The United States acted independently, however.

During this period of our history, Americans watched events in Europe closely and cheered efforts to overthrow tyrannical governments. But we did nothing to undermine existing governments. When disputes arose, they were settled amicably. In fact, American foreign relations in the nineteenth century include several important "firsts":

1. The United States and Britain agreed to the principle of an unfortified border between the United States and

Canada, this being the longest national boundary on which such a condition exists.

2. The United States and Britain used arbitration successfully for the settlement of some of their disputes, thus becoming the first great nations in modern times to agree to let an impartial group of "umpires" settle their problems.

In addition to this, other efforts were made during and after the nineteenth century which illustrate American interest in world affairs:

1. All through this era, Americans had great interest in fostering friendship in the Western Hemisphere. We took part in Pan American movements in the 1880s and even began to depart from Washington's advice about permanent alliances by urging a permanent union to improve trade and cultural exchanges.
2. When an international conference was called at The Hague in Holland, our representatives attended and helped to establish the Permanent Court of International Arbitration. A few years later, President Theodore Roosevelt suggested that another conference be held at the Hague. It was held in 1907 and international problems were discussed.
3. After Wilson's unsuccessful efforts to secure American membership in the League of Nations, the United States still was concerned with peace and international friendship. A disarmament conference was held in Washington in the 1920s and brought about a limited "naval holiday," which meant that the nations involved would agree to limit their navies to prescribed sizes.
4. In 1928, a treaty called the Kellogg-Briand Pact was drawn up, outlawing war as part of any nation's policy.

Were there no dark spots upon America's dealings with other nations? All nations, like all human beings, have their imperfections. American participation in the Mexican War of the 1840s and the Spanish-American War of 1898 has been regarded as unnecessary and even aggressive. And American methods used in aiding Panama in its rebellion against Colombia in order to clear the way for acquiring the Canal Zone to build the isthmian canal are similarly regarded. Also, in the years between 1898 and the 1920s, many Americans came to regard the Caribbean Sea as an American lake. This attitude was used to justify our intervention in the affairs of Central American and Caribbean nations on many occasions.

Shortly before World War II began, American policy toward permanent alliances slowly changed. Several conferences held with the nations of Latin America produced mutual defense promises. The most important of these, the 1938 Declaration of Lima, pledged the nations of the Western Hemisphere to consider joint action for defense, if necessary.

When World War II broke out, the United States became a full-fledged ally of dozens of nations fighting against German and Japanese aggression. During the war, President Roosevelt made much use of the presidential power known as the "executive agreement" power. In the past, such power usually had covered fairly unimportant matters, but it now was transformed into use for vital dealings with other nations.

Under this authority, President Roosevelt exchanged fifty American warships for some British bases even before we had entered the war. He also embargoed (forbade) trade in strategic goods with Japan, sent American troops to Iceland, and ordered the United States Navy to fire on German submarines on sight. This was done before war was declared, partly under the "executive agreement" power and partly under the commander-in-chief power.

This policy was criticized as an attempt to "get around" the war powers of Congress, and the President was accused of trying to bring the nation into the war. His defenders declared that President Roosevelt had not exceeded his powers, since President McKinley, President John Adams, and many other chief executives had undertaken military or naval action without specific permission from Congress on the basis of their responsibilities as commander-in-chief of the American armed services.

When war was declared in December, 1941, America made a giant step into world politics, a step from which it has not retreated since. Many agreements were made with our wartime allies, mostly on the "executive agreement" basis. The most famous of these were the agreements made at the Yalta Conference in 1945. President Roosevelt, Prime Minister

Churchill of Great Britain, and Joseph Stalin of the Soviet Union met in the Russian town of Yalta on the Black Sea. Here, many decisions were made which shaped the future course of world history. Stalin was promised grants of land in China and from the Japanese in return for Russia's entrance into the war against Japan. Other decisions were made which later were used by Stalin to secure control of part of Eastern Europe for his Russian empire. The Yalta agreements were condemned severely as an abuse of presidential power because they gave so many advantages to the Soviet Union.

THE UNITED NATIONS

Even before the end of the war, the United States and its allies had been calling themselves the United Nations. In early 1945, before the surrender of Germany or Japan, a group of delegates met in San Francisco to draft the UN charter. This brought the world peace organization into existence in October, 1945.

The UN is made up of six major branches, each of which has special functions:

1. The Secretariat is headed by a secretary-general elected by all members and charged with the administrative duties of the UN.
2. The General Assembly is a kind of world legislature in which each nation has one vote. At first there were 50 members, but by 1978 membership had reached 149. The General Assembly is not a powerful organization constitutionally but, because it is the debate forum for nations of the world, its recommendations have considerable influence.
3. The Security Council consists of fifteen members, five of which are permanent (Great Britain, the United States, the Soviet Union, France, and China). The other ten members are chosen by the General Assembly for two-year terms. The Security Council has the power to call for the use of force in order to ward off a threat to peace. This has been done on several occasions, the most important being in 1950 in South Korea.
4. The International Court of Justice grew out of the conferences held at The Hague which we have already men-

tioned. It has fifteen judges and decides on international disputes submitted to it by interested and directly concerned nations.

5. The Trusteeship Council is an agency set up to administer areas of the world where the people have not become self-governing. Such areas are called "trust territories" and have been administered by such nations as France, Italy, Great Britain, Australia, Belgium, and the United States. Many nations have come into being out of the trust territory system; for example, Ghana, Somalia, Togo, Cameroon, Burundi, Rwanda, and Papau New Guinea. The United States is the only country still administering a trust territory.
6. The Economic and Social Council, also known as ESOSOC, is the agency dealing with the problems of hunger, disease, refugees, drug traffic, labor conditions, and other areas of human misery. Through its various departments, living conditions have improved greatly in many areas of the undeveloped world. There are many specialized agencies attached to the UN or otherwise affiliated with it which do a great deal of work for the social, economic, educational, medical, nutritional, and other needs of the world's peoples. There is the FAO, Food and Agricultural Organization of the United Nations; WHO, World Health Organization; and UNESCO, United Nations Educational, Scientific and Cultural Organization.

Much beneficial work has been done by the UN in its short life. It has interceded in disputes between nations such as India and Pakistan, Israel and the Arab world, Russia and Hungary, and Russia and Turkey. Peace-keeping forces have been used to reduce international tensions, particularly in the Mediterranean and in the Middle East. UN members contributed blue-helmeted young men to stand between Israelis and Palestinian guerrillas in Lebanon in 1978 and to prevent further outbreaks of hostilities. Sometimes the UN has succeeded in maintaining peace, sometimes not. But failure does not take away from the generosity of the effort.

It is in other areas besides disputes between nations that the UN, through its specialized agencies, has been most effective. Millions of refugees have been fed and sheltered and countless millions of children have been cared for, inoculated,

United Nations Photo

The General Assembly, meeting in regular session in the United Nations Building in New York.

clothed, and educated through UN efforts. Above all, nations have learned to cooperate and communicate for mutual goals to a greater extent because of the existence of a permanent body which has allowed them to associate freely and frequently.

Since the foundation of the UN, the United States has contributed generously for all its activities. For 1977, the American figure was slightly under $100 million, or twenty-five percent of the UN's total budget. The UN's budget of approximately $400 million is large, of course, but compared to the hundreds of billions spent by the world's nations on arms, naval vessels, and missiles, it is an insignificant sum.

FOREIGN AID

Most American assistance to the rest of the world has not been funneled through the UN. Much aid has been given directly to nations in need since the end of World War II. During the years after the war, Americans took a hard look at the misery caused by the war and by the generally low standards of living throughout the world. A proposal to solve these problems was made by Secretary of State George C. Marshall in 1947.

The Marshall Plan, as it was called, was a suggestion for assisting all war-torn nations (even Communist-dominated ones) to get back on their economic feet. The United States would provide grants or loans to any nation applying for such aid. The Communist countries rejected the idea, but sixteen other countries accepted it. Since that time, the idea has been expanded to cover almost any nation in need.

The plan was carried out under a number of different names and by many different programs created by acts of Congress. The popular name for this program has been simply "foreign aid," although the more accurate name for it in 1948 was ECA or Economic Cooperation Administration. There were several changes between then and 1961 when the name AID (Agency for International Development) came to be applied. These agencies have dispensed tens of billions of dollars during the course of their work to scores of nations and organizations all over the world. From 1946 to 1977, counting all economic aid, military assistance, and loans, the United States provided $230 billion to the world's nations. Among the biggest beneficiaries of this assistance were India ($9.5 billion), South Korea ($12.6 billion), South Vietnam ($23.4 billion), France ($8.4 billion), and Great Britain ($8.7 billion).[1] There were also grants or loans to such nations as Burundi, Mali, Chad, Nepal, Dahomey, and to dozens of others whose names are unfamiliar to us still.

The United States also has assisted other nations through easy trade policies. The Trade Development and Assistance Act of 1954, for instance, provided for the sale of American surplus agricultural products to underdeveloped nations. The United States paid the cost of transportation and sold the food at very low prices. The money received by the United States

---

1. *Congressional Record*, 5 August 1977, pp. S13840-41.

was left in the underdeveloped country and used for further aid to that country.

Foreign-aid programs have not been universally popular in the United States (or in other countries, for that matter). The whole point of the programs has been to help other countries help themselves. Critics have pointed out, however, that in some cases where the United States has given aid, the citizens of those countries have been paying lower taxes to their governments than have Americans on comparable salaries. On a few occasions, members of Congress have tried to terminate foreign-aid programs entirely, but have lacked sufficient votes to do so. Still, Congress has invariably reduced the amount of money requested by the President year after year. Sometimes, the amount requested has been cut by as much as twenty percent.

Aside from the assistance American aid has given to the needy of the world, the most important feature of the work has been the lesson in sharing which it taught to all peoples. Following the American example, West Germany, France, Sweden, Israel, Britain, Taiwan, Japan, and many other nations have undertaken their own versions of foreign-aid programs, and have relieved the United States of some of its burden.

The aid distributed between 1946 and 1977 breaks down into the ratio of sixty percent economic and forty percent military assistance. This last form of aid was made necessary by a condition which can be summed up in two words: "cold war."

MILITARY ALLIANCES

When World War II ended, Americans hoped that peace was secured at least for their generation. This was not to be. Joseph Stalin, dictator of the Soviet Union, went back on his promises to respect the independence of Russia's neighbors and soon began to annex one state after another to his greedy empire. Albania, Poland, Hungary, Rumania, Bulgaria, Czechoslovakia, and Yugoslavia fell to Communist rule, always with the help of Russian troops.

Promises made during and after the war were ignored by Stalin. One of these concerned Berlin, which was to be divided

Flip Schulke from Black Star

American and East German soldiers observe each other across the Berlin Wall. The Communists built the wall dividing the city in November, 1961, in order to stop the flow of refugees into the free western sector.

into four sectors administered by Britain, France, Russia, and the United States. Berlin was situated deep in the Russian zone of Germany and, to force the Western nations out of the city, Stalin ordered all roads and canals to be sealed off. The "Berlin Blockade," as this was called, lasted for almost a year (1948–1949). Instead of admitting defeat, the Western nations flew food and other supplies into the city in a magnificent airlift which demonstrated their willingness to oppose Stalin's faithless conduct.

Communist aggression did even more. It forced the free world to take a look at itself to see how well prepared it was to meet the threat. By the creation of NATO, the North Atlantic Treaty Organization, in 1949, a dozen nations tied themselves to each other by a binding pledge which declared that "an armed attack on one or more of the Parties is deemed to include an armed attack on the territory of any of the Parties in Europe or North America."

Within the next few years, NATO increased in size to fifteen nations. They were the United States, Great Britain, France, Belgium, Canada, Denmark, Luxembourg, Norway,

Portugal, Iceland, Greece, Turkey, Italy, the Netherlands, and West Germany.[2]

Now, the free nations of Europe and North America were united in their determination to prevent further Communist aggression. Since they were not actually shooting at each other, the antagonists were said to be fighting a "cold war." The two sides developed their methods of dealing with each other.

The West conceived a plan known as "containment," by which the free nations would ring the Communist world with allies or at least neutral ("nonaligned") powers, promising that any attack upon these could lead to armed conflict. American forces were distributed all over the world. By the end of the 1970s, there were 490,000 American military personnel serving outside the country, the largest numbers being in the Federal Republic of (West) Germany, Japan and Okinawa, South Korea, Great Britain, and the Philippines. These service personnel, along with millions of allied soldiers, showed the Communist nations that any aggression would be costly.

The Communist plan was designed to subvert neighboring states in order to win them over to the Communist camp. Using civil war, guerrilla warfare, propaganda, and economic and military assistance, Russians and other Communists chipped away at the containment efforts of the free nations. Through a civil war fought bitterly for years, the Republic of China fell to the Communists in late 1949, and in the following year North Korea's Communist army invaded South Korea. When this occurred, President Truman replied by sending troops to South Korea and won UN approval for his course of action. Aggression in Korea did not pay either for the North Koreans or for the Communist Chinese, who entered the war when it became apparent that Allied forces might capture North Korea. Elsewhere in Asia, Communists attempted to take over the vast island nation of Indonesia, but the people rose up and, led by anti-Communists, overthrew their pro-Communist leaders and adopted a free choice of government.

The most serious confrontation in the postwar world between Communism and anti-Communism occurred in Indo-

2. It should be noted that France disassociated itself from NATO in 1967, although it still remains a member of the Western bloc.

china. Communists and anti-imperialists had fought to free Indochina from French control for years, finally achieving their goal in 1954. Indochina then was partitioned into four countries: North Vietnam, South Vietnam, Laos, and Cambodia. North Vietnam was under Communist control and, using the argument that it was trying to establish one nation, carried on a long war of infiltration, terrorism, and eventually outright invasion against South Vietnam. President Eisenhower sent military aid and advisers to the South, and this was followed by President Kennedy's decision to send U.S. combat troops there. As the war escalated, President Johnson ordered more American troops into the Southeast Asian theater, their numbers finally exceeding 540,000. President Nixon made a number of moves in this area, withdrawing almost all American troops in his first four years of office, but during the same period invading Cambodia and aiding invasions of Laos by South Vietnamese troops. He also ordered massive bombing of the leading cities of North Vietnam and the mining of seaports there. Peace negotiations, which had been started and broken off several times under Johnson and Nixon, were at last concluded in 1973.

The United States kept its part of the peace agreements by withdrawing its troops from South Vietnam. The Communists from North Vietnam and within South Vietnam itself increased their pressure on the South Vietnamese armed forces. Poorly governed, the South Vietnamese could not stand without U.S. support. After years of war, the shattered South simply gave up; its army fell to pieces and its government fled. The war ended in 1975. Communist North Vietnam then began integrating North and South Vietnam into one Communist state. Opposition was silenced and contacts with the outside world were kept to a minimum. The best evidence of what was going on came from refugees known as "boat people." Fleeing the new order in small boats, thousands of Vietnamese braved the storms of the Pacific to escape the political tempests in their homeland. A number perished because the nations to which they fled would sometimes turn them away.

No single reason can be given for the success of Communism in Southeast Asia, nor for the failure of the United States to stem it there. The Communists had many advantages, including the powerful factor of nationalism, on their side. They claimed to be fighting for an Indochina free of foreign influences. As for the Americans, this was the longest war in American history and, unlike the other wars of the twentieth century, it produced a great amount of opposition and disharmony. The American people may just have grown weary of the conflict, and may have become convinced that the results were not worth the price of any more lives lost or money spent. Again, all the causes for this setback cannot be seen yet, and scholars will be busy for years to come trying to fathom the reasons for the Communist victory.

On the domestic scene, the war in Vietnam played an important role. It split the nation: demonstrations, riots, and political turmoil being its bitter fruit. It was challenged in the courts, in Congress, and in the streets. At least two political careers were overwhelmingly affected by it. In 1968, a massive Communist attack (the "Tet" offensive) contributed to Lyndon Johnson's decision to withdraw from consideration for another presidential term. And President Nixon's use of American funds for secret and allegedly illegal bombings of Cambodia played a part in his ultimate downfall in 1974.

In Asia, the United States entered SEATO (Southeast Asia Treaty Organization) with Pakistan, Thailand, Australia, France, Britain, the Philippines, and New Zealand. Created in 1954, this organization was dedicated to peace through defense in the Pacific. Disagreements among the members, partially over American conduct of the Vietnam War, weakened this alliance greatly both in spirit and in strength. In 1976, the members decided that SEATO was no longer a useful tool in the effort to build a defense against Communism, and it was scrapped.

Considering the defeat of Vietnam and the demise of SEATO, it might be thought that Americans had abandoned Asia. This was not the case at all. American interest was just as high, but in a different direction.

The Nixon administration played a key role in setting American policy in Asia beginning in 1969. In that year the President expressed what is now called the "Nixon Doctrine." He promised that the United States would live up to its commitments to Asian countries. However, he also stated that in the event of invasion in the usual military sense (that is, without the use of nuclear weapons), the endangered nation would have to supply the manpower to meet the threat.

UPI

President Richard Nixon and Chinese Premier Chou En-lai at the farewell banquet on the eve of Nixon's departure from his historic visit to China in 1972.

Another direction came in 1972, when President Nixon announced that he was going to the People's Republic of China for a state visit. The Nixon initiative was a shock to all the world, not only because China and the United States had been hostile since the Communists took power twenty years before, but also because China had been a closed country, withdrawn from participation in world affairs. It represented the first step toward the establishment of a regular diplomatic relationship between China and the most powerful of the world's free nations, and it therefore had important international effects. The Soviet Union, although supposedly of the same Communist background as China, was in reality hostile toward and extremely insecure about its giant neighbor. The hostility came from rivalry over which nation should control the Communist movement in Asia, and the insecurity arose over China's huge population and its constant threat to Soviet borders. Thus, China's emergence into the world, brought about by American diplomacy, may have been as important as the "opening" of Japan to world participation in the last century.

Presidents Ford and Carter and other American leaders followed up the 1972 initiative in later years. In 1979, President Carter and Chinese Vice-Premier Deng Xiaoping signed a treaty that normalized relations between the United States and China. This historic treaty, which also called for economic and cultural cooperation, generated much suspicion in the Soviet Union.

In the Middle East, Communist policy was based on supplying the enemies of Israel with weapons and advisors to help them defeat the new Jewish state. Even with Russian help, however, the Arab countries were not successful in taking over their smaller neighbor. The "Six-Day War" of 1967 was a disastrous defeat for Egypt, Syria, and their allies. The Israelis conquered and occupied portions of Jordan, Syria, and Egypt. In 1973, in an attempt to win back those territories, the Arabs launched a surprise attack on Israel on Yom Kippur, a Jewish holy day. But Israel was able to mobilize quickly, and soon Israeli forces had pushed across the Suez Canal deep into Egypt and had occupied territory just miles from the Syrian capital of Damascus. At that point, both the Soviet Union and the United States, which was supplying arms to Israel, used their influence with the antagonists and a cease-fire was arranged. But problems did not stop with the fighting. The Arab countries and the Soviet Union demanded that Israel return all territories occupied during the 1967 and 1973 wars; the Israelis claimed that the territories were necessary to secure their borders against future attacks. In an attempt to bring worldwide pressure to bear on Israel, the Arab countries refused to sell oil to any nation which supported the Israeli position. As a result, there were severe fuel shortages in Western Europe and Japan. The United States also suffered from the boycott, and Congress and the nation began a long debate on how to deal with the energy crisis.

The Arab countries had discovered a potent weapon in the oil boycott, one which gave them a powerful lever in world affairs. When the boycott ended, the OPEC (Organization of Petroleum Exporting Countries) nations found that they had still another weapon, in price increases. Raising these to new highs, the oil producers drastically altered the financial order of the world. For decades, the rich industrial nations had relied on cheap oil to run their economies. This ended in the mid-1970s, and a whole new set of circumstances had to be faced. Alternative sources of oil were sought. The United States, with its great oil fields in Alaska, and Great Britain, with its North

The White House

President Jimmy Carter met with Egyptian President Anwar Sadat, left, and Israeli Prime Minister Menachem Begin, right, at Camp David, Maryland, in 1978 to establish a framework for peace between the two countries.

Sea wells, seemed to gain a slight advantage. But oil consumption in the United States continued to increase, as did dependence on foreign oil. Developing alternatives to oil became a goal in itself, but by the end of the 1970s no source of energy as inexpensive or as plentiful as foreign oil had been found. So Americans continued to import, hoping that some technological breakthrough would bail them out of a desperate position which few wanted even to think about.

In the meantime, the political situation in the Middle East improved. Despite opposition from other Arab countries, President Anwar Sadat of Egypt courageously opened diplomatic relations with Israel late in 1977, exchanging visits with Israeli Prime Minister Menachem Begin. Then, in the summer of 1978, the two leaders met in the United States, at the presidential retreat at Camp David, Maryland. After days of intense negotiations, assisted by President Carter, they reached agreement on a framework for a permanent peace treaty between the two nations. Many problems remained, notably the refusal of other Arab countries to participate in a settlement, but nevertheless the "Camp David Summit" represented a triumph for the three national leaders involved and for the cause of peace in the Middle East.

The Western Hemisphere was not neglected in the years following World War II, either by the Communists or the Americans. In 1947, the United States and its southern neighbors signed the Rio Pact, a mutual defense treaty binding twenty nations to resist aggression. The following year, the Organization of American States (OAS) came into being to provide an agency that could take quick action to avert Communist revolution. In 1965, a revolt occurred in the Dominican Republic. It appeared that a Communist plot was in the making, and within a few days more than 20,000 American troops were in the country. They were later joined by soldiers from other Latin American nations. OAS mediators arranged elections which were successfully held and resulted in the establishment of a new, democratically elected government.

American interest in Latin America took many forms during the postwar years, not all of them legal or moral. A Select Committee of the Senate held hearings and released a number of findings based on the seventy-five witnesses it heard. The conclusions were that American agencies, including the CIA and the Attorney-General's office, knew of and even encouraged assassination or at least ouster plots to eliminate leaders considered dangerous to American interests. The most famous cases were plots against Cuba's Fidel Castro, which failed, and against Rafael Trujillo of the Dominican Republic, which succeeded.[3]

Deploring the thought of assassination and other subversive means, Americans nevertheless were faced with the sad fact that Communists have used assassination frequently. Vietcong terrorists employed this tactic with great success against anti-Communist Vietnamese during the 1960s. In fact, an estimated six thousand civilians, such as teachers and medical experts, were assassinated in South Vietnam

---

3. *Alleged Assassination Plots Involving Foreign Leaders*, Report No. 94-465 (Washington: U.S. Government Printing Office, 1975), pp. 4, 5, 154.

between 1959 and 1964.[4] Latin America is one of the most assassination-prone areas of the world, and not just the highest leaders suffer either. An estimated five hundred persons died by assassination in Argentina alone during a ten-month period in the mid-1970s. During the 1960s and 1970s, some three thousand persons were assassinated in Guatemala.[5]

These figures of illegal and immoral conduct by other people do not absolve those few Americans in the federal government during the 1960s and 1970s who contemplated such means to further American interests, but they should put in perspective the problems facing U.S. foreign policy makers in the modern world. Presidents Ford and Carter have denounced illegal tactics, and Congress has taken steps to supervise federal agencies such as the CIA more closely.

From a more positive angle, Americans began negotiations with Panama for turning over the Panama Canal to that nation. Two treaties were negotiated, guaranteeing the neutrality of the canal and giving ultimate control to the Republic of Panama in the year 2000, subject to the right of the United States to protect the canal if necessary. The treaties raised great controversy in this country, and both were passed by only one vote when ratified by the Senate in 1978.

Another example of positive American help is the program known as the Alliance for Progress. This program, begun in 1961, was designed to raise the living standards of Latin Americans through large-scale aid. The aid has gone into the building of roads, schools, hospitals, and other worthwhile projects. By these means, trade was encouraged and good jobs secured by healthier and better educated Latin Americans.

Help like this has eliminated much human misery all over the world. Not all of it has been in the form of cold, impersonal loans or gifts. Thousands of young and old American men and women have volunteered to serve humanity overseas in various relief agencies. The most famous of these is

---

4. Andrew R. Molvan, *Human Factors Considerations of Undergrounds in Insurgencies*, Pamphlet No. 550-104 (Washington: Department of the Army, 1966), p. 170.
5. Murray Clark Havens et al., *Assassination and Terrorism* (Manchaca, Tex.: Sterling Swift, 1975), p. 163.

the Peace Corps, with volunteers in dozens of countries. (President Carter's mother Lillian, a nurse, served with the Peace Corps in India during her "retirement" years.) Other agencies—public, private, and religious—have recruited more thousands of dedicated people for their work. As they teach children, heal the sick, or instruct farmers in better ways of increasing their agricultural output, these people are the best ambassadors any country could have.

DISARMAMENT

World War II was barely over when the United States began to seek disarmament as a means of reducing the possibility of future wars. Disarmament was discussed in hundreds of meetings, held by dozens of committees. No success was achieved in limiting conventional arms, but by 1963 some progress had been made in the limitation of nuclear weapons testing. In that year, Russia, Great Britain, and the United States signed the Treaty of Moscow or Limited Nuclear Test Ban Treaty, which outlawed the testing of nuclear weapons above ground or in outer space. The treaty soon was approved by more than one hundred nations. However, it was rejected by France and Communist China; these nations continued to test their superweapons in the atmosphere in an attempt to "catch up" with the older nuclear powers, Britain, Russia, and the United States.

Other smaller successes have been scored in the field of arms control. In 1963, both Russia and the United States agreed not to use their rocket facilities for placing nuclear weapons in space. An earlier agreement, made in 1959, banned nuclear weapons and even military bases in Antarctica.

Following his journey to Communist China in 1972, President Nixon went to Russia in an effort to bring to life a new spirit of cooperation between the leading powers. Russian-American agreements in the areas of space and medical research were followed in 1972 by Senate ratification of a treaty to limit the number of offensive missiles the United States and Russia could have. This treaty, the fruit of the famous SALT (Strategic

Arms Limitation Talks) meetings, was a major breakthrough in arms control. Negotiations for further agreements continued in the administrations of Presidents Ford and Carter. In 1979, Soviet President Leonid I. Brezhnev and President Carter met in Geneva, Switzerland, to sign a second strategic arms control treaty. By the year's end, the U.S. Senate, still entangled in a fierce debate over SALT II's contribution to U.S. security, had not yet voted on the treaty.

In 1975, Russia and the United States, joined by more than thirty other nations, signed agreements regarding human rights and international security at Helsinki, Finland. The Helsinki agreement seemed to be a good first step toward international recognition that each individual nation had responsibilities toward guaranteeing basic rights to their citizens. Unfortunately, Communist countries such as Russia and Czechoslovakia were not serious about extending to their citizens such rights as freedom of speech, of the press, and of emigration to other lands.

When he took office in 1977, President Jimmy Carter added a new stress to United States foreign policy, one which most Americans applauded widely. This was Carter's emphasis on the need for Americans to speak out in defense of human rights around the world. Oppression in Russia, Turkey, South Africa, and other nations was condemned by the President without regard for whether those nations were allies or adversaries.

By admitting wrongdoing by federal government leaders in the recent and the remote past, President Carter, like President Ford before him, purged the nation of past guilt and gave it a moral position from which it might assume a less authoritative but perhaps a more effective leadership in world affairs. This new attitude was best summed up by a recent U.S. ambassador to the United Nations, now a Senator, Daniel P. Moynihan:

> It is time that the American spokesman comes to be feared in international forums for the truths he might tell. It is past time that we ceased to apologize for an imperfect democracy. Find its equal....

AFTER-CHAPTER REVIEW

REVIEW QUESTIONS

1. Define the following names, terms, or ideas.

Treaty of Versailles	NATO
Monroe Doctrine	Nixon Doctrine
"executive agreements"	cold war
Yalta Conference	Treaty of Moscow
ECOSOC	Alliance for Progress
"containment" doctrine	French Alliance of 1778
OAS	Helsinki agreement
Peace Corps	SALT agreement

2. Vocabulary building.

isolationism   embargo   trustee

3. Review of the text.

   a. Describe the conduct of foreign policy by the United States, using the Treaty of Versailles as an example.
   b. Draw up an outline history of American foreign relations from independence to the present day.
   c. Review the peace and disarmament efforts made by the United States from the end of World War I to the present day.
   d. Prove the following statement: American Presidents often have used troops without a congressional declaration of war.
   e. What are the purposes of the United Nations? How is this body organized? Is it effective? What are the functions of each part of the UN?
   f. Outline the defense agreements made between the United States and other nations of the world.

DISCUSSION AND PROJECTS

1. Questions for discussion.

   a. Discuss: The United States of America can be called an "Empire for Liberty."

b. What are some of the themes which have characterized America's policies toward the rest of the world from George Washington's day to the present? Explain and evaluate these.
c. Discuss the future of the UN.
d. Discuss the part played by terror and assassination in international events.
e. Discuss the responsibility of each nation for the human rights of citizens of every other nation.

2. Debate topics.

a. Resolved: Let's give the House of Representatives a voice in ratifying treaties.
b. Resolved: The UN's accomplishments no longer justify continued American support and this nation should withdraw from it.

3. Opinion poll.

Should the President's role in foreign affairs be reduced?

BIBLIOGRAPHY

Barron, John. "Espionage: The Dark Side of Detente," *Reader's Digest*, January 1978.

Brezezinski, Zbigniew. "U.S. Foreign Policy: The Search for Focus," *Foreign Affairs*, July 1973.

Chace, James. "America's Newest Strategy of Containment," *Harper's*, January 1978.

Chace, James. "How Moral Can We Get?" *New York Times Magazine*, 22 May 1977.

"Eight Experts Size Up U.S. Future in a Dangerous World," *U.S. News & World Report*, 27 June 1977.

"Foreign Aid Keeps Growing—Despite All the Complaints," *U.S. News & World Report*, 1 November 1976.

Lewy, Guenter. "Vietnam: New Light on the Question of American Guilt," *Commentary*, February 1978.

McDowell, Bart. "The Panama Canal Today," *National Geographic*, February 1978.

Rostow, Eugene V. "Eight Foreign Policies for the United States—Which Is Yours?" *New York Times Magazine*, 23 April 1972.

Rowan, Carl T. "China, Russia, and the United States: The Triple-Power Balance," *Reader's Digest*, March 1978.

Zagoria, Donald S. "Why We Can't Leave Korea," *New York Times Magazine*, 2 October 1977.

Appendix

THE MAYFLOWER COMPACT

In The Name of God, Amen. We, whose names are underwritten, the Loyal Subjects of our dread Sovereign Lord King James, by the Grace of God, of Great Britain, France, and Ireland, King, Defender of the Faith, etc. Having undertaken for the Glory of God, and Advancement of the Christian Faith, and the Honour of our King and Country, a Voyage to plant the first colony in the northern Parts of Virginia; Do by these Presents, solemnly and mutually in the Presence of God and one another, covenant and combine ourselves together into a civil Body Politick, for our better Ordering and Preservation, and Furtherance of the Ends aforesaid; And by Virtue hereof do enact, constitute, and frame, such just and equal Laws, Ordinances, Acts, Constitutions, and Offices, from time to time, as shall be thought most meet and convenient for the general Good of the Colony; unto which we promise all due Submission and Obedience. In Witness whereof we have hereunto subscribed our names at Cape Cod the eleventh of November, in the Reign of our Sovereign Lord King James of England, France, and Ireland, the eighteenth and of Scotland, the fifty-fourth. Anno Domini, 1620.

THE AMERICAN'S CREED

I believe in the United States of America as a government of the people, by the people, for the people, whose just powers are derived from the consent of the governed; a democracy in a republic; a sovereign nation of many sovereign states; a perfect union, one and inseparable, established upon those principles of freedom, equality, justice, and humanity for which American patriots sacrificed their lives and fortunes.

I therefore believe it is my duty to my country to love it, to support its Constitution, to obey its laws, to respect its flag, and to defend it against all enemies.

William Tyler Page

THE DECLARATION OF INDEPENDENCE

July 4, 1776
The Unanimous Declaration of the Thirteen United States of America

When in the Course of human events, it becomes necessary for one people to dissolve the political bands which have connected them with another, and to assume among the Powers of the earth, the separate and equal station to which the Laws of Nature and of Nature's God entitle them, a decent respect to the opinions of mankind requires that they should declare the causes which impel them to the separation.

We hold these truths to be self-evident, that all men are created equal, that they are endowed by their Creator with certain unalienable Rights, that among these are Life, Liberty and the pursuit of Happiness. That to secure these rights, Governments are instituted among Men, deriving their just powers from the consent of the governed. That whenever any Form of Government becomes destructive of these ends, it is the Right of the People to alter or to abolish it, and to institute new Government, laying its foundation on such principles and organizing its powers in such form, as to them shall seem most likely to effect their Safety and Happiness. Prudence, indeed, will dictate that Governments long established should not be changed for light and transient causes; and accordingly all experience hath shown, that mankind are more disposed to suffer, while evils are sufferable, than to right themselves by abolishing the forms to which they are accustomed. But when a long train of abuses and usurpations, pursuing invariably the same Object evinces a design to reduce them under absolute Despotism, it is their right, it is their duty, to throw off such Government, and to provide new Guards for their future security.—Such has been the patient sufferance of these Colonies; and such is now the necessity which constrains them to alter their former Systems of Government. The history of the present King of Great Britain is a history of repeated injuries and usurpations, all having in direct object the establishment of an absolute Tyranny over these States. To prove this, let Facts be submitted to a candid world.

He has refused his Assent to Laws, the most wholesome and necessary for the public good.

He has forbidden his Governors to pass Laws of immediate and pressing importance, unless suspended in their operation till his Assent should be obtained; and when so suspended he has utterly neglected to attend to them.

He has refused to pass other Laws for the accommodation of large districts of people, unless those people would relinquish the right of Representation in the Legislature, a right inestimable to them and formidable to tyrants only.

He has called together legislative bodies at places unusual, uncomfortable, and distant from the depository of their Public Records, for the sole purpose of fatiguing them into compliance with his measures.

He has dissolved Representative Houses repeatedly, for opposing with manly firmness his invasions on the rights of the people.

He has refused for a long time, after such dissolutions, to cause others to be elected; whereby the Legislative Powers, incapable of Annihilation, have returned to the People at large for their exercise; the State remaining in the mean time exposed to all the dangers of invasion from without, and convulsions within.

He has endeavoured to prevent the population of these States; for that purpose obstructing the Laws of Naturalization of Foreigners; refusing to pass others to encourage their migration hither, and raising the conditions of new Appropriations of Lands.

He has obstructed the Administration of Justice by refusing his Assent to Laws for establishing Judiciary Powers.

He has made Judges dependent on his Will alone, for the

tenure of their offices, and the amount and payment of their salaries.

He has erected a multitude of New Offices, and sent hither swarms of Officers to harass our People, and eat out their substance.

He has kept among us, in times of peace, Standing Armies without the Consent of our legislature.

He has affected to render the Military independent of and superior to the Civil Power.

He has combined with others to subject us to a jurisdiction foreign to our constitution, and unacknowledged by our laws; giving his Assent to their acts of pretended legislation:

For quartering large bodies of armed troops among us;

For protecting them, by a mock Trial, from Punishment for any Murders which they should commit on the Inhabitants of these States;

For cutting off our Trade with all parts of the world;

For imposing taxes on us without our Consent;

For depriving us in many cases, of the benefits of Trial by Jury;

For transporting us beyond Seas to be tried for pretended offences;

For abolishing the free System of English Laws in a neighboring Province, establishing therein an Arbitrary government, and enlarging its Boundaries so as to render it at once an example and fit instrument for introducing the same absolute rule into these Colonies;

For taking away our Charters, abolishing our most valuable Laws, and altering fundamentally the Forms of Governments;

For suspending our own Legislature, and declaring themselves invested with Power to legislate for us in all cases whatsoever.

He had abdicated Government here, by declaring us out of his Protection and waging War against us.

He has plundered our seas, ravaged our Coasts, burnt our towns, and destroyed the lives of our people.

He is at this time transporting large armies of foreign mercenaries to compleat the works of death, desolation and tyranny, already begun with circumstances of Cruelty and perfidy scarcely paralleled in the most barbarous ages, and totally unworthy the Head of a civilized nation.

He has constrained our fellow Citizens taken Captive on the high Seas to bear Arms against their Country, to become the executioners of their friends and Brethren, or to fall themselves by their Hands.

He has excited domestic insurrections amongst us, and has endeavoured to bring on the inhabitants of our frontiers, the merciless Indian Savages, whose known rule of warfare, is an undistinguished destruction of all ages, sexes and conditions.

In every stage of these Oppressions We have Petitioned for Redress in the most humble terms: Our repeated Petitions have been answered only by repeated injury. A Prince, whose character is thus marked by every act which may define a Tyrant, is unfit to be the ruler of a free People.

Nor have We been wanting in attention to our British brethren. We have warned them from time to time of attempts by their legislature to extend an unwarrantable jurisdiction over us. We have reminded them of the circumstances of our emigration and settlement here. We have appealed to their native justice and magnanimity, and we have conjured them by the ties of our common kindred to disavow these usurpations, which, would inevitably interrupt our connections and correspondence. They too have been deaf to the voice of justice and of consanguinity. We must, therefore, acquiesce in the necessity, which denounces our Separation, and hold them, as we hold the rest of mankind, Enemies in War, in Peace Friends.

We therefore, the Representatives of the United States of America, in General Congress, Assembled, appealing to the Supreme Judge of the world for the rectitude of our intentions, do, in the Name and by Authority of the good People of these Colonies, solemnly publish and declare, That these United Colonies are, and of Right ought to be Free and Independent States; that they are Absolved from all Allegiance to the British Crown, and that all political connection between them and the State of Great Britain, is and ought to be totally dissolved; and that as Free and Independent States, they have full Power to levy War, conclude Peace, contract Alliances, establish Commerce, and to do all other Acts and Things which Independent States may of right do. And for the support of this Declaration, with a firm reliance on the Protection of Divine Providence, we mutually pledge to each other our Lives, our Fortunes and our sacred Honor.

John Hancock

New Hampshire
Josiah Bartlett,
Wm. Whipple,
Matthew Thornton.

Connecticut
Roger Sherman,
Sam'el Huntington,
Wm. Williams,
Oliver Wolcott.

Georgia
Button Gwinnett,
Lyman Hall,
Geo. Walton.

New York
Wm. Floyd,
Phil. Livingston,
Frans. Lewis,
Lewis Morris.

Pennsylvania
Robt. Morris
Benjamin Rush,
Benja. Franklin,
John Morton,
Geo. Clymer,
Jas. Smith
Geo. Taylor,
James Wilson,
Geo. Ross.

Massachusetts Bay
Saml. Adams,
John Adams,
Robt. Treat Paine,
Elbridge Gerry.

Delaware
Caesar Rodney,
Geo. Read,
Tho. M'Kean.

North Carolina
Wm. Hooper,
Joseph Hewes,
John Penn.

Maryland
Samuel Chase,
Wm. Paca,
Thos. Stone,
Charles Carrol of Carrolton.

Rhode Island
Step. Hopkins,
William Ellery.

Virginia
George Wythe,
Richard Henry Lee,
Th. Jefferson,
Benj. Harrison,
Ths. Nelson, Jr.,
Francis Lightfoot Lee,
Carter Braxton.

South Carolina
Edward Rutledge,
Thos. Heyward, Junr.,
Thomas Lynch, Junr.,
Arthur Middleton.

New Jersey
Richd. Stockton,
Jno. Witherspoon,
Fras. Hopkinson,
John Hart,
Abra. Clark.

THE CONSTITUTION OF THE UNITED STATES

We the people of the United States, in order to form a more perfect union, establish justice, insure domestic tranquility, provide for the common defense, promote the general welfare, and secure the blessings of liberty to ourselves and our posterity, do ordain and establish this Constitution for the United States of America.

ARTICLE I

Section 1.

1. All legislative powers herein granted shall be vested in a Congress of the United States, which shall consist of a Senate and House of Representatives.

Section 2.

1. The House of Representatives shall be composed of members chosen every second year by the people of the several States, and the electors in each State shall have the qualifications requisite for electors of the most numerous branch of the State legislature.
2. No person shall be a Representative who shall not have attained to the age of twenty-five years, and been seven years a citizen of the United States, and who shall not, when elected, be an inhabitant of that State in which he shall be chosen.
3. Representatives and direct taxes shall be apportioned among the several States which may be included within this Union, according to their respective numbers, *which shall be determined by adding to the whole number of free persons, including those bound to service for a term of years, and excluding Indians not taxed, three fifths of all other persons.** The actual enumeration shall be made within three years after the first meeting of the Congress of the United States, and within every subsequent term of ten years, in such manner as they shall by law direct. The number of Representatives shall not exceed one for every thirty thousand, but each State shall have at least one Representative; and until such enumeration shall be made, the State of New Hampshire shall be entitled to choose three, Massachusetts eight, Rhode Island and Providence Plantations one, Connecticut five, New York six, New Jersey four, Pennsylvania eight, Delaware one, Maryland six, Virginia ten, North Carolina five, South Carolina five, and Georgia three.
4. When vacancies happen in the representation from any State, the executive authority thereof shall issue writs of election to fill such vacancies.

---

*Italics indicate passage has been affected by subsequent amendments to the Constitution.

5. The House of Representatives shall choose their Speaker and other officers, and shall have the sole power of impeachment.

Section 3.

1. The Senate of the United States shall be composed of two Senators from each State, *chosen by the legislature thereof,* for six years; and each Senator shall have one vote.

2. Immediately after they shall be assembled in consequence of the first election, they shall be divided as equally as may be into three classes. The seats of the Senators of the first class shall be vacated at the expiration of the second year, of the second class at the expiration of the fourth year, and of the third class at the expiration of the sixth year, so that one third may be chosen every second year; *and if vacancies happen by resignation, or otherwise, during the recess of the legislature of any State, the executive thereof may make temporary appointments until the next meeting of the legislature, which shall then fill such vacancies.*

3. No person shall be a Senator who shall not have attained to the age of thirty years, and been nine years a citizen of the United States, and who shall not, when elected, be an inhabitant of that State for which he shall be chosen.

4. The Vice-President of the United States shall be President of the Senate, but shall have no vote, unless they be equally divided.

5. The Senate shall choose their other officers, and also a President pro tempore, in the absence of the Vice-President, or when he shall exercise the office of the President of the United States.

6. The Senate shall have the sole power to try all impeachments. When sitting for that purpose, they shall be on oath or affirmation. When the President of the United States is tried, the Chief Justice shall preside; and no person shall be convicted without the concurrence of two thirds of the members present.

7. Judgment in cases of impeachment shall not extend further than to removal from office, and disqualification to hold and enjoy any office of honor, trust, or profit under the United States; but the party convicted shall, nevertheless, be liable and subject to indictment, trial, judgment, and punishment, according to law.

Section 4.

1. The times, places, and manner of holding elections for Senators and Representatives shall be prescribed in each State by the legislature thereof; but the Congress may at any time by law make or alter such regulations, except as to the places of choosing Senators.
2. The Congress shall assemble at least once in every year, *and such meeting shall be on the first Monday in December, unless they shall by law appoint a different day.*

Section 5.

1. Each house shall be the judge of the elections, returns, and qualifications of its own members, and a majority of each shall constitute a quorum to do business; but a smaller number may adjourn from day to day, and may be authorized to compel the attendance of absent members, in such manner, and under such penalties, as each house may provide.
2. Each house may determine the rules of its proceedings, punish its members for disorderly behavior, and, with the concurrence of two thirds, expel a member.
3. Each house shall keep a journal of its proceedings, and from time to time publish the same, excepting such parts as may in their judgment require secrecy; and the yeas and nays of the members of either house on any question shall, at the desire of one fifth of those present, be entered on the journal.
4. Neither house, during the session of Congress, shall, without the consent of the other, adjourn for more than three days, nor to any other place than that in which the two houses shall be sitting.

Section 6.

1. The Senators and Representatives shall receive a compensation for their services, to be ascertained by law and paid out of the Treasury of the United States. They shall, in all cases except treason, felony, and breach of the peace, be privileged from arrest during their attendance at the session of their respective houses, and in going to and returning from the same; and for any speech or debate in either house they shall not be questioned in any other place.
2. No Senator or Representative shall, during the time for which he was elected, be appointed to any civil office under the authority of the United States, which shall have been

created, or the emoluments whereof shall have been increased, during such time; and no person holding any office under the United States shall be a member of either house during his continuance in office.

Section 7.

1. All bills for raising revenue shall originate in the House of Representatives; but the Senate may propose or concur with amendments as on other bills.

2. Every bill which shall have passed the House of Representatives and the Senate shall, before it becomes a law, be presented to the President of the United States; if he approves he shall sign it, but if not he shall return it, with his objections, to that house in which it shall have originated, who shall enter the objections at large on their journal and proceed to reconsider it. If after such reconsideration two thirds of that house shall agree to pass the bill, it shall be sent, together with the objections, to the other house, by which it shall likewise be reconsidered, and if approved by two thirds of that house, it shall become a law. But in all such cases the votes of both houses shall be determined by yeas and nays, and the names of the persons voting for and against the bill shall be entered on the journal of each house respectively. If any bill shall not be returned by the President within ten days (Sundays excepted) after it shall have been presented to him, the same shall be a law, in like manner as if he had signed it, unless the Congress by their adjournment prevent its return, in which case it shall not be a law.

3. Every order, resolution, or vote to which the concurrence of the Senate and House of Representatives may be necessary (except on a question of adjournment) shall be presented to the President of the United States; and before the same shall take effect, shall be approved by him, or being disapproved by him, shall be repassed by two thirds of the Senate and House of Representatives, according to the rules and limitations prescribed in the case of a bill.

Section 8.

1. The Congress shall have power to lay and collect taxes, duties, imposts and excises, to pay the debts and provide for the common defence and general welfare of the United States; but all duties, imposts and excises shall be uniform throughout the United States;

2. To borrow money on the credit of the United States;

3. To regulate commerce with foreign nations, and among the several States, and with the Indian tribes;

4. To establish a uniform rule of naturalization and uniform laws on the subject of bankruptcies throughout the United States;

5. To coin money, regulate the value thereof, and of foreign coin, and fix the standard of weights and measures;

6. To provide for the punishment of counterfeiting the securities and current coin of the United States;

7. To establish post-offices and post-roads;

8. To promote the progress of science and useful arts by securing for limited times to authors and inventors the exclusive right to their respective writings and discoveries;

9. To constitute tribunals inferior to the Supreme Court;

10. To define and punish piracies and felonies committed on the high seas, and offences against the laws of nations;

11. To declare war, grant letters of marque and reprisal, and make rules concerning captures on land and water;

12. To raise and support armies, but no appropriation of money to that use shall be for longer term than two years;

13. To provide and maintain a navy;

14. To make rules for the government and regulation of the land and naval forces;

15. To provide for calling forth the militia to execute the laws of the Union, suppress insurrections, and repel invasion;

16. To provide for organizing, arming, and disciplining the militia, and for governing such part of them as may be employed in the service of the United States, reserving to the States respectively the appointment of the officers, and the authority of training the militia according to the discipline prescribed by Congress;

17. To exercise exclusive legislation in all cases whatsoever over such district (not exceeding ten miles square) as may, by cession of particular States and the acceptance of Congress, become the seat of the Government of the United States, and to exercise like authority over all places purchased by the consent of the legislature of the State in which the same shall be, for the erection of forts, magazines, arsenals, dockyards, and other needful buildings; and

18. To make all laws which shall be necessary and proper for carrying into execution the foregoing powers, and all other powers vested by this constitution in the Government of the United States, or in any department or officer thereof.

Section 9.

1. The migration or importation of such persons as any of the States now existing shall think proper to admit shall not be prohibited by the Congress prior to the year one thousand eight hundred and eight, but a tax or duty may be imposed on such importation, not exceeding ten dollars for each person.

2. The privilege of the writ of *habeas corpus* shall not be suspended, unless when in cases of rebellion or invasion the public safety may require it.

3. No bill of attainder or *ex post facto* law shall be passed.

4. *No capitation or other direct tax shall be laid, unless in proportion to the census or enumeration hereinbefore directed to be taken.*

5. No tax or duty shall be laid on articles exported from any State.

6. No preference shall be given by any regulation of commerce or revenue to the ports of one State over those of another; nor shall vessels bound to or from one State be obliged to enter, clear, or pay duties in another.

7. No money shall be drawn from the Treasury but in consequence of appropriations made by law; and a regular statement and account of the receipts and expenditures of all public money shall be published from time to time.

8. No title of nobility shall be granted by the United States; and no person holding any office of profit or trust under them shall, without the consent of the Congress, accept of any present, emolument, office, or title, of any kind whatever, from any king, prince, or foreign State.

Section 10.

1. No State shall enter into any treaty, alliance, or confederation; grant letters of marque and reprisal; coin money; emit bill or credit, make anything but gold and silver coin a tender in payment of debts; pass any bill of attainder, *ex post facto* law, or law impairing the obligation of contracts, or grant any title of nobility.

2. No State shall, without the consent of Congress, lay any imposts or duties on imports or exports, except what may be absolutely necessary for executing its inspection laws; and the net produce of all duties and imposts, laid by any State on imports or exports, shall be for the use of the Treasury of the United States; and all such laws shall be subject to the revision and control of the Congress.

3. No State shall without the consent of Congress, lay any duty of tonnage, keep troops or ships of war in time of peace, enter into any agreement or compact with another State, or with a foreign power, or engage in war, unless actually invaded or in such imminent danger as will not admit of delay.

ARTICLE II

Section 1.

1. The executive power shall be vested in a President of the United States of America. He shall hold his office during the term of four years and, together with the Vice-President, chosen for the same term, be elected as follows:

2. Each State shall appoint, in such manner as the legislature thereof may direct, a number of electors, equal to the whole number of Senators and Representatives to which the State may be entitled in the Congress; but no Senator or Representative, or person holding an office of trust or profit under the United States, shall be appointed an elector.

3. *The electors shall meet in their respective States and vote by ballot for two persons, of whom one at least shall not be an inhabitant of the same State with themselves. And they shall make a list of all the persons voted for, and of the number of votes for each; which list they shall sign and certify, and transmit sealed to the seat of the government of the United States, directed to the President of the Senate. The President of the Senate shall, in the presence of the Senate and House of Representatives, open all the certificates, and the votes shall then be counted. The person having the greatest number of votes shall be the President, if such number be a majority of the whole number of electors appointed; and if there be more than one who have such majority, and have an equal number of votes, then the House of Representatives shall immediately choose by ballot one of them for President; and if no person have a majority, then from the five highest on the list the said House shall in like manner choose the President. But in choosing the President the votes shall be taken by States, the representation from each State having one vote; a quorum for* *this purpose shall consist of a member or members from two thirds of the States, and a majority of all the States shall be necessary to a choice. In every case, after the choice of the President, the person having the greatest number of votes of the electors shall be the Vice-President. But if there should remain two or more who have equal votes, the Senate shall choose from them by ballot the Vice-President.*

4. The Congress may determine the time of choosing the electors and the day on which they shall give their votes, which day shall be the same throughout the United States.

5. No person except a natural-born citizen or a citizen of the United States at the time of the adoption of this Constitution, shall be eligible to the office of President; neither shall any person be eligible to that office who shall not have attained to the age of thirty-five years, and been fourteen years a resident within the United States.

6. In case of the removal of the President from office, or of his death, resignation, or inability to discharge the powers and duties of the said office, the same shall devolve on the Vice-President, and the Congress may by law provide for the case of removal, death, resignation, or inability, both of the President and Vice-President, declaring what officer shall then act as President, and such officer shall act accordingly until the disability be removed or a President shall be elected.

7. The President shall, at stated times, receive for his services a compensation which shall neither be increased nor diminished during the period for which he shall have been elected, and he shall not receive within that period any other emolument from the United States or any of them.

8. Before he enter on the execution of his office he shall take the following oath or affirmation:

> "I do solemnly swear (or affirm) that I will faithfully execute the office of President of the United States, and will to the best of my ability, preserve, protect, and defend the Constitution of the United States."

Section 2.

1. The President shall be commander-in-chief of the army and navy of the United States, and of the militia of the several States when called into actual service of the United States; he may require the opinion, in writing, of the principal officer in each of the executive departments, upon any subject relating to the duties of their respective offices, and he shall have power to grant reprieves and pardons for offences against the United States, except in cases of impeachment.

2. He shall have power, by and with the advice and consent of the Senate, to make treaties, provided two thirds of the Senators present concur; and he shall nominate, and, by and with the advice and consent of the Senate, shall appoint ambassadors, other public ministers and consuls, judges of the Supreme Court, and all other officers of the United States, whose appointments are not herein otherwise provided for, and which shall be established by law; but the Congress may by law vest the appointment of such inferior officers, as they think proper, in the President alone, in the courts of law, or in the heads of departments.

3. The President shall have power to fill up all vacancies that may happen during the recess of the Senate, by granting commissions which shall expire at the end of their next session.

Section 3.

1. He shall from time to time give to the Congress information of the state of the Union, and recommend to their consideration such measures as he shall judge necessary and expedient; he may, on extraordinary occasions, convene both houses, or either of them, and in case of disagreement between them with respect to the time of adjournment, he may adjourn them to such time as he shall think proper; he shall receive ambassadors and other public ministers; he shall take care that the laws be faithfully executed, and shall commission all the officers of the United States.

Section 4.

1. The President, Vice-President, and all civil officers of the United States shall be removed from office on impeachment for and conviction of treason, bribery, or other high crimes and misdemeanors.

ARTICLE III

Section 1.

1. The judicial power of the United States shall be vested in one Supreme Court, and in such inferior courts as the Congress may from time to time ordain and establish. The judges, both of the supreme and inferior courts, shall hold their offices

during good behavior, and shall, at stated times, receive for their services a compension which shall not be diminished during their continuance in office.

Section 2.

1. The judicial power shall extend to all cases, in law and equity, arising under this Constitution, the laws of the United States, and treaties made, or which shall be made, under their authority; to all cases affecting ambassadors, other public ministers and consuls; to all cases of admiralty and maritime jurisdiction; to controversies to which the United States shall be a party; to controversies between two or more States; *between a State and citizens of another State;* between citizens of different States; between citizens of the same State claiming lands under grants of different States, and between a State, or the citizens thereof, and foreign States, citizens, or subjects.

2. In all cases affecting ambassadors, other public ministers and consuls, and those in which a State shall be party, the Supreme Court shall have original jurisdiction. In all the other cases before mentioned the Supreme Court shall have appellate jurisdiction, both as to law and fact, with such exceptions and under such regulations as the Congress shall make.

3. The trial of all crimes, except in cases of impeachment, shall be by jury; and such trial shall be held in the State where the said crimes shall have been committed; but when not committed within any State, the trial shall be at such place or places as the Congress may by law have directed.

Section 3.

1. Treason against the United States shall consist only in levying war against them, or in adhering to their enemies, giving them aid and comfort. No person shall be convicted of treason unless on the testimony of two witnesses to the same overt act, or on confession in open court.

2. The Congress shall have power to declare the punishment of treason, but no attainder of treason shall work corruption of blood or forfeiture except during the life of the person attained.

ARTICLE IV

Section 1.

1. Full faith and credit shall be given in each State to the public acts, records, and judicial proceedings of every other

State. And the Congress may by general laws prescribe the manner in which such acts, records, and proceedings shall be proved, and the effect thereof.

Section 2.

1. The citizens of each State shall be entitled to all privileges and immunities of citizens in the several States.

2. A person charged in any State with treason, felony, or other crime, who shall flee from justice, and be found in another State, shall, on demand of the executive authority of the State from which he fled, be delivered up, to be removed to the State having jurisdiction of the crime.

3. *No person held to service or labor in one State, under the laws thereof, escaping into another, shall, in consequence of any law or regulation therein, be discharged from such service or labor, but shall be delivered up on claim of the party to whom such service or labor may be due.*

Section 3.

1. New States may be admitted by the Congress into this Union; but no new State shall be formed or erected within the jurisdiction of any other State; nor any State be formed by the junction of two or more States, or parts of States, without the consent of the legislatures of the States concerned as well as of the Congress.

2. The Congress shall have power to dispose of and make all needful rules and regulations respecting the territory or other property belonging to the United States; and nothing in this Constitution shall be so construed as to prejudice any claims of the United States or of any particular State.

Section 4.

1. The United States shall guarantee to every State in this Union a republican form of government, and shall protect each of them against invasion, and on application of the legislature, or of the executive (when the legislature cannot be convened), against domestic violence.

ARTICLE V

1. The Congress, whenever two thirds of both houses shall deem it necessary, shall propose amendments to this Constitution, or, on the application of the legislatures of two thirds of the several States, shall call a convention for proposing amendments, which in either case shall be valid to all intents and purposes as part of this Constitution, when ratified by the legislatures of three fourths of the several States, or by conventions in three fourths thereof, as the one or the other mode of ratification may be proposed by the Congress; provided that no amendment which may be made prior to the year one thousand eight hundred and eight shall in any manner affect the first and fourth clauses in the ninth section of the first article; and that no State, without its consent, shall be deprived of its equal suffrage in the Senate.

ARTICLE VI

1. All debts contracted and engagements entered into, before the adoption of this Constitution, shall be as valid against the United States under this Constitution as under the Confederation.
2. This Constitution, and the laws of the United States which shall be made in pursuance thereof, and all treaties made, or which shall be made, under the authority of the United States, shall be the supreme law of the land; and the judges in every State shall be bound thereby, anything in the Constitution or laws of any State to the contrary notwithstanding.
3. The Senators and Representatives before mentioned, and the members of the several State legislatures, and all executive and judicial officers, both of the United States and of the several States, shall be bound by oath or affirmation to support this Constitution; but no religious test shall ever be required as a qualification to any office or public trust under the United States.

ARTICLE VII

1. The ratification of the conventions of nine States shall be sufficient for the establishment of this Constitution between the States so ratifying the same.

> Done in convention by the unanimous consent of the States present, the seventeenth day of September, in the year of our Lord one thousand seven hundred and eighty-seven, and of the independence of the United States of America

the twelfth. In witness whereof, we have hereunto subscribed our names.

G.⁰ Washington—Presid. and deputy from Virginia

AMENDMENTS

The first ten amendments to the Constitution are known as the Bill of Rights and became effective on December 15, 1791.

I.
Congress shall make no law respecting an establishment of religion, or prohibiting the free exercise thereof; or abridging the freedom of speech or of the press; or the right of the people peaceably to assemble, and to petition the government for a redress of grievances.

II.
A well-regulated militia being necessary to the security of a free state, the right of the people to keep and bear arms shall not be infringed.

III.
No soldier shall, in time of peace, be quartered in any house without the consent of the owner, nor in time of war, but in a manner to be prescribed by law.

IV.
The right of the people to be secure in their persons, houses, papers, and effects, against unreasonable searches and seizures, shall not be violated, and no warrants shall issue but upon probable cause, supported by oath or affirmation, and particularly describing the place to be searched, and the persons or things to be seized.

V.
No person shall be held to answer for a capital or otherwise infamous crime, unless on a presentment or indictment of a grand jury, except in cases arising in the land or naval forces or in the militia when in actual service in time of war or public danger; nor shall any person be subject for the same offence to be twice put in jeopardy of life or limb; nor shall be compelled in any criminal case to be witness against himself, nor be deprived of life, liberty, or property, without due process

of law; nor shall private property be taken for public use without just compensation.

VI.

In all criminal prosecutions the accused shall enjoy the right to a speedy and public trial, by an impartial jury of the State and district wherein the crime shall have been committed, which district shall have been previously ascertained by law, and to be informed of the nature and cause of the accusation; to be confronted with the witnesses against him; to have compulsory process for obtaining witnesses in his favor, and to have the assistance of counsel for his defense.

VII.

In suits at common law, where the value in controversy shall exceed twenty dollars, the right of trial by jury shall be preserved, and no fact tried by a jury shall be otherwise reexamined in any court of the United States, than according to the rules of the common law.

VIII.

Excessive bail shall not be required, nor excessive fines imposed, nor cruel and unusual punishments inflicted.

IX.

The enumeration in the Constitution of certain rights shall not be construed to deny or disparage others retained by the people.

X.

The powers not delegated to the United States by the Constitution, nor prohibited to the States, are reserved to the States respectively, or to the people.

XI. *(Effective January 8, 1798.)*

The judicial power of the United States shall not be construed to extend to any suit in law or equity, commenced or prosecuted against one of the United States by citizens of another State, or by citizens or subjects of any foreign state.

XII. *(Effective September 25, 1804.)*

The electors shall meet in their respective States and vote by ballot for President and Vice-President, one of whom, at least, shall not be an inhabitant of the same State with themselves; they shall name in their ballots the person voted for as President, and in distinct ballots the person voted for as Vice-President, and they shall make distinct lists of all persons voted for as President and of all persons voted for as Vice-President, and of the number of votes for each, which lists they shall sign and certify, and transmit sealed to the seat of the government of the United States, directed to the President of the Senate. The President of the Senate shall, in the presence of the Senate and House of Representatives, open all the certificates and the votes shall then be counted. The person having the greatest number of votes for President shall be the President, if such number be a majority of the whole number of electors appointed; and if no person have such majority, then from the persons having the highest numbers not exceeding three on the list of those voted for as President, the House of Representatives shall choose immediately, by ballot, the President. But in choosing the President the votes shall be taken by States, the representation from each State having one vote; a quorum for this purpose shall consist of a member or members from two thirds of the States, and a majority of all the States shall be necessary to a choice. And if the House of Representatives shall not choose a President whenever the right of choice shall devolve upon them, before the *fourth day of March* next following, then the Vice-President shall act as President, as in the case of the death or other constitutional disability of the President.

The person having the greatest number of votes as Vice-President shall be the Vice-President, if such number be a majority of the whole number of electors appointed; and if no person have a majority, then from the two highest numbers on the list the Senate shall choose the Vice-President; a quorum for the purpose shall consist of two thirds of the whole number of Senators, and a majority of the whole number shall be necessary to a choice. But no person constitutionally ineligible to the office of President shall be eligible to that of Vice-President of the United States.

XIII. *(Effective December 18, 1865.)*

Section 1. Neither slavery nor involuntary servitude, except as a punishment for crime whereof the party shall have been duly convicted, shall exist within the United States or any place subject to their jurisdiction.

Section 2. Congress shall have power to enforce this article by appropriate legislation.

XIV. *(Effective July 28, 1868.)*

Section 1. All persons born or naturalized in the United States, and subject to the jurisdiction thereof, are citizens of the United States and of the State wherein they reside. No State shall make or enforce any law which shall abridge the privileges or immunities of citizens of the United States; nor shall any State deprive any person of life, liberty, or property, without due process of law; nor deny to any person within its jurisdiction the equal protection of the laws.

Section 2. Representatives shall be apportioned among the several States according to their respective numbers, counting the whole number of persons in each State, excluding Indians not taxed. But when the right to vote at any election for the choice of electors for President or Vice-President of the United States, Representatives in Congress, the executive and judicial officers of a State, or the members of the legislature thereof, is denied to any of the male inhabitants of such State, being twenty-one years of age, and citizens of the United States, or in any way abridged, except for participation in rebellion, or other crime, the basis of representation therein shall be reduced in the proportion which the number of such male citizens shall bear to the whole number of male citizens twenty-one years of age in such State.

Section 3. No person shall be a Senator or Representative in Congress, or elector of President and Vice-President, or hold any office, civil or military under the United States or under any State, who, having previously taken an oath as a member of Congress, or as an officer of the United States, or as a member of any State legislature, or as an executive or judicial officer of any State, to support the Constitution of the United States, shall have engaged in insurrection or rebellion against the same, or given aid or comfort to the enemies thereof. But Congress may, by a vote of two thirds of each house remove such disability.

Section 4. The validity of the public debt of the United

States, authorized by law, including debts incurred for payment of pensions and bounties for services in suppressing insurrection or rebellion, shall not be questioned. But neither the United States nor any State shall assume or pay any debt or obligation incurred in aid of insurrection or rebellion against the United States, or any claim for the loss or emancipation of any slave; but all such debts, obligations and claims shall be held illegal and void.

Section 5. The Congress shall have power to enforce, by appropriate legislation, the provisions of this article.

XV. *(Effective March 30, 1870.)*

Section 1. The right of citizens of the United States to vote shall not be denied or abridged by the United States or by any State on account of race, color, or previous condition of servitude.

Section 2. The Congress shall have power to enforce this article by appropriate legislature.

XVI. *(Effective February 25, 1913.)*
The Congress shall have power to lay and collect taxes on incomes, from whatever source derived, without apportionment among the several States, and without regard to any census or enumeration.

XVII. *(Effective May 31, 1913.)*
The Senate of the United States shall be composed of two Senators from each State, elected by the people thereof, for six years; and each Senator shall have one vote. The electors in each State shall have the qualifications requisite for electors of the most numerous branch of the State legislature.

When vacancies happen in the representation of any State in the Senate, the executive authority of such State shall issue writs of election to fill such vacancies: *Provided,* That the legislature of any State may empower the executive thereof to make temporary appointments until the people fill the vacancies by election as the legislature may direct.

This amendment shall not be so construed as to affect the election or term of any Senator chosen before it becomes valid as part of the Constitution.

XVIII. *(Effective January 29, 1919.)*

Section 1. *After one year from the ratification of this article the manufacture, sale, or transportation of intoxicating liquors within, the importation thereof into, or the exportation thereof from the United States and all territory subject to the jurisdiction thereof for beverage purposes is hereby prohibited.*

Section 2. *The Congress and the several States shall have concurrent power to enforce this article by appropriate legislation.*

Section 3. *This article shall be inoperative unless it shall have been ratified as an amendment to the Constitution by the legislatures of the several States, as provided in the Constitution, within seven years from the date of the submission hereof to the States by Congress.*

XIX. *(Effective August 26, 1920.)*
The right of citizens of the United States to vote shall not be denied or abridged by the United States or by any State on account of sex.

Congress shall have power to enforce this article by appropriate legislation.

XX. *(Effective February 6, 1933.)*

Section 1. The terms of the President and Vice-President shall end at noon on the 20th day of January, and the terms of Senators and Representatives at noon on the 3rd day of January, of the years in which such terms would have ended if this article had not been ratified; and the terms of their successors shall then begin.

Section 2. The Congress shall assemble at least once in every year, and such meeting shall begin at noon on the 3rd day of January, unless they shall by law appoint a different day.

Section 3. If, at the time fixed for the beginning of the term of the President, the President-elect shall have died, the Vice-President-elect shall become President. If a President shall not have been chosen before the time fixed for the beginning of his term, or if the President-elect shall have failed to qualify, then the Vice-President-elect shall act as President until a President shall have qualified; and the Congress may by law provide for the case wherein neither a President-elect nor a Vice-President-elect shall have qualified, declaring who shall then act as President, or the manner in which one who is to act shall be selected, and such person shall act accordingly until a President or Vice-President shall have qualified.

Section 4. The Congress may by law provide for the case of the death of any of the persons from whom the House of Representatives may choose a President whenever the right of choice shall have devolved upon them, and for the case of the death of any of the persons from whom the Senate may choose a Vice-President whenever the right of choice shall have devolved upon them.

Section 5. Sections 1 and 2 shall take effect on the 15th day of October following the ratification of this article.

Section 6. This article shall be inoperative unless it shall have been ratified as an amendment to the Constitution by the legislatures of three-fourths of the several States within seven years from the date of its submission.

XXI. *(Effective December 5, 1933.)*

Section 1. The eighteenth article of amendment to the Constitution of the United States is hereby repealed.

Section 2. The transportation or importation into any State, territory, or possession of the United States for delivery or use therein of intoxicating liquors, in violation of the laws thereof, is hereby prohibited.

Section 3. This article shall be inoperative unless it shall have been ratified as an amendment to the Constitution by conventions in the several States, as provided in the Constitution, within seven years from the date of the submission hereof to the States by the Congress.

XXII. *(Effective February 26, 1951.)*

Section 1. No person shall be elected to the office of the President more than twice, and no person who has held the office of President, or acted as President, for more than two years of a term to which some other person was elected President shall be elected to the office of President more than once.

But this Article shall not apply to any person holding the office of President when this article was proposed by the Congress, and shall not prevent any person who may be holding the office of President, or acting as President, during the term within which this Article becomes operative from holding the office of President or acting as President during the remainder of such term.

Section 2. This article shall be inoperative unless it shall have been ratified as an amendment to the Constitution by the legislatures of three-fourths of the several States within seven years from the date of its submission to the States by the Congress.

XXIII. *(Effective March 29, 1961.)*

Section 1. The District constituting the seat of Government of the United States shall appoint in such manner as the Congress may direct:

A number of electors of President and Vice-President equal to the whole number of Senators and Representatives in Congress to which the District would be entitled if it were a State, but in no event more than the least populous State; they shall be in addition to those appointed by the States, but they shall be considered, for the purposes of the election of President and Vice-President, to be electors appointed by a State; and they shall meet in the district and perform such duties as provided by the twelfth article of amendment.

Section 2. The Congress shall have power to enforce this article by appropriate legislation.

XXIV. *(Effective January 23, 1964.)*

Section 1. The right of citizens of the United States to vote in any primary or other election for President or Vice-President, or for Senators or Representatives in Congress, shall not be denied or abridged by the United States or any State by reason of failure to pay any poll tax or other tax.

Section 2. The Congress shall have power to enforce this article by appropriate legislation.

XXV. *(Effective February 23, 1967.)*

Section 1. In case of the removal of the President from office or of his death or resignation, the Vice-President shall become President.

Section 2. Whenever there is a vacancy in the office of the Vice-President, the President shall nominate a Vice-President who shall take office upon confirmation by a majority vote of both Houses of Congress.

Section 3. Whenever the President transmits to the President *pro tempore* of the Senate and the Speaker of the House of Representatives his written declaration that he is unable to discharge the powers and duties of his office, and until he transmits to them a written declaration to the contrary, such powers and duties shall be discharged by the Vice-President as Acting President.

Section 4. Whenever the Vice-President and a majority of either the principal officers of the executive departments or of such other body as Congress may by law provide, transmit to the President *pro tempore* of the Senate and the Speaker of the House of Representatives their written declaration that the President is unable to discharge the powers and duties of his office, the Vice-President shall immediately assume the powers and duties of the office as Acting President.

Thereafter, when the President transmits to the President *pro tempore* of the Senate and the Speaker of the House of Representatives his written declaration that no inability exists, he shall resume the powers and duties of his office unless the Vice-President and a majority of either the principal officers of the executive departments or of such other body as Congress may by law provide, transmit within four days to the President *pro tempore* of the Senate and the Speaker of the House of Representatives their written declaration that the President is unable to discharge the power and duties of his office. Thereupon Congress shall decide the issue, assembling within forty-eight hours for that purpose if not in session. If the Congress within twenty-one days after receipt of the latter written declaration, or, if Congress is not in session, within twenty-one days after Congress is required to assemble, determine by two-thirds vote of both Houses that the President is unable to discharge the powers and duties of his office, the Vice-President shall continue to discharge the same as Acting President; otherwise, the President shall resume the powers and duties of his office.

XXVI. *(Effective June 30, 1971.)*

Section 1. The right of citizens of the United States, who are eighteen years of age or older, to vote shall not be denied or abridged by the United States or any state on account of age.

Section 2. The Congress shall have power to enforce this article by appropriate legislation.

INDEX